IMPORTANT TELEPHONE NUMBERS

Veterinarian: _____

Address: _____

Telephone: _____

Emergency clinic or
  veterinary hospital: _____

Poison control center: _____

ASPCA (humane shelter): _____

YOUR CAT'S RECORDS

Name _____ Breed _____ Breeder _____

Tom _____

Birthdate _____ Registration number _____ Queen _____

	7–14 wks.	6 mos.	1 yr.	2 yrs.	3 yrs.	4 yrs.	5 yrs.	6 yrs.	6–15 yrs.
FVR-C-P									
Rabies									
Feline leukemia									
Stool sample									
FLV test									
FTLV test									
FIP test									

FVR-C-P	Rhinotracheitis, calicivirus, panleukopenia (distemper). A kitten series and *yearly* boosters throughout life are needed for protection.
Rabies	Vaccination at four to six months and *yearly* boosters are required by state laws.
Leukemia	First-time vaccination requires two doses given two to three weeks apart and a third dose given two to four months later. After that, a single dose per year is recommended.

Stool sample   Feces should be checked whenever vaccinations are given. Bring a fresh sample to be examined.

FLV test   Feline leukemia virus test (see page 47).

FTLV test   Feline T-Lymphocytic virus test (see page 75).

FIP test   Feline infectious peritonitis test (see page 149). If you plan to breed your cat or if the illnesses described are present, the FLV, FTLV, and FIP tests should be done.

Surgery	Date	Follow-up

Problem or illness	Date	Medication used	Doctor was seen	Used home treatment	Resolved without medicine

In heat	Date bred	Mate: FLV-free?	Owner: FTLV-free?	FIP-free?	Number of kittens	Kitten mortality

The
CAT
CARE
Book
REVISED AND UPDATED

Other Books by
Sheldon L. Gerstenfeld, V.M.D.

The Bird Care Book
The Dog Care Book

Zoo Clues (for children)

The CAT CARE Book

REVISED AND UPDATED

All you need to know to keep
your cat healthy and happy

Sheldon L. Gerstenfeld, V.M.D.

Addison-Wesley Publishing Company, Inc.
Reading, Massachusetts   Menlo Park, California   New York
Don Mills, Ontario   Wokingham, England   Amsterdam   Bonn
Sydney   Singapore   Tokyo   Madrid   San Juan

Many of the designations used by manufacturers and sellers to distinguish their products are claimed as trademarks. Where those designations appear in this book and Addison-Wesley was aware of a trademark claim, the designations have been printed in initial capital letters (i.e., DL-Methionine).

The author and publisher have tried to ensure the accuracy of the information in this book. Readers should nevertheless verify all information with their veterinarians. Neither the publisher nor the author may be held responsible for any damage, direct or indirect, that may be caused or exacerbated by treatment described in this book.

Library of Congress Cataloging-in-Publication Data

Gerstenfeld, Sheldon L., 1943–
    The cat care book / Sheldon L. Gerstenfeld.—Rev. and updated.
        p.   cm.
    Rev. ed. of: Taking care of your cat. 1979.
    Includes index.
    ISBN 0-201-09569-6
    1. Cats—Diseases. I. Gerstenfeld, Sheldon L., 1943–   Taking
care of your cat. II. Title.
SF985.G47   1989
636.8′089—dc19   88-39579
                                                                          CIP

Cover design by Hannus Design Associates
Cover photo by L. Grant/FPG
Text design by Sally Carson, Carson Design
Set in 10-point Cheltenham by Compset, Inc., Beverly, MA

BCDEFGHIJ-DO-89
Second printing, October 1989

To my dear wife, Traudi, whose love and whole being have expanded my creativity and my sensitivity of the world.

To my dear parents, Sidney and Isabelle, who encouraged their son to pursue his dream to be an "animal doctor."

To our dear Pepe, who has passed on. He brightened our lives for fourteen wonderful years and will always be remembered.

Acknowledgments

The sincere help and encouragement of many people made the writing of this book a most pleasurable experience.

First and foremost, I thank my wife, Traudi, for her very helpful comments and patience, and for providing a loving and creative environment.

Ann Dilworth accepted the manuscript with those three little words that mean so much to an author—"We love it!" The raw manuscript evolved into its most effective form thanks to the teamwork of Doe Coover, Martha Drumm, and Tess Palmer. They helped me rearrange, reword, and delete, studying every word and paragraph until they could almost recite the text verbatim! Lois Hammer deserves a lot of credit for turning my "doctor's handwriting" into a typewritten beauty. John Hackmaster did the marvelous medical illustrations, and Beth Anderson finalized my original cartoons. John Bell, Cyrisse Jaffee, Laura Noorda, Lori Foley, Robert Shepard, and many others were helpful in creating this revised edition.

Five colleagues took time from very busy schedules to review the manuscript and offer suggestions: Dr. Gus Thornton, Dr. Jean Holzworth, Dr. Donald Patterson, Dr. Anne Jeglum, and Dr. Al Kissileff. Encouragement and suggestions were also enthusiastically provided by Jack Neifert.

All my patients' owners deserve a great deal of credit for caring so well and so responsibly for their pets. Their hopes, fears, and needs and their development into well-informed pet owners formed the foundation for this book.

Finally, I want to thank my patients themselves for giving me their unquestioning love and trust.

S. L. G.

To the Reader

This book can be of great help to you and your cat. Several veterinarians have reviewed the text and have agreed on the medical care suggested for each problem. Nevertheless, the recommendations may not always work. Here are some qualifications for you to bear in mind:

1. If your cat is under the care of a veterinarian who gives advice contrary to that given in the book, follow your veterinarian's advice. Your veterinarian can take into account the individual characteristics of your cat.
2. You know your cat best. If you believe you should seek professional help for your cat for any reason, do so.
3. If you think your cat has or might have an allergy to a medication, call your veterinarian for advice.
4. If your cat's problem persists beyond a reasonable period, make an appointment with your veterinarian.

Contents

Introduction

Owning a cat is a big responsibility. As the owner, you provide essential care for your animal—whether it be a Persian cat of royal breeding or a stray who followed you home one day—live a happy and healthy life. With the information in this book, you will be able to take good care of your pet at home and ensure that professional veterinary care is obtained when it is needed. You will also save time and money.

The writing of this book was a labor of love. I am thankful that I was able to become a veterinarian, to help injured and ill pets, and to be a source of information, comfort, and reassurance for many, many pet owners.

I have been very fortunate in veterinary practice. My pet owners have become *active* partners with me in sharing the responsibility for their pets' well-being and health. **The Cat Care Book** is the result of this wonderful experience.

Your veterinarian is a busy person. A typical day may include reuniting a child with her cat, Jaws, who has mended from serious automobile injuries; watching as an owner gives his diabetic dog its first life-sustaining injection of insulin; performing one or two "Marcus Welby"–type heroics (without a commercial break); giving several well-pet exams, which cover vaccinations and routine tests; and diagnosing and treating illnesses and injuries that require immediate attention. Your veterinarian also sees many minor medical problems that could be called "unnecessary" visits. In human medicine, up to 70 percent of first visits to the doctor have been termed "unnecessary." There is no reason to believe that our pets' illnesses or injuries are any different. You can save money and time and provide the best care for your pet by learning to treat many of your pet's medical problems at home and by learning when it *is* important to visit or telephone your veterinarian. I'm very proud of my pet owners when they handle minor medical problems efficiently at home. They know that I am around if they need reassurance or advice. I'm equally proud when they recognize *early* that their pet's problem requires my help. The step-by-step Decision Charts in **The Cat Care Book** will provide you with enough information to make sound judgments about most of your cat's medical problems.

To help you become an active partner, an aware pet owner, a good consumer, and a constructive critic, the chapters in Part I provide the following useful information:

Selecting a Cat

Taking care of a pet actually starts *before* you choose one (or two). This chapter will help you select and find the proper pet for your lifestyle, and it emphasizes the *responsibility* of pet ownership.

The Owner's Home Physical Exam: Your Cat's Body and How It Works

You'll be fascinated at the similarities between a person's body and a cat's body. This chapter also shows you how to examine your pet at home.

Keeping Your Cat Healthy, Happy, & Obedient

Many illnesses and injuries are the result of long-term abuse or lack of proper maintenance. Preventive care—grooming, training, good nutrition, annual vaccinations, checking for parasites, and dental care—will keep your pet healthy. The section entitled How Do I Know When My Cat Is Sick? describes some general signs that may be the first indication that your pet is not feeling well.

Going to the Veterinarian

Finding a competent and interested veterinarian and being a cooperative, aware, and concerned owner are important for your cat's health. You should understand and appreciate the procedures that may be necessary for your veterinarian to diagnose and properly treat your pet's health problem.

Your Cat's Home Pharmacy

A first aid kit is a must, and this chapter will help you stock it with the most effective medications for minor medical problems. Included are hints on uses, dosages, and possible side effects for a variety of over-the-counter medications.

Part II provides specific guidance for sixty one of your cat's most common medical problems. This section is designed for quick and easy reference. First, identify your pet's primary symptom—for instance, coughing, vomiting, or straining to urinate. To find a discussion of the problem, look it up in the Contents or the Index.

Emergency Procedures

Chapter 6 details the best way to approach injured animals and the things you can do during those first vital minutes that could mean the difference between life and death.

Accidents and Injuries

This chapter goes into common injuries sustained by cats, listing any appropriate home treatment and what to expect from your veterinarian.

Common Problems and Diseases

Each of the medical problems in this section includes a general discussion, suggestions for home treatment, and pointers to show you when a telephone call or visit to your veterinarian is needed. Information on what to expect at the veterinarian's office is also given to help you be aware of appropriate care. The Decision Charts that accompany each problem provide step-by-step instructions to help you decide whether to use home treatment or to seek professional advice. No medication suggested in this section should be used without knowledge of its dosage and side effects. Most medicines are discussed in Chapter 5, Your Cat's Home Pharmacy. First aid information for handling the most common cat emergencies is provided. Your handling of the emergency at home and your knowledge about what to expect at the veterinarian's office may combine to save your pet's life. Prevention of injuries is also discussed.

Breeding and Reproduction

Breeding, pregnancy, delivery, and nursing are fully discussed. Step-by-step charts on delivery and nursing will give you easy instructions to follow if your help—or the veterinarian's help—is needed.

Genetics and Hereditary Diseases
Cancer

These two chapters provide you with the latest information on advances in these important health areas.

Death and Euthanasia

It is painful to lose the unselfish love and companionship that a pet provides. When that pet is suffering and there is no hope for a cure, euthanasia should be considered an act of love and mercy. It is a very difficult decision to make and should be considered only after discussion with your family and your veterinarian.

Grieving for a pet that has died can be difficult, but it is a normal process. This chapter offers some steps to help you and your children endure the death of a beloved pet.

I know you will find the book informative and helpful in taking care of your cat. I hope you will also find it enjoyable and interesting reading.

Philadelphia, Pennsylvania   S. L. G.

PART I

You and Your Cat

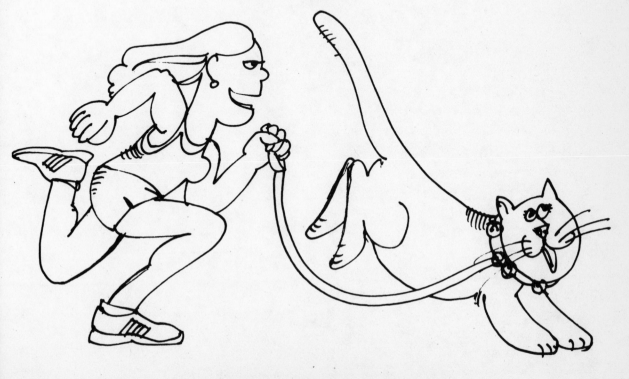

CHAPTER

1

Selecting a Cat

One of the greatest pleasures human beings can experience is to share their home with a pet. Having a cat or dog can keep you closer to nature. It should also kindle your spirit of reverence for all life on earth, from the ant on your picnic table to your brothers and sisters in every country. Cats and dogs are an unfailing source of companionship during times of sadness or joy. They have a sense of timing, of humor, seen in few human comedians. You'll always remember their body movements, facial expressions, and "one-liners," even after their bodies have departed and their spirits have become part of your memories. A kitten or puppy is a wonderful aid in teaching a child (and even some adults) about responsibility, patience, love, understanding, and self-control.

No other animal on earth has enjoyed such varied public relations as the cat. Cats have been both vilified and deified throughout history. Their association with witchcraft gave them a bad reputation during the seventeenth century, but ancient Egyptians revered them. Many others have had similar feelings. A French philosopher once said that there are only two aesthetically perfect things in the world—the clock and the cat. Lafe Hill (*Town and Country,* March 1979) quotes Colette:

> [*The cat*] *is the animal to whom the Creator gave the biggest eye, the softest fur, the most supremely delicate nostrils, a mobile ear, an unrivaled paw, a curved claw, borrowed from a rose tree. . . . I am indebted to the cat for a particular kind of honorable deceit, for a greater control over myself, for a characteristic aversion to brutal sounds, and for the need to keep silent for long periods of time.*

JOY AND RESPONSIBILITY

With the joy of owning a cat, however, comes *responsibility.* The lack of responsibility and lack of planning for owning or breeding a pet can be witnessed on the streets and in the humane shelters. Millions upon millions of cats are put to death each year; the reasons range from "too much trouble" or "too much money" to "the kids went to college" or "the kitten's not cute any more."

Owning a cat takes a commitment of time (as much as ten to fifteen years) and money. You and your family should ask yourselves the following questions before deciding on the new family member:

Do We Have Time for a Cat?

Who will have the responsibility for feeding the cat and caring for its toilet needs? Does the breed need daily grooming?

Can We Afford to Keep a Cat Healthy and Well Nourished?

The purchase price is small change compared to the maintenance fees: food, accessories, veterinary care, boarding, and kitty litter.

Food and accessories	$250–$400 per year
Veterinary care	$100–$300 per year
Boarding	$7–$15 per day
Kitty litter (if house cat)	$100–$150 per year

These figures are estimates and will vary in different regions, but they provide a model for figuring your pet's expenses for the year. Be sure that you have a little extra money set aside for unforeseen problems.

Do We Have Room for a Cat?

Will it be convenient to have a house cat? an indoor-outdoor cat?

Do We Want a Male or a Female?

See Breeding and Reproduction (page 236) for a discussion that should help with this decision.

What Are Our Favorite Breeds?

Selecting a pedigreed or nonpedigreed cat is a personal choice. Nonpedigreed cats are like us—a product of mixed breeding. For the most part, these unions produce wonderful and beautiful offspring.

Pedigreed cats (the term means that there is a record, a pedigree, of the kitten's ancestors for three or more generations) that are raised by responsible private breeders are excellent specimens of their breed. The good breeder looks for outstanding physical and mental qualities, such as soundness, beauty, and good temperament, and is continually trying to improve the line. Responsible breeders prepare their cats for breeding (see Breeding and Reproduction, page 236) so that healthy and vigorous kittens are produced.

There are thirty-six breeds recognized by cat associations. You can become familiar with the breeds that interest you by attending cat shows or talking to a neighbor who owns the breed that you like. The following specialty magazines are another excellent source of information:

Cat Fancy	*Cat Fanciers' Almanac*	*Cats*
P.O. Box 6050	Cat Fanciers' Association	P.O. Box 37
Mission Viejo, CA 92690	1309 Allaire Avenue	Port Orange, FL 32029
(714) 240-6001	Ocean, NJ 07719	(904) 788-2770
	(201) 531-2390	

Your veterinarian can supply advice on the breeds that interest you and help you to answer the final three questions:

What are the positive and negative characteristics of the breed?
Can such a cat adapt to our family?
What are the hereditary or common problems of the breed?

FINDING THE RIGHT CAT FOR YOU

If you have decided that you can afford the time and money to own a cat (and I hope you can), where can you go to select the new member of your family? If a specific breed appeals to you, ask your veterinarian for a list of reputable breeders in the area. The Cat Fanciers' Association lists more than 30,000 cat breeders throughout the United States and Canada. You can also check the daily newspapers or the specialty magazines.

If you want a pedigreed pet, avoid outlets. The breeding that produces outlet kittens is often indiscriminate, with no regard for good physical and mental characteristics. Crowding, malnutrition, intestinal parasites, and stress make the kittens vulnerable to many viral and bacterial diseases. The most critical period in the formation of a cat's personality is the first sixteen weeks of life. Outlet kittens are given little love and attention during this time—a tragedy that can affect them for the rest of their lives.

Breeders' home-raised kittens are generally healthy and well socialized because reputable breeders usually follow a standard procedure before breeding, during pregnancy, and at nursing that will give the newborns every chance at a healthy and long life. The new kittens are also checked, vaccinated, and wormed (if necessary) by a licensed local veterinarian. Most important, they are handled gently and given lots of love during the critical socialization period.

Breeders' kittens actually cost less, in most cases, than outlet pets, since the breeder does not have high advertising costs and overhead (shipping costs, rent, and employees' salaries). The breeder is in it not because of the money but because of a love for fine physical and mental specimens of the breed.

Mixed-breed cats can be found through newspaper ads, through the neighborhood pipeline, through notices on veterinarians' bulletin boards, or at the local humane shelters. There can be drawbacks to getting a nonpedigreed kitten. Since the mother may not have had good prenatal care, the kittens have more "youngster" problems, such as external and internal parasites, and their future temperament is harder to predict unless you can see the home where they were raised and the temperament of the parents. But these are correctable problems, given the help of your veterinarian and a lot of tender loving care and proper training. Remember, "mixed breeds are beautiful!"

The best time to form a human bond with a cat is when the cat is very young, from seven to twelve weeks old. (Anything younger should still be with its mother.) But don't forget that adult cats, especially at humane shelters, are begging for homes, too. That's where "Morris the Cat" of television fame was found.

To help overcome the "They're *all* so cute, which should we take?" syndrome, go through the following checklist:

Is This a Good Breeder and a Good Cattery?

Of course, your veterinarian's recommendation is usually adequate, but your own observations are important. A good breeder will keep the kennel clean and orderly. He or she will also be active in cat shows and be interested in improving the breed. Do the owners seem to love their cats? Does the breeder want to know about *you,* your family, and your lifestyle? A good breeder will not sell cats to just anyone. Visit several breeders. This will give you a "feel" for the breed and more information. Be sure to telephone for an appointment. Private catteries are part of the breeder's home, and this fact should be respected.

Can We Meet the Kitten's Parents?

Meeting the mother and father will give you some idea of the eventual size and temperament of the kittens. The cat's parents should be friendly and outgoing, not vicious or shy. They should be FLV and FTLV negative.

"This Is the One We Want!"

Select a kitten that seems physically healthy, with

- No eye or nose discharges
- No black debris in the ears*
- A healthy, glossy coat with no hair loss or reddened, scabby areas
- No fleas* or ticks
- Pink gums
- No coughing
- Firm bowel movements
- No lump at the belly button (this would indicate an umbilical hernia, which can be corrected with surgery, or, if small, can be left untreated)

Also, select one that is temperamentally well balanced.

- Friendly
- Responds to your attention
- Doesn't mind being held

BUYING A KITTEN

Besides the new kitten, what else should you receive from the breeder at the time of payment? He or she should ask you to take your new pet to a veterinarian of your choice within two days of purchase. The breeder should also offer to let you return the kitten for a refund if it is not in good health.

Purchase Papers

You should receive a **written bill of sale** stating: (1) the aforementioned privilege of return; (2) the date of purchase and any conditions of sale; (3) the price paid; (4) the registration numbers and names of the parents; (5) the litter or individual registration number of the kitten; and (6) its date of birth and description, including breed, sex, and color.

You should also receive **registration papers.** If the breeder has not yet received the papers (sometimes this happens), be sure that the bill of sale states this fact and indicates that the papers will be sent when they are received by the

---

*The presence of fleas or ear mites doesn't necessarily disqualify a kitten for purchase.

breeder. You should never be asked to pay extra for the kitten's registration papers—you have a *right* to them.

Note: In some instances, the breeder may indicate that the kitten is not for breeding purposes and will ask you to sign an agreement to this effect. One copy of the agreement goes to the registry. Breeders are within their rights to ask this.

Instructions for Care

The breeder should also give you **written instructions on feeding and care.** Dates of any wormings that have taken place, and the type of medicine used, should be included. You should also receive a statement, signed by a veterinarian, of all vaccinations given and the date of the next scheduled vaccination.

When you take your new kitten home, be sure that it has plenty of time for rest. Have a litter box, bedding (a blanket or soft pillow), food, and water awaiting your new arrival. Be gentle and patient and always keep in mind your *size*. After all, the kitten has been brought to a strange home to live with "giants," who cannot communicate directly and who have new rules. Follow the breeder's instructions for feeding and care until you see your veterinarian. Be sure that you are present when your kitten is with small children. Kittens can suffer severe injuries and even death from being dropped, hit, or squeezed by a child.

Registries

After the first cat show was held in England in 1871, breeding cats for certain physical and temperamental qualities, and registering the cats produced, became important. There are several registries in this country, and more abroad, each with its own standards and specifications for the breeds.

The Cat Fanciers' Association (C.F.A.), founded in 1906, is the largest registry in the United States. The C.F.A. has registered more than one-half million cats since its inception, and it sponsors some 200 annual shows across the country. The American Cat Association registers over 10,000 cats a year and sponsors about 75 national cat shows. In addition, there are the Cat Fanciers' Federation, the American Cat Fanciers' Association, the International Cat Association, and United Cat Federation. In Canada, the Canadian Cat Association is a major registry. The Federation International Feline d'Europe is a primary European association. Addresses follow.

Cat Fanciers' Association
1309 Allaire Avenue
Ocean, NJ 07712
(201) 531–2390

Cat Fanciers' Federation
402 McKeige Court
Donelson, TN 37214
(615) 883–7137

American Cat Association
8101 Katherina Avenue
Panorama, CA 91402
(818) 782–6080

American Cat Fanciers' Association
P.O. Box 203
Point Lookout, MO 65726
(417) 334–5430

United Cat Federation
1521 Stonewood Court
San Pedro, CA 90731
(213) 519–7178

International Cat Association
P.O. Box 2988
Harlingen, TX 78551
(512) 428–8046

Canadian Cat Association
52 Dean Street
Brampton, Ontario
CANADA L6W 1M6
(416) 459–1481

Federation International Feline d'Europe
c/o Mme. Claudine Rossi
No. 33, Rue Duquesnoy
Brussels
BELGIUM

INTRODUCING NEW CATS

Kittens usually make friends easily and are quickly liked or tolerated by established household cats. There may be some hissing and posturing, but the kitten will quickly become part of the cat family.

A new adult cat should be kept separate from the resident cat(s) for a few days. Alternate the cats among the rooms so that they will become familiar with one another's odors. Use the techniques for avoiding fear-induced aggression when introducing the cats (page 168).

Of course, your veterinarian should examine the new cat *before* you bring it home.

PET HEALTH INSURANCE

All owners should have health and accident insurance for their cats. Such insurance has received the widespread support and participation of the veterinary community and the confidence of the pet-owning public.

An unexpected costly veterinary bill can severely strain your family finances. Veterinary bills of $500 to $2,000 are not uncommon. The insurance policies provide payment for office calls, prescriptions, surgery, hospitalization, lab fees, radiographs (X-rays), and treatments. There are some exclusions, such as routine vaccinations and teeth cleaning.

Talk to your veterinarian or call the following insurance underwriter:

Veterinary Pet Insurance
    1–800–VPI–PETS (California)
    1–800–USA–PETS (National)

Get health insurance for your cat!

2

The Owner's Home Physical Exam

YOUR CAT'S BODY AND HOW IT WORKS

A veterinarian often hears a pet owner's surprised exclamation, "You mean that my pet has [diabetes, jaundice, leukemia, etc.]? Why, I didn't even know that [cats, dogs, parakeets, etc.] had a [pancreas, liver, kidney, etc.]!" Yes, pets *do* have the same organs in the same locations, and those organs can malfunction. The same diseases are seen in humans, dogs, and cats—and even in birds, guinea pigs, and snakes.

There is nothing more awe-inspiring than the way a body is put together (*anatomy*) and the way the parts function by themselves and in cooperation with the rest of the body (*physiology*). Even that fly or ant that visits your picnic lunch has a heart and intestines. So what does all this have to do with your cat's health? Health (yours and your pet's) is precious. You should know how the body is put together and how it functions so that you can respect it and do your best to prevent illness. For example, giving your cat a ball of string to play with is disrespectful to its stomach and intestines because, if the string is swallowed, it can cause vomiting, bloody diarrhea, or constipation. A more serious, life-threatening complication, such as an intestinal obstruction, can also occur.

You and your cat share more similarities than differences. You have less body hair, no tail, and a thumb, and you walk on two legs; but this is just about where the physical differences end. People do have more complex thinking centers in their brains (which, it seems, they often don't use very well), but cats leave human beings far, far behind in the development of the senses of smell, hearing, and sight. Many people go through life without developing these senses to their greatest ability—and some never use them at all. So who is "smarter" in "feeling" life—you or your cat?

The normal appearance and functions of your pet's body should be studied so that by using the Decision Charts and by doing a brief physical exam, you will be better prepared to know when to treat your cat at home and when to see your veterinarian.

It's a good idea to examine healthy cats about once every six months. If your cat doesn't seem to feel well (see How Do I Know When My Cat Is Sick? page 31), it's advisable to run through it again.

SKIN

A wrapping of fur is not all there is to your cat's skin. It is also a factory for vitamin D production; it protects the internal parts from injury, bacteria, and viruses; and it contains a sensory system that is unsurpassed in efficiency. The network of skin nerve cells goes to work when your cat is cold, has a cut, or receives a pat on the head. In cold weather, the hairs stand erect and form air pockets that will insulate against the cold.

Healthy skin and hair coats are flexible, glossy, and free of excessive oiliness, redness, dandruff, scabs, eruptions, or parasites (see page 177). There should be no areas of hair loss. Each cat has its own shedding cycle, which may change from year to year. Some pets shed a small amount all the time, while others may lose large clumps at various intervals. Don't be concerned unless the Skin-Problem Chart indicates a problem. Cats may have a normal receding hairline in front of both ears. This is the area of the *temporal gland,* a scent gland thought to be used for marking territory by rubbing the forehead against an object. To check for growths or blemishes run your hand against the hair coat.

Pets can have freckles, concentrations of cells containing the brown pigment called *melanin.* These can be found anywhere on the skin and even in the mouth. Be sure to check the skin's special alterations: the mammary glands, the footpads, the claws, supracaudal organ (an oil gland located on the top of the tail base), and whiskers.

The *mammary glands* are located on the abdomen. As shown in the accompanying picture, there are five pairs of nipples. The glands of nursing females enlarge and produce milk tailor-made for their new kittens. Females experiencing a false pregnancy (see page 241) can have enlarged breasts and can produce milk. Once your female cat has passed seven years of age, routinely *palpate* (feel gently) each gland to check for lumps (see page 194). See your veterinarian if you find any.

Check your cat's paws. The thick, pigmented, tough *footpads* are excellent shock absorbers. The pads are named for their location. Pets have sweat glands in the footpad area. If your cat gets excited at the veterinarian's office, you may see sweaty pawprints on the exam table. Check the spaces between the digits. Since your cat walks barefoot and this is a very moist area, the interdigital area can be easily irritated and infected by briars, stones, foxtail, sand, and salt (for melting snow).

The claws are used for getting traction and digging. A cat is able to retract and extend its nails for use as excellent offensive and defensive weapons. However, your pet's nails should be trimmed (see page 61), because cats keep their nails sharp and mark their territory by scratching. Having your cat declawed (see page 170), trimming its nails, or supplying it with a scratching post can save your furniture.

Some cats develop *stud tail,* formed when the supracaudal organ secretes a greasy, brownish material, which scales, crusts, and mixes with matted hair on the top of the tail base. It is seen most often in confined, uncastrated male cats, hence the name. Treatment consists of clipping the area and washing it with soap and water. Cleaning the area daily with alcohol seems to control the problem, and outdoor romps in the sunshine seem to be beneficial.

Whiskers (*tactile hairs*) are long, stiff hairs located on the muzzle, upper eye-

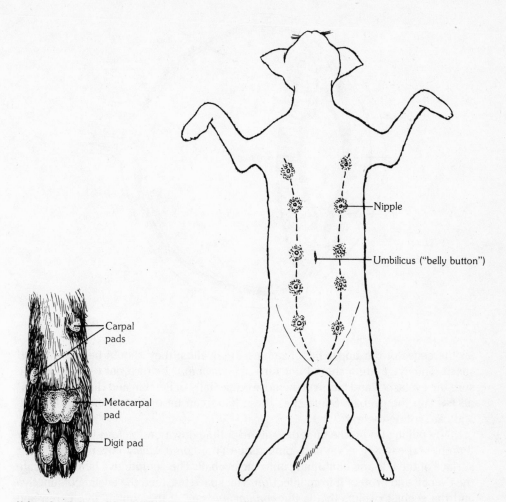

Carpal pads

Metacarpal pad

Digit pad

Nipple

Umbilicus ("belly button")

lids, cheeks, and legs. They are used as feelers and are especially handy for navigation at night or in dark areas.

EYES

No other organ in your cat's body contains such an intricate and complex mechanism in such a small structure as the eye. Without their eyes, your pet's ancestors would not have been able to avoid predators or to capture their food.

The first parts seen when examining your pet's eyes are the upper and lower eyelids—specialized curtains that protect the eyes. Eyelashes are located primarily

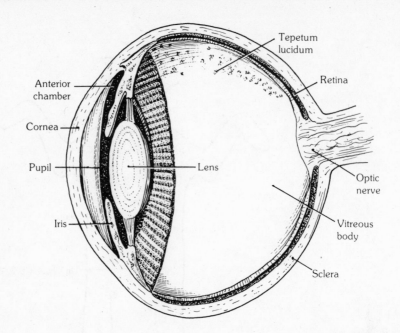

Anterior chamber

Cornea

Pupil

Iris

Tepetum lucidum

Retina

Lens

Optic nerve

Vitreous body

Sclera

on the edges of the upper lids. Examine the eyelids; they should be smooth and sharp. The eye margin should not turn in (*entropion*) or turn out (*ectropion*). Be sure the eyelashes and hairs on the nose (especially of Persian and Himalayan cats) do not rub the eyeball. Sometimes these hairs can be distorted and misdirected and can irritate the eye.

By pulling up on the upper eyelid or pulling down on the lower lid with your thumb, you can see a smooth, pink tissue (the *conjunctiva*) covering the inner surface of the lids and continuing onto the eyeball. The conjunctiva helps lubricate the eyeball and protect it from infection. The space between the eyelid conjunctiva and the eyeball conjunctiva is the *conjunctival sac.* If the conjunctiva is red and swollen or if there is a green or yellowish discharge, an inflammation of the tissue is present (see page 198).

Cats have a structure called the *third eyelid,* or *nictitating membrane,* which contributes to tear formation and distribution. It is light pink and is located at the inner corner of the eye. In sick pets, and sometimes even in healthy pets, the third eyelid may cover more than half the eye. "My pet's eyeball has disappeared," is sometimes the first thought of an owner who sees the third eyelid covering the eye. Don't worry—the eye is still resting comfortably under the membrane.

The *cornea* is the clear "front window" of the eye that bends the incoming light rays. The cornea can lose its clarity if it becomes inflamed or injured. Hairs and twigs can injure the cornea, especially in pop-eyed cats.

The *sclera* is the fibrous coat that gives the eyeball its Ping-Pong-ball shape and dull white color (this is often called the "white" of the eye). The sclera frequently takes on a yellow color (*jaundice*) in cats with liver problems.

The *iris* controls the amount of light entering the back of the eye and gives your pet's eye its color. The black hole in the center of the iris is the *pupil*. It *dilates* (gets larger) to let more light enter in dim light and *constricts* (gets smaller) in bright light. Shining a bright light in one eye should constrict both pupils. The pupils should be the same shape and size.

Light rays enter the eye's fluid-filled *anterior chamber,* pass through the pupil, and are further bent by the lens as they continue their journey through the *vitreous body,* a transparent, jellylike substance that keeps the eyeball firm. The light rays finally hit the "heart" of the eye—the *retina* at the back. This membrane has over 100 million light-sensitive cells, called *rods* and *cones.* These cells set off a flurry of electrochemical activity that transmits the image to your cat's brain by way of the *optic nerve* in about two-thousandths of a second. That's traveling!

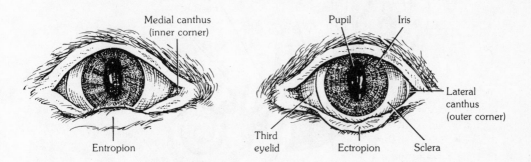

Your cat's retina contains a remarkable wedge of reflector tissue, the *tapetum lucidum.* The tapetum makes it possible for your cat to see better than humans in dim light. Light rays are reflected off the tapetum and back to the light-sensitive cells. The bright green eye reflection seen in dim light is the tapetum.

Cataracts, white opacities that block the light's passage through the eye, can be seen by shining a bright light in the pupil of affected pets. A normal aging process called *senile cataracts,* in which the pupil of older pets takes on a blue-white hue, does not interfere with vision. Senile cataracts, or *nuclear sclerosis,* is caused by a rearrangement of the fibers and a loss of water in the older lens.

Tears cover the eye with each blink. They keep the eyes moist and help protect them from foreign objects, bacteria, and viruses. Tears are formed by the secretion of glands located around the inner lids and behind the third eyelid. They drain from the eye through a canal system that runs from the *medial canthus* of the eye to the nostrils. (This is why your nose runs when you cry.) The blockage of these canal openings by debris or by an eyelid turning in (*entropion*) can cause excessive tearing (*epiphora*) and brown staining of the hair around the eye.

15

EARS

Not long ago, we came home to a very strange sight. All our cats had gathered around the refrigerator and were completely entranced by its bottom. On moving the refrigerator, we found cockroaches! The high-pitched communication of bugs or rodents that falls on our "deaf" ears is music to a cat.

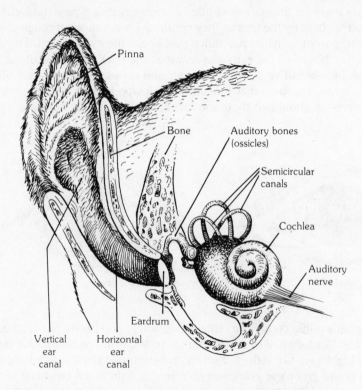

Pinna

Bone

Auditory bones
(ossicles)

Semicircular
canals

Cochlea

Auditory
nerve

Eardrum

Vertical
ear
canal

Horizontal
ear
canal

A cat's superb hearing ability begins with the sound-gathering flap called the *pinna.* The inner surface of the pinna and the beginning of the ear canal (which you can see) should be a light pink. You may see a small amount of yellow wax and a few hairs at the canal opening. These act like flypaper, trapping dust, insects, or other potential irritants and guarding against infection. If this area is reddened, foul-smelling, or has a puslike or brown, waxy discharge, an ear infection may be present (see page 202). Your veterinarian can check the rest of the ear with an *otoscope,* a special instrument equipped with a light source and magnifying lens.

The ear canal is L-shaped, going down (*vertical canal*) and then in (*horizontal canal*). The *eardrum* is at the end of the horizontal canal. Sound waves (the cockroach talk, for example) travel down the canal and beat against the eardrum—like a stick beating a drum. The cockroach-talk vibrations are amplified in the *middle ear* by three small bones called the *auditory ossicles,* which pass the sound on to the *inner ear's* snail-shaped and fluid-filled *cochlea* via the *oval window* (a vibrating membrane). The waves produced in the cochlea are converted to electrical messages that travel to your pet's brain via the *auditory nerve.* Your cat interprets the message as cockroach talk and sits in front of the refrigerator, patiently waiting for a roach snack.

Above the cochlea are three small, fluid-filled *semicircular canals.* These loops of tubing contribute to your cat's remarkable sense of balance. If your cat starts to fall, fluid in one of the canals is displaced. Hair cells in the canals detect the change and immediately inform the cat's brain, which orders muscles to tighten and keep your cat upright.

THE CIRCULATORY SYSTEM

The hardest worker in your cat's body is the heart. It is a top-of-the-line, four-chambered model (just like the human heart) that actually consists of two pumps. The right side of the heart receives the blue blood (depleted of oxygen) that has already dropped off its cargo of oxygen and nutrients and has returned with waste products, such as carbon dioxide, by way of the veins. This blue blood is pumped through the lungs to receive fresh oxygen and to remove the carbon dioxide. The blood then returns to the left side of the heart and is pumped out through the arteries to the trillions of cells in your pet's body.

The normal heart beats about 120 times per minute in a resting cat. You can feel the heart beat by placing the palm of your hand against your pet's chest, near the left elbow (see Taking Your Cat's Heartbeat, page 18). You may hear the "lub-dup" of the normal heart valves closing by placing your ear there. Panting, breathing, and purring may make it difficult for you to hear even with a stethoscope, which you can purchase at a medical supply store. The heart receives its oxygen by way of two branching *coronary arteries* that are about the width of a piece of spaghetti. Fortunately, cats do not have heart attacks (sudden blocking of the coronary arteries), but after eight years of age they often develop a problem with the heart *valves* (flaps that control the passage of blood through the heart's chambers): The valves do not close properly, and the heart must work harder to pump the blood. It may even fail unless treated with digitalis-like drugs. Your veterinarian (or even you, by using your stethoscope) will detect a heart *murmur* when the valves are closing improperly. A "zsa" sound may be heard between the "lub-dup" of the regular heartbeat: "lub-zsa-dup." The regurgitation of blood around "sick" valves is responsible for the "zsa" sound. Not *all* heart murmurs are serious problems. Your veterinarian is the best judge. *Cardiomyopathy* (a disorder of the heart's muscle tissue) is another typical cat problem.

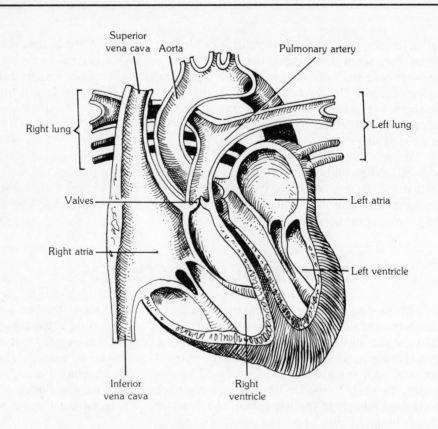

Superior vena cava · Aorta · Pulmonary artery · Right lung · Left lung · Valves · Left atria · Right atria · Left ventricle · Inferior vena cava · Right ventricle

The *pulse* and *capillary refill time* will give you some indication of how well the heart and blood vessels are working to maintain your pet's blood pressure (see Taking Your Cat's Pulse, which follows). When you press a finger against your pet's gum and then lift it away, the white area should return to the normal pink color in one second. This indicates that the capillaries are refilling with blood.

TAKING YOUR CAT'S HEARTBEAT

- Place your palm over your cat's left chest wall.
- Hold this position for fifteen seconds and count the number of beats felt in that time.
- Multiply the number by four. EXAMPLE: 30 beats in 15 seconds = 30 × 4 = 120 beats per minute.
  Note: A normal cat heart rate should fall in the range between 80 and 175.

TAKING YOUR CAT'S PULSE

- Place your fingers lightly in the middle of your pet's upper inner thigh.
- Hold this position for fifteen seconds and count the number of beats felt in that time.
- The number of pulse beats should equal the number of heartbeats.
  Note: The pulse should be easier to detect if the heart is pumping strongly, and fainter if the heart is pumping weakly (as in shock).

What are the *capillaries*? These microscopic vessels serve as the unloading dock for new goods (oxygen, nutrients, antibodies, hormones) and the loading dock for the waste products, such as carbon dioxide. The capillaries are like tiny streams that connect two large rivers (arteries and veins). The capillaries are so tiny that *red blood cells* (the delivery trucks loaded with oxygen) have to travel single file through them. The *white blood cells,* which are important in preventing and fighting infections, and *platelets,* which are vital to patching leaky blood vessels and initiating the clotting mechanism, also flow through these tiny streams. The fluid that keeps all the cells and other components floating is called *plasma.*

The *lymphatic system* is a great helper to the heart and blood vessels. It filters out invaders and transports to the bloodstream, in a watery substance called *lymph,* the *antibodies* and *lymphocytes* produced in *lymph nodes.* These components protect your pet's body against invaders such as bacteria, viruses, and even cancer cells. Three pairs of lymph nodes that may be examined are the *tonsils, prescapular nodes,* and *popliteal* nodes. These may enlarge during infections or in *lymphosarcoma* (*leukemia,* see page 261). They may be difficult to find, so on your next visit ask your veterinarian to show you where they are. The tonsils are housed in pouches—one on each side of the throat entrance. They are the throat's watchdogs (or watchcats!), ready to gobble up any bacteria or viruses with bad intentions. Tonsils rarely have to be removed. Enlargement of the tonsils is usually not a good reason for removing them.

THE RESPIRATORY SYSTEM

Cats, like people, need to gather oxygen from the air and to expel carbon dioxide (a waste product of metabolism). The *respiratory system,* consisting of the nose, mouth, larynx, trachea, bronchi, lungs, diaphragm, and chest muscles, makes it all possible.

The normal *rate of respiration* is ten to thirty breaths per minute. *Panting,* an increased respiratory rate (as high as 300 breaths per minute), is the primary way that your cat can sweat and thus lower body temperature. Panting is seen in hot

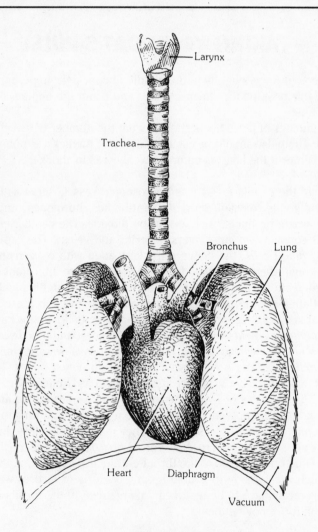

weather, after exercise, with lung disease, and even with pain or excitement. Notice also your pet's respiratory *rhythm*. The chest should expand (*inspiration*) and contract (*expiration*) with no difficulty.

A dry, hot nose or a moist, cold nose is not a reliable way to determine your pet's health, but the discharge, if any, might be an indicator of illness. Normally, there is a slight, clear, watery secretion from your cat's nostrils. A bloody or thick yellowish, white, or greenish nasal discharge is abnormal.

A light pink color to the gums indicates that your pet is getting enough oxygen. A blue or muddy red color to the tongue and gums indicates a serious problem in the respiratory or cardiovascular system. Pale gums may indicate anemia.

The *larynx* (Adam's apple or voice box) can be felt as a hard structure at the top of the windpipe—the same location as the human voice box. The larynx produces your cat's snarls and meows by vibrations of the *vocal cords*. The purr is thought to originate from vibrations of the "false" vocal cords.

Air passes through the larynx into the breathing tubes—the windpipe (*trachea*) and its smaller divisions, the *bronchi*. The air is warmed and filtered of dust, bacteria, and viruses by the microscopic hairs and mucus in these tubes until the air finally reaches its destination—the lungs. Your veterinarian uses a stethoscope to hear the passage of air in the breathing tubes and lungs. *Percussion of the chest* is useful in an examination of the respiratory system.

All that dirty air passing down the breathing tubes must be cleaned. The mucus that traps the dust, bacteria, and viruses is expelled through your pet's *cough reflex*. Occasionally, your cat will cough up some mucus. Although owners frequently confuse this with vomiting (expelling food from the digestive system), it's just normal "housecleaning" (see Coughs, page 208), so don't get alarmed.

The lungs don't have any muscles. They expand only when your cat's chest expands and the *diaphragm* (a muscular divider between the chest and abdomen) moves backward. This creates a slight vacuum in the chest, and air is sucked into the lungs. When your cat exhales, the lungs collapse and blow out the carbon dioxide. If air leaked into the vacuum chamber (a condition called *pneumothorax*), or if a tear in the diaphragm allowed intestines to enter the chest cavity (a condition termed *diaphragmatic hernia*), your pet would have a very difficult time breathing. These conditions happen frequently when pets are hit by cars (see page 116).

THE DIGESTIVE SYSTEM

The most finicky and most delicate part in your pet's body *has* to be the digestive system. Throughout your cat's lifetime it will remind you both that it won't stand for any foolishness. Spicy foods, bones, bad-tasting mice, pieces of wood, and any other garbage will cause a fit of vomiting and/or diarrhea that will send you running to the Decision Charts!

Your cat's digestive system is a food processor par excellence. It puts the Cuisinart to shame! Not only does the digestive system chop, pulverize, blend, grind, and emulsify food, but it converts carbohydrates, fats, and proteins into easily digested molecules that are then handed over to the bloodstream and lymphatic system for delivery to your cat's cells for energy, growth, and tissue repair.

Digestion begins when food enters your cat's mouth. The tongue positions the food for the shredding and tearing action of the teeth and mixes the food with the saliva to start the digestion of carbohydrates.

Open your cat's mouth as described on page 90. Your cat's tongue, which should be pink, has hard spiny projections similar to those on a wire brush. The tongue, in fact, does act as your cat's own built-in wire brush for pulling out loose hairs. The tongue also has taste buds that are aided by a primitive gland (*vomeronasal gland*) located in back of the upper front teeth. Occasionally, you may see your cat "taste" by first licking (such as when a male cat licks a female's vulva) and then flicking the tongue behind its upper front teeth, thereby distributing the taste to the sensitive vomeronasal gland, which can't be seen.

Your pet's teeth are used for protection and for grasping, cutting, and crushing food. Your kitten doesn't have teeth at birth. The "baby" (*deciduous*) teeth appear between two and five weeks of age. The permanent teeth begin replacing the "baby" teeth at four months of age. Cats have four types of teeth: *incisors, canines, premolars,* and *molars.* The teeth should be white, and the gum line should be pink, not swollen or red (see Mouth Odor, page 212).

Some cats fail to lose all their "baby" teeth (especially an incisor or canine) by eight months of age. In that case, you may see a double tooth. The "baby" tooth should be surgically removed, because it produces a good location for food entrapment and infection and may cause misalignment of the adult teeth.

A normal bite in cats has the upper incisors slightly overlapping the lower incisors. A slight overbite (a more marked overlapping) or an underbite (the lower incisors overlapping the upper incisors) doesn't seem to cause any problems.

The rest of the digestive system cannot be seen, but with practice you may be able to palpate some of the organs. Remember, palpate *gently* to avoid injury.

After your cat swallows, the food enters a muscular tube, the *esophagus,* through which it is transported to the stomach by coordinated waves called *peristalsis.* Because they eat odd things and fail to chew, cats can occasionally get blockages in the esophagus, caused by bones, fishhooks, small toys, and so forth. Early diagnosis and treatment are a must since a perforation in the esophagus can cause a fatal pneumonia. Persistent gulping, difficulty in swallowing, regurgitating (not vomiting) food ("it just seems to come right back out"), and excessive salivation are some early signs.

The stomach is the chief active partner in the digestive system, churning food and making it acceptable for the intestines. When your pet's stomach is full of food (or full of gas), it may feel like a doughy bag (feel behind the last rib on the left side). A kitten's stomach can distend considerably after a meal, and this is not necessarily a sign of disease or worms.

The liver is the largest organ in your pet's body, but it is located so that it cannot be palpated well in the normal cat. It nestles under the rib cage, probably because it has hundreds of jobs to do and can't be interrupted. The liver makes the proteins that provide energy for your cat's graceful leaps, manufactures the clotting agents that stop the bleeding of a cut, and is very important in fat and sugar metabolism. In addition, the liver is the "great detoxifier"—purifying toxins and drugs in your cat's system—and it recycles the bodies of dead red blood cells.

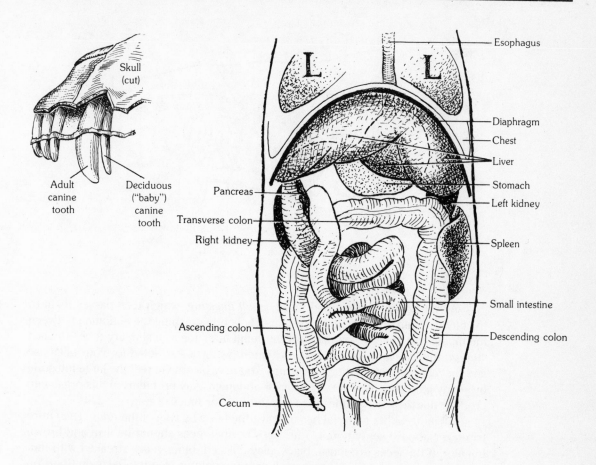

Some of its products are used to make new red blood cells; others are used to make *bile,* the green digestive juice stored in the *gall bladder* that, at mealtime, is released to the intestine through the bile duct to help break large fat molecules into smaller ones. Liver disease or the rapid destruction of red blood cells will release large amounts of bile into the bloodstream, producing *jaundice* and staining the eyes, gums, and skin yellow.

The *pancreas* resides behind your cat's stomach and also can't be palpated easily. The first job that the pancreas undertakes is to neutralize the acids in the soupy gruel that the stomach passes on to the intestines. These acids are no laughing matter; they could inflict serious damage to the intestines if not neutralized. Your cat's pancreas also produces an impressive array of enzymes that are important in sugar, fat, and protein digestion. If the pancreas becomes inflamed (as in *pancreatitis*), some of these enzymes leak from the cells into the bloodstream. The pancreas is best known, however, for its manufacture of *insulin,* which ensures that all your pet's cells get *glucose,* a simple sugar, for their energy needs.

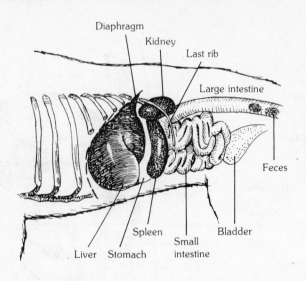

All nutrients are absorbed in the *small intestine,* which then passes them to the bloodstream and lymphatic systems. By gently grasping the abdomen between the thumb and fingers, you may feel the small intestine as a slippery tube. The last stop on the way is the *large intestine,* where water is extracted for your pet's use and the *feces* (the stool) become firmer. You may be able to feel the large intestine by gently palpating high in the posterior abdomen. Any problems in this organ can produce diarrhea, sometimes mixed with blood or mucus (see page 220).

All indigestible material has to leave the body by way of the *anus.* The entire trip takes about twenty hours. Your pet's normal feces should be firm and brown in color. If the feces are loose, black, clay-colored, bloody; are streaked with mucus; have a foul odor; or are extremely large in volume, see the Decision Chart on page 229. Anal sacs are discussed on page 228.

THE UROGENITAL SYSTEM

Your pet's urinary system is the main waste-disposal plant. The paired kidneys clean and filter the blood continuously as it passes through them. They help regulate the amount of salt, potassium, and water needed in the body. The excess is passed on with the waste products of metabolism through two tiny tubes called *ureters* to the storage tank, the *bladder.* When your pet's bladder fills with enough urine, a signal is sent to the brain for your pet to head for the litter box or ask to be let out. The urine exits to the outside by a thin tube called the *urethra,* located in the vagina of the female and the penis of the male.

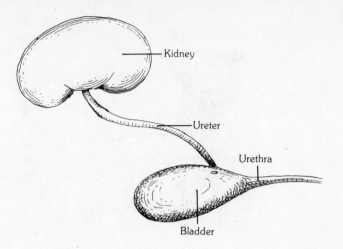

The one important time for you to examine your pet's urinary system at home is if your cat is straining to urinate or has blood in the urine (see page 230). A large bladder accompanied by frequent attempts to urinate is a very serious problem. The bladder is located in the posterior abdomen between the rear legs. Using *very* gentle pressure, with your left hand on the left posterior abdomen and your right hand on the right posterior abdomen, you may feel a firm, round ball that varies in size from a Ping-Pong ball to an orange. During your next visit, you should ask your veterinarian to show you how to palpate the bladder.

The sperm factories of your male cat are the *testes.* There should be two testes located within paired sacs called the *scrotum.* The testicles should be present in the scrotum at birth. If only one testicle is present, your pet is called a *monorchid;* if neither testicle is in the scrotum, your pet is a *cryptorchid.* This condition is hereditary (see page 251) and may be the source of a tumor in later life (see page 249). Pick up your male cat's tail. The scrotum with the paired testicles is located about one-half inch below the anus. They're very sensitive, so handle them gently. The two are generally the same size and shape in the normal male cat. A small lump may be felt on the back end of both testes. This is the *epididymis,* a storehouse for the sperm.

When your male cat ejaculates, millions of sperm (enough to repopulate the whole world) travel through the *vas deferens* to the urethra, where a very special fluid from the *bulbourethral glands* mixes with the sperm. This special fluid contains proteins, fats, sugars, and enzymes to nourish and protect the fragile sperm on their hazardous journey out of the penis and up the female's reproductive system to meet the egg.

The penis and vagina serve both urinary and reproductive systems. Your male cat's penis can be examined, but first you must find it. It lies within a fold of skin

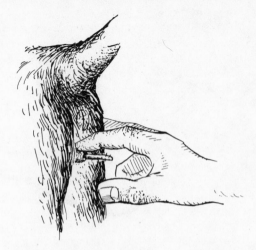

called the *prepuce,* or sheath, located just below the scrotum. Push forward on the prepuce and out pops a pink penis with small barbs, or *papillae,* on the tip. These papillae are thought to stimulate the female and to initiate ovulation. They are probably responsible for the ear-piercing howls of the female during mating and for her swat at the male when mating ends.

The only readily visible portions of the female cat's reproductive system are the soft, pliable *labia* (lips of the *vulva*) that form a vertical slit a few inches below the anus. By gently separating the lips, you can see the pink *vestibule* of the vagina. Urine exits through the urethral orifice located inside the vestibule.

Again, the internal parts of the female cat's reproductive system are the same as in the human: ovaries, fallopian tubes (or *oviducts*), uterus, cervix, and vagina. The paired ovaries produce eggs and female hormones. The eggs are delivered to

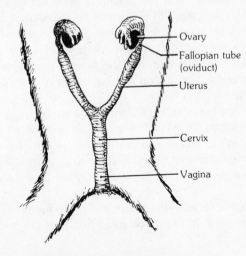

Ovary
Fallopian tube (oviduct)
Uterus
Cervix
Vagina

the thick-walled uterus through the small, coiled fallopian tubes. After ejaculation, the male's tadpole-like microscopic sperm, their tails whipping furiously, must swim a long distance (equivalent to humans swimming about thirty miles), up the vagina and through the opening of the muscular cervix. Once in the uterus, the sperm may or may not make contact with the eggs waiting there.

THE MUSCULOSKELETAL SYSTEM

Without the support and protection of bones, your cat would collapse into a pile of fur and skin. Most of the two essential minerals, calcium and phosphorus, are stored in, inventoried by, and distributed when needed from the bones. Without calcium, your pet's heart could not beat, nor could the nerves conduct messages. When your cat is pregnant or nursing, the need for both these minerals is at a peak,

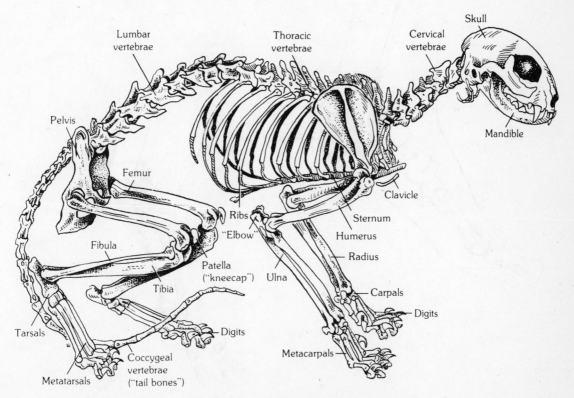

to aid in the growth of the fetuses and in milk production (see page 40). Furthermore, old, tired red and white blood cells must be "retired," so replacements are constantly manufactured by the bones' spongy marrow and sent out into the bloodstream.

The grouping of the 230-or-so bones and the joints, under command of the nervous and muscular systems, makes it possible for your cat to climb, jump, and scratch its fleas. The joints connecting the *cervical* (neck) bones are so flexible that your cat can lick itself everywhere but the back of the head.

Cats walk on their "fingertips" and "tiptoes." If you got down in this position, you would find that almost all your bones, muscles, tendons, and ligaments are in the same positions as your pet's. For example, in this position, your heel would be sticking up in the air. Well, so does the "heel" of your cat's rear legs.

The most important time to examine your pet's musculoskeletal system is when you see a lameness (see page 174). If your pet has a lame front leg, its head

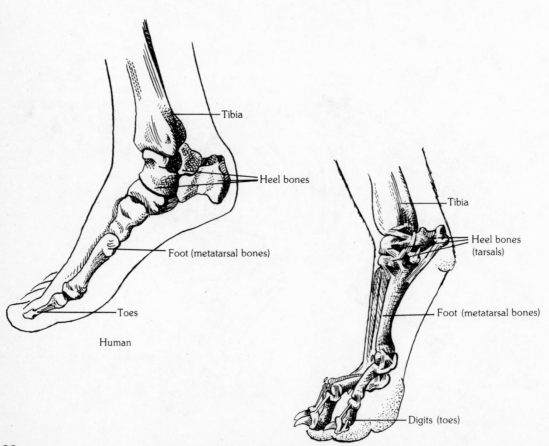

Tibia

Heel bones

Foot (metatarsal bones)

Toes

Human

Tibia

Heel bones (tarsals)

Foot (metatarsal bones)

Digits (toes)

To be checked	Human equivalent	How to examine
Digits, pads, and spaces between	Toes and fingers	Press on each bone and move each joint
Metacarpal bones and *metatarsal* bones	Bones between the fingers and wrist and between the toes and ankle	Press the length of each bone
Carpal bones and *tarsal* bones	Wrist and ankle	Press on each bone and move each joint
Achilles tendon	Attached between heel bone and muscle	Make sure the tendon is taut
Radius, ulna, tibia, and *fibula*	Forearm bones and lower leg bones	Press the length of each bone
Elbow joint	Same	Press on each bone and move each joint
Patella	Kneecap	Press each bone and move the joint
Humerus and *femur*	Upper arm bone and upper leg bone	Press the length of each bone
Shoulder joint and hip joint	Same	Move the humerus and femur back and forth in their respective joints
Scapula	Shoulder blade	Press on each bone
Cervical bones	Neck	Press each bone and move the neck up and down
Spine	Same	Press the length of the spine and all projections (*dorsal spines*)

will bob up when that leg touches the ground; the head will bob down when a sore rear leg touches the ground. A shorter stride and lighter touch are usually seen in the sore leg.

If you notice a lame leg, take the cat's temperature first, because in cats the cause is often a bite wound that has formed an abscess. In that case a fever of 104°F to 105°F may be seen (see page 192). If the temperature is normal, start the exam. You will be looking for swelling or pain by gently pressing on the bones with your finger or moving a joint. Your pet will exhibit pain by crying or pulling the leg away. If you think you've found a painful area, repeat that part of the exam to see if you get the same reaction.

To examine the individual areas of your cat's skeletal system, you may find it helpful to locate your own corresponding bones and/or joints first. The chart on the preceding page is a handy guide to follow. Remember to be gentle.

That finishes the skeletal system exam. If your cat exhibits pain at any point, by crying out and/or pulling away, gently repeat that step of the exam to double-check the reaction.

The muscles, after receiving messages from the nerves, move the bones, blink the eyes, and twitch the tail. These are the skeletal muscles that your cat can consciously move. Two special types of muscles work day and night involuntarily. The heart (*cardiac*) muscle contracts with less than one-half-second rest between beats throughout your cat's life. Smooth muscle tissue, which moves food along the digestive tract day and night, is also primarily involuntary.

THE NERVOUS SYSTEM

Your cat's brain, the "central computer," coordinates the heavy traffic of messages received from inside and outside the body with the activities the body can perform, via the network of nerves and the spinal cord. The brain is the "top cat." In fact, it *is* your cat. The nervous system, one of the primary controllers of the body's activities, can adjust your pet's body very quickly to environmental and internal changes.

THE ENDOCRINE SYSTEM

People's and cats' bodies alike contain small chemical factories tucked away in obscure corners. These are the *endocrine glands,* whose specialty products are *hormones* (from the Greek word meaning "to arouse to activity"). Hormones regulate chemical reactions. The endocrine system primarily regulates processes of long duration, such as growth and reproduction.

Malfunctions of endocrine glands, such as *diabetes* (see page 158), *hyperthyroidism* (page 164), *hypothyroidism* (see page 164), and *Cushing's syndrome* are seen frequently in pets. *Note:* Continuous, long-term corticosteroid therapy can cause serious problems, including Cushing's syndrome. Many disorders cause characteristic skin changes. See your veterinarian if your cat is over eight years of age and has symmetrical hair loss or bald spots but does not scratch. The skin in these areas often becomes brown. Most endocrine disorders are treatable. Your veterinarian will have to perform blood tests and a urinalysis to make the specific diagnosis.

HOW DO I KNOW WHEN MY CAT IS SICK?

The following signs should indicate to you that something is not right:

- Your cat's behavior changes—it becomes withdrawn and less active.
- Your cat exhibits a change in appetite that lasts for a few days. Loss of appetite (*anorexia*) or increased appetite (*polyphagia*) may indicate disease.
- Your cat is urinating more or less than normal.
- Your cat exhibits either vomiting or diarrhea for an extended period. Fluid is lost during vomiting and diarrhea, and *dehydration* (depletion of body water), a serious situation, can result.

Is Your Cat Dehydrated?

Pick up a fold of skin in the middle back area. If it snaps back rapidly, your pet is not dehydrated. If it stays up or returns slowly, dehydration is present. Do not test the skin in the neck area; this is normally loose in many animals and will give you false results. If dehydration is present, your doctor will find the underlying cause and will give fluids *intravenously* (in the blood vessel) or *subcutaneously* (under the skin) to replace the water lost.

Is Your Cat in Pain?

Lameness, a stiff neck, reluctance to get up or lie down, or tense abdominal muscles are indicators that your pet is in pain.

What Is Your Cat's Temperature?

A normal temperature is from 101.0°F to 102.5°F. Anything higher indicates a problem that needs professional attention (see Fever, page 149, for more information). To use a thermometer, follow these steps:

TAKING YOUR CAT'S TEMPERATURE

- Use a *rectal* thermometer, which has a rounded, stubby tip. Shake it down first by holding it between your thumb and index finger and snapping your wrist.
- Apply Vaseline or mineral oil to the bulb.
- Restrain the cat (see page 97). *Note:* It is advisable to have someone hold the back end of your pet while you hold the tail and the thermometer, so that your pet cannot move from side to side or up and down and break the thermometer.
- Lift the tail, gently slide the thermometer into the anus, and leave it in for three minutes.
- Remove the thermometer and read the mercury level.

3

Keeping Your Cat Healthy, Happy, & Obedient

A cat that is groomed regularly, fed properly, and trained well; travels nicely; and sees its veterinarian on schedule for vaccinations, parasite control, and dental care should have a happy and healthy life.

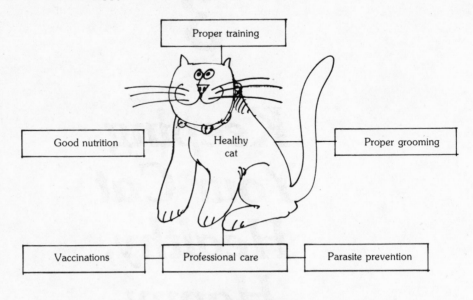

NUTRITION

What is good nutrition, and why is it so important? Nutrition is the process of using or transforming food into living tissue. Without a complete and balanced diet, your cat will not grow properly, reproduce, maintain the health of all its body tissues, or fight infection.

The "Great Food Hunt"

Your cat's hunt for a complete and balanced daily food intake is made much easier than its ancestor's hunt of thousands of years ago, thanks to commercial pet foods. The sound of the can opener or the jumbling of the dry food in the box will awaken the beast inside your cat—it will run from the comfy carpet near the fireplace to the kitchen to devour its neatly packaged and completely nutritious "prey." Your cat's ancestors had to go "shopping." The game they caught provided everything: protein from muscle tissue; fats, vitamins, and minerals from organs and bones; carbohydrates extracted from the vegetable and cereal matter left in the game's digestive tract. Vegetables and cereal starches aren't required by cats, but they do provide calories and bulk.

Years of research and development by the major pet-food companies have produced complete and balanced foods for your modern cat. These products, which are excellent from weaning to old age, eliminate the need for homemade diets that are time-consuming and expensive to prepare and may lack important nutritional requirements. The following discussion will focus on (1) the composition of food, (2) the types of pet foods, (3) how much to feed at different stages of your cat's life, and (4) the advantages and disadvantages of each type of commercial pet food.

FOOD FOR THOUGHT

Fuel needed to keep the heart pumping, the chest expanding, and the legs climbing is provided by the breakdown of carbohydrates, fats, and proteins. The amount of energy provided by molecules is measured in *kilocalories* (or *calories*). Fats provide the most energy per molecule. Carbohydrates, proteins, fats, vitamins, minerals, and water must be supplied in adequate and balanced amounts. Pregnant or lactating cats, growing kittens, and all heavily exercised pets may require up to twice as much energy as the inactive pet.

Carbohydrates

Use	For energy
	For bulk (indigestible cellulose)
	Fiber absorbs water; this bulk stimulates intestinal movements and can prevent constipation.
	Spares proteins; since carbohydrate is used for quick energy, protein can be used for body growth and repair.
Sources	Primarily well-cooked cereal grains, cellulose, starch, sugars

35

Amount needed	No more than 30 percent (on a dry-weight basis)

Note: The milk sugar *lactose* may cause diarrhea in many kittens and adult cats, since the amount of *lactase*, an enzyme that breaks up the sugar molecule, may be low. The large lactose molecule pulls water into the intestines and causes diarrhea.

Remedy: Use little or no milk or milk products if diarrhea develops. Try yogurt, which has a lower lactose content.

Proteins

Proteins are composed of *amino acids,* some of which (*essential* amino acids) cannot be manufactured by the body and must be supplied in the food. Eggs, soybeans, milk, fish meal, and muscle meat contain all the essential amino acids and are therefore said to be of high biological value.

Use	For growth
	Healthy tissue repair and maintenance
	Formation of antibodies that fight infection
	Formation of enzymes and hormones that help in body's chemical reactions
Sources	Meat, eggs, fish, vegetables (especially soybeans), milk and milk products, yeast
Amount needed	About 25 to 30 percent (on a dry-weight basis); kittens need 35 to 40 percent

Note: Do not feed raw egg white

This binds up *biotin* (a B vitamin), which is necessary for growth, but cooked eggs or raw yolks are very good protein sources.

Do not feed raw fish

Raw fish (especially freshwater, such as carp) contains *thiaminase,* an enzyme that destroys the B vitamin, *thiamine.*

Thiamine deficiency causes a serious nervous system disorder.

A reversible condition called *dilated cardiomyopathy* is caused by a deficiency of an amino acid called *taurine,* found naturally in clam juice. Your cat's food should have taurine in it.

Fats

Use	Provide more than twice as much energy per molecule as carbohydrates or protein (9.1 calories per gram)
	Transport vitamins A, D, E, K (the fat soluble vitamins)
	Provide fatty acids (e.g., linoleic) for a healthy skin and hair coat
	An important taste factor (such as marbling in steak)
Sources	Commercial cat food has generally adequate amounts.
Amount needed	About 25 to 30 percent
	Note: If your cat has a dry, lusterless hair coat and scaly skin, consult your doctor. Sometimes the addition of vegetable oil (corn or safflower) is beneficial, but excess oil in the diet can decrease the food intake and retard growth.
	Consult your doctor before starting supplements.
	Note: Do not use cod liver oil as a routine supplement.

Vitamins

Chemically known as *coenzymes,* vitamins are essential for life but are needed in very small quantities. A balanced diet should not let a deficiency develop.

Use	For normal body functioning
Sources	Supplemented commercial pet food has generally adequate amounts.
	Note: Be sure that the food is supplemented with all vitamins, especially A, B (thiamine), and E
	A deficiency of vitamin A (a problem with cats fed dog food, which is too low in many components) is thought to start degeneration in the cat's eye.
	Thiamine deficiency can result from feeding your cat raw fish or unsupplemented cat foods.
	Vitamin E deficiency causes *pansteatitis* (a painful inflammation of the fatty tissue; it is seen in cats fed red-meat tuna with no vitamin E supplementation).

Prolonged diarrhea or vomiting can cause a loss of water *and* water soluble vitamins (such as the B vitamins), which should be replaced with supplements.

Minerals

Use   For normal body functioning
For bone development

Sources   Commercial cat foods have adequate amounts of sodium, potassium, iron, and calcium.

Note: Do not use unprescribed calcium-phosphorus preparations.

If the calcium-to-phosphorus ratio is altered by unneeded supplements or by an all-meat diet (too high in phosphorus), severe skeletal problems will occur.

If you are feeding your cat a low-magnesium diet, make sure that it is supplemented by the manufacturer with additional potassium (see Hypokalemic Polymyopathy Syndrome, page 79).

Water

Water is essential. It is obtained from the process of *metabolism* (especially of fats) of the food and liquids that your cat ingests. Your cat also needs constant access to clean, fresh drinking water.

Cats need about 30 milliliters (one ounce) of water per pound of body weight daily. Lactation, fever, hot weather, exercise, and water loss from vomiting or diarrhea will increase your pet's need. Dry foods (only 10 percent moisture) will increase your pet's water intake, while canned foods (75 percent moisture) will decrease the amount of water it drinks. *Note:* Do *not* allow your pet to drink water from unsanitary sources, such as stagnant pools or streams and toilet bowls.

YOUR CAT'S FOOD

	Dry	Semimoist	Moist (canned)
Advantages	Most economical	Convenient to feed	Very palatable
	Easy to feed	Very palatable	
	Excellent for self-feeding (see below)	Easily stored	
	Easily stored	No refrigeration needed	
	No refrigeration needed	Convenient to use when traveling	
Disadvantages	None	Expensive	Expensive
		Good taste may lead to overeating	Must refrigerate leftovers
			Spoils if left in bowl all day
			Good taste may lead to overeating
How to feed	Self-feeding—leave daily ration in bowl; cat will eat whenever hungry	Divide daily ration into two equal feedings for less chance of digestive upset	Divide daily ration into two equal feedings
	May be moistened with water or with semimoist or canned food		May be mixed with dry food (up to 25 percent of total daily intake)

Feeding Your Kitten

A kitten's caloric needs are twice those of an adult cat. The protein requirement is about 50 percent greater. The major pet-food companies have special kitten foods that meet these standards. If you cannot obtain the kitten foods, the adult maintenance foods should be supplemented with proteins of high biological value (cooked eggs, yogurt, cooked liver, milk, and milk products). If the milk and milk products cause diarrhea, discontinue their use.

Feeding Your Adult Cat

Adult cats need about forty calories per pound every day.

Weight (in pounds)	Calories needed	Daily feeding (in ounces)		
		Dry	Semimoist	Moist (canned)
4	160	1½	1½	5
6	240	2½	2½	8
8	320	3⅓	3⅓	10
10	400	4	4	13
12	480	5	5	16
14	560	6	6	18

These feeding recommendations are estimates that will vary according to your cat's activity, metabolic rate, and growth. Even the environmental temperature is a factor. An alert, active cat that is neither fat nor thin and has a glossy haircoat is being fed properly.

Feeding Your Pregnant Cat

The pregnant cat's nutritional needs (energy and protein requirements) will not increase drastically until the last trimester of pregnancy, which begins on the thirty-fifth day. The fastest growth and calcification of the fetus occurs during this period.

At two weeks, start to increase its food intake by 20 percent. Supplements of cooked eggs, cooked liver, cooked muscle meat, milk, and yogurt are good. At delivery time, the food intake will be 50 to 60 percent higher than the maintenance level.

A high-protein commercial food or supplemental proteins of high biological value (cooked eggs, cooked liver and meats, milk, or yogurt) are very important in late pregnancy to assure a good milk supply.

As pregnancy progresses, the fetuses occupy a large area of the abdomen. The mother's digestive tract will be able to handle only smaller, more frequent feedings.

Feeding Your Lactating Cat

A well-balanced commercial cat food should supply adequate nutrients. Your cat's appearance and milk production are the best indicators of nutritional status; if you notice any change, try supplementing the diet with high-protein foods such as milk products and cooked eggs. *Note:* Supplements of vitamins and minerals *should* be given to heavily lactating cats with large litters.

Although the content of the mother cat's diet won't alter much, the amounts eaten will. A general rule is to feed an additional 100 calories per pound of kitten (you can weigh the babies on an ounce or gram scale). By the end of the nursing period, the mother may be eating three times the prebreeding level (see Nursing Period, page 245).

Feeding Your Old Cat

Time passes very quickly. Soon you'll find that the little ball of fur you played with on the livingroom rug twelve years ago is slow in getting around and stays close by your side as if every minute counted. In old age, everything in the cat's system becomes less efficient. Fewer calories are needed because your old pal is less active and the metabolic rate is slower. The digestive process and absorption of food take longer. If your cat is getting fat, you are supplying too many calories, so decrease the daily ration. If your cat is not a self-feeder, smaller, more frequent feedings will help the old cat digest and absorb the food better.

VACCINATIONS

In 1879, Louis Pasteur coined the word *vaccination* (from the Latin word for "cow"), when he realized that his research was based on the same principle that Edward Jenner, an English physician, had observed almost 100 years earlier. Dr. Jenner found that cowpox could be used to protect humans against smallpox. Pas-

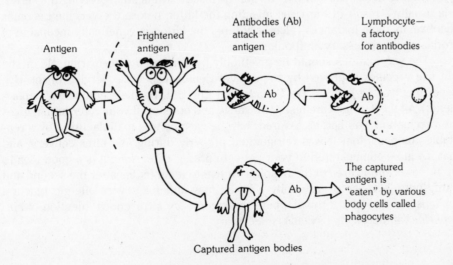

Antigen

Frightened antigen

Antibodies (Ab) attack the antigen

Lymphocyte— a factory for antibodies

Ab

Ab

Ab

The captured antigen is "eaten" by various body cells called phagocytes

Captured antigen bodies

teur went on to develop a rabies *vaccine* by drying the spinal cords (thus making the virus noninfectious) of rabbits infected with the rabies virus.

Years later it was discovered that the invading agents, viruses and bacteria (also called *antigens*), cause the body's lymphocytes to produce *antibodies* that fight these foreign invaders. It was also discovered that antigens could be chemically modified to lose their disease-producing quality while still triggering the production of antibodies to fight the disease. The chemically modified antigens together are called an *attenuated vaccine*, and this is what your pet receives in the injections from the veterinarian.

The body's *amnestic response* ("memory") is the basis for the series of vaccinations given to kittens and for the yearly boosters. Each time a vaccination is given, the body "remembers" its prior experience with these antigens and therefore produces a successively higher number of antibodies (thus affording more protection). Boosters, usually given at yearly intervals, are essential to keep the "memory" (and the antibodies) at peak level.

Your pet's immune system must be in good working order to respond to the vaccine. Any stress, such as the presence of external or internal parasites or malnutrition, can decrease your cat's manufacture of antibodies. Treating the parasites (see page 48) and correcting the malnutrition (see page 45) are essential for successful vaccinations.

Kittens receive actual antibodies (*passive immunity*) to *panleukopenia* (destruction of the white blood cells) while still in the uterus and from the "first milk." These antibodies help protect your kitten for six to twelve weeks after birth. Although the antibodies can sometimes interfere with the vaccine, the kitten series of vaccinations should still be initiated at an early age. The last shot should be given at twelve to sixteen weeks.

On rare occasions a kitten can get the disease while still receiving the series. It is usually a result of the virus infecting the kitten before the vaccine becomes effective. In some instances (also very rare) the kitten is genetically incapable of producing the necessary antibodies.

The vaccinations should be given only by a *licensed* veterinarian. He or she will use vaccines approved by the Animal Health Inspection Service of the U.S. Department of Agriculture (in Canada and England, by their equivalent departments). All the vaccines are tested for safety and potency. If your veterinarian gives the vaccination, you can be assured that the vaccine was manufactured by a reputable company, that it was refrigerated properly during and after delivery, and that it will be administered to your pet with proper care. *Note:* It is a good idea to sit in the reception area of the hospital for five to ten minutes after the second and third shots, because occasionally a kitten may suffer a severe allergic reaction (collapse and shock). If this happens, an emergency intravenous injection of *epinephrine* (and possibly oxygen) is necessary.

Calicivirus

What is the nature of the illness?	A virus that primarily attacks the mouth and lungs
	Infects only cats
What are the signs?	Fever
	Weakness
	Loss of appetite
	Ulcers on the tongue, nostrils, or roof of mouth (*hard palate*)
	Heavy breathing
	Watery discharge from eyes and nose
	Sneezing
	Drooling
How is it spread?	Airborne transmission
	Direct contact
What is the treatment?	Antibiotics, fluids, vitamins, and forced feeding are usually necessary.
	Inhalation therapy may loosen the nasal and tracheal congestion and increase the cat's appetite.
	Good nursing and supportive therapy are very important.
How is it prevented by vaccination?	An attenuated vaccine usually given in the same inoculation with the rhinotracheitis vaccine
	Boosters are necessary every six to twelve months.
	Note: If the drops are used, sneezing may occur in four to seven days after innoculation; no treatment is necessary.

Panleukopenia
(Feline distemper, "cat plague," infectious enteritis)

What is the nature of the illness?	A virus that primarily attacks the bone marrow and intestines (it does not cause "bad temper")
	Note: Highly contagious
	The death rate in infected, unvaccinated young cats is over 90 percent.

What is the nature of the illness? (cont.)	Seen in all members of the cat family, from lions to house cats
What are the signs?	High fever (104°F to 105°F)
	Loss of appetite
	Weakness
	Vomiting
	Diarrhea (sometimes bloody)
	Note: Some kittens may die suddenly with no outward signs of illness.
How is it spread?	Direct contact with the saliva, urine, feces, or vomit of an infected cat.
	Infected fleas and flies harbor the virus and contaminate surfaces.
What is the treatment?	Antibiotics, fluids, vitamins, blood transfusions, antivomiting and antidiarrheal medications, and forced feeding are all generally essential for maintaining life.
	A disinfected environment is essential to avoid recontamination.
How is it prevented by vaccination?	An attenuated vaccine first given at seven to nine weeks of age; the last after twelve weeks (kitten series)
	Boosters are necessary every twelve months.

Pneumonitis

What is the nature of the illness?	A bacteria that primarily attacks the eye lining (conjunctiva) and the lining of the nose
	Infects only cats; fairly rare
What are the signs?	*Conjunctivitis* (inflammation of the eye lining)
	Sneezing
	Watery or puslike discharge from the eyes and nose
How is it spread?	Airborne transmission
	Direct contact
What is the treatment?	Antibiotics, fluids, vitamins, and forced feeding are usually necessary.

Inhalation therapy may loosen the nasal and tracheal congestion and increase the cat's appetite.

Good nursing and supportive therapy are very important.

How is it prevented by vaccination?

Vaccination is not very effective because it does not produce a high level of antibodies and the antibody level is elevated for only a short time.

Rabies

What is the nature of the illness?

A viral disease that attacks the brain

Seen in all warm-blooded animals, especially skunks, raccoons, foxes, bats, coyotes, dogs, and cats

Note: Infectious to humans

What are the signs?

Change in behavior

Extreme restlessness

Dilated pupils

Extreme shyness or aggressiveness

Tendency to bite anything in its way

Paralysis of throat, causing voice changes, salivation, and an inability to eat and drink

Paralysis of the lower jaw

Generalized paralysis, coma, and death

How is it spread?

The bite of a rabid animal (virus-laden saliva enters the wound)

Airborne transmission in caves inhabited by bats has been reported.

What is the treatment?

Animals are not treated because of the public health danger and the high (almost 100 percent) mortality rate.

A few humans have reportedly been cured by intensive supportive therapy.

How is it prevented by vaccination?

Attenuated vaccines are used.

The first vaccination is given between three and six months of age; boosters are given at one year and annually thereafter.

Rhinotracheitis

What is the nature of the illness?	A herpes virus that primarily attacks the eye lining (conjunctiva) and upper breathing tubes (trachea)
	Infects only cats
What are the signs?	Fever
	Loss of appetite
	Watery or puslike discharge from eyes and nose
	Weakness
	Sneezing
	Coughing
	Drooling
	Breathing through the mouth (nose is stuffed up)
	Note: Pregnant cats may abort.
How is it spread?	Airborne transmission
	Direct contact
What is the treatment?	The virus is inactivated easily by disinfection or a dry environment.
	Antibiotics, fluids, vitamins, and forced feeding are usually necessary.
	Inhalation therapy may loosen the nasal and tracheal congestion and increase the cat's appetite.
	Good nursing and supportive therapy are very important.
How is it prevented by vaccination?	An attenuated vaccine given by injection or in eye drops
	Two inoculations are necessary in kittens, the last given after twelve weeks of age.
	Boosters are necessary every six to twelve months.
	Note: If the drops are used, sneezing may occur about four to seven days after inoculation; no treatment is necessary.

Feline Leukemia Virus

What is the nature of the illness?	A contagious virus that attacks any cell in the cat's body
	It can cause a blood cancer (leukemia) and tumors in almost any tissue or organ. It more commonly attacks the cat's immune system and must be suspected and investigated whenever a cat develops anything but the simplest of problems.
What are the signs?	The leukemia virus, which suppresses the immune system, is an important infectious agent in a wide variety of cat diseases: tumors (lymphosarcoma); anemias; and secondary infections such as toxoplasmosis, hemobartonella (red blood cell parasite), feline infections, peritonitis, chronic mouth sores, recurring abscesses, nonhealing skin wounds, and chronic respiratory disease. It is also responsible for reproductive problems such as infertility and abortion. It is suspected, and a test is performed, whenever a cat develops anything but the simplest problem.
How is it spread?	Direct contact with the saliva, urine, or feces of infected cats; through the mother's milk or uterus to unborn kittens
How is it diagnosed?	A simple blood test will indicate if the virus has reached the bone marrow (IFA test) or is present in the circulation (ELISA test).
	A cat that tests positive should be retested at one- to three-month intervals. Cats can "fight off" the virus.
What is the treatment?	The type of secondary infection will determine the treatment (for example, antibiotics for bacterial infection). For lymphosarcoma, see Cancer (page 255).
How is it prevented by vaccination?	The feline leukemia vaccination is recommended for all healthy cats nine weeks of age or older; yearly boosters are recommended.
	A feline leukemia virus diagnostic test is a good idea before the first vaccination. The vaccine is of no known value to a cat with existing feline leukemia virus infection.

PARASITES

A parasite obtains its nutrition from your pet and gives nothing in return except possible illness. This one-sided relationship has been under attack by concerned pet owners, veterinarians, pet-food manufacturers, and pharmaceutical companies.

As a concerned pet owner, you will find that reading this section and the Decision Charts will make you aware of whether your cat has a parasite problem, whether you can treat it at home or need to visit your veterinarian, and how to prevent the parasite from finding a home on or in your pet's body. First, let me dispel a few old wives' tales:

1. Garlic does *not* cure worms.
2. Cats do *not* transmit pinworms to children.
3. Candy does *not* cause worms.
4. Worms do *not* always cause disease (many pets live nicely with their parasites).
5. Thinness or constant hunger does *not* always indicate worm problems.

The worm medicine sold in pet stores and grocery stores should *not* be used unless your pet has roundworms and your veterinarian has advised you to use it. Since other intestinal parasites may be present, it is wiser to have your doctor check for other worms with a fecal sample. In most cases, the adult cat has developed an immunity to the worms (*ascarids*) killed by this medication, so once-a-month worming is not necessary. One stool sample that is negative for worm eggs does *not* mean that your pet has no worms—the worms may not be shedding their eggs at test time.

Veterinary medicine, the pharmaceutical companies, the pet-food companies,

and concerned pet owners, through good diagnostic methods, specific medicines, and sound hygiene and nutrition, have made it possible for today's pets to live almost free of parasites on or in their bodies.

Heartworms
(Dirofilaria)

Who gets them?	Dogs, foxes, and wolves mainly, but there has been an increase of reported cases in cats
	Note: Human infections have been reported but are rare. Humans seem immune to the dog heartworm.
	A worldwide problem, heartworms are prevalent in warm and tropical areas and in any heavily mosquito-infested areas.
What do they look like?	Slender, white roundworms that are five to twelve inches long
How are they spread?	Transmitted by the mosquito
What is their life cycle?	After biting an infected animal, the mosquito hosts the *microfilaria* (noninfective larvae) in its sucking apparatus, where they become infective in two weeks.
	A subsequent bite injects the larvae (baby worms) into the skin of another animal.
	The larvae migrate through the body and grow into mature worms in the right heart chambers.
	The worms produce new microfilaria and release them into the bloodstream, where another mosquito picks them up.
Are there any signs to look for?	Weight loss despite a healthy appetite
	Anemia
	Coughing
	Vomiting
	Heavy breathing
	Tendency to tire easily
	Swollen abdomen and legs
	Severe heart, lung, and liver damage leading to death

How are they diagnosed? A blood test measuring adult cuticular antigens in the serum is necessary. Radiographs, an electro-cardiogram, an echocardiogram, and a tracheal wash may be done.

What is the treatment? Intravenous injections of *thiacetarsamide* kill the adult worms in the heart.

Your veterinarian may take chest X-rays and perform an electrocardiogram to see the health of the lungs and heart before treatment.

The liver and kidneys will be checked by blood tests before, during, and after treatment, since the chemical can damage these organs and the dead worms can lodge there.

Careful monitoring during hospitalization will minimize the chance of complications.

If everything has gone well, another drug is given about two months later to kill the microfilaria in the bloodstream.

Can they be prevented? Avoid mosquito-infested areas.

Keep your pet screened from mosquitoes at night.

Diethylcarbamazine works well to prevent the maturation of larvae into adult worms (a blood test is a prerequisite for this treatment).

Note: In general, heartworms are not a feline parasite, but their presence should be investigated in cats with a history of chronic vomiting or respiratory problems.

Hookworms

Who gets them? Cats and dogs; cats and kittens seem more resistant, however

Note: A few cases of development to the adult stage in the human intestine have been reported.

What do they look like? They are usually too small to be seen with the naked eye.

How are they spread? The larvae penetrate the skin or are swallowed.

Kittens can be infected while in the uterus or by larvae passing in the mother's milk.

Are there any signs to look for?	Severe anemia
	Weakness
	Bloody diarrhea
How are they diagnosed?	Check successive stool samples.
What is the treatment?	Medication is necessary.

Note: Medication kills only the adults in the intestine, not the larvae migrating through the body, so two or more wormings are necessary to kill all the parasites.

Hookworm larvae can *encyst* (form cysts) in the muscles and survive for long periods of time, and medication is not effective against this stage.

| Can they be prevented? | Keep your cat's environment sanitary. |

Remove feces from your yard.

Wash concrete runs often, with salt or sodium borate (borax), if possible, which may be helpful in killing the eggs and larvae.

Note: These chemicals can damage or kill grass and other vegetation.

Protozoan-Coccidia

| Who gets them? | Cats and dogs |

Note: Mature animals usually build up immunity to this parasite.

What do they look like?	They are too small to be seen with the naked eye.
How are they spread?	Infected animals shed the parasite in their feces.
Are there any signs to look for?	Bloody diarrhea
How are they diagnosed?	Check successive stool samples.
What is the treatment?	Sulfa drugs are effective. Also, an immunity develops over time.
Can they be prevented?	Good sanitation is essential.

Protozoan-Toxoplasmosis

| Who gets them? | Cats and dogs |

Note: Highly infectious to humans, and birth defects can result from infection

What do they look like?	They are too small to be seen with the naked eye.
How are they spread?	The *oocysts* ("egg-sac" stage) are introduced by eating infected raw meat, rodents, or birds, or by handling the feces of infected animals.
What is their life cycle?	The parasite multiplies in the wall of the intestine.
	Sometimes the parasite will spread to other parts of the body.
Are there any signs to look for?	Fever
	Loss of appetite
	Weight loss
	Weakness
	Vomiting
	Diarrhea
	Breathing difficulties
	Coughing
	Anemia
	Jaundice
	Note: Most infections do not develop signs, or the signs are very mild.
	Note: Pregnant cats may abort.
How are they diagnosed?	Special stool and antibody tests
What is the treatment?	Sulfa drugs are effective.
Can they be prevented?	Do not feed your cat raw or undercooked meat.
	Keep your cat indoors.
	Clean the litter box daily using a 7 percent ammonia solution.
	Pregnant women should wear gloves when changing cat litter or gardening where a cat may defecate.
	Wash your hands well after handling raw meat.

Protozoan-Giardia

Who gets them?	Cats, dogs, all animals
	Note: Has the potential to infect humans
What do they look like?	They are too small to be seen with the naked eye.

How are they spread?	Feces of an infected animal
Are there any signs to look for?	Chronic, nonresponsive diarrhea, especially in kittens under six months of age

Note: Some cats may be carriers and show no signs. Humans with giardia have diarrhea, abdominal cramps, bloating, and sometimes fever and nausea.

How are they diagnosed?	The cysts may not be seen on a fecal examination. The best test is the *trichrome stain* of *fresh* feces.
What is the treatment?	*Metronidazole* or *furazolidone*
Can they be prevented?	Since it is spread by fecal contamination of food, water, and the environment, prompt disposal of cat litter and thorough cleaning of the sanitary pans are very important. Also, keep your cat indoors.

Giardia has been found in the water supply of some areas and has caused illness in humans and animals.

Roundworms
(Ascarids)

Who gets them?	Cats and dogs

Note: Young children (especially under age four) may become infected with the larvae (a rare disease, called *visceral larva migrans*), which can move to the eye, liver, lungs, or brain, causing blindness, pneumonia, or other problems.

What do they look like?	White, round worms, coiled into disks that may grow three to four inches long

They may appear in the stool or in vomit.

How are they spread?	The worm eggs are introduced by licking infected ground or eating infected insects or mice.

Kittens can be infected by larvae passed in the mother's milk.

What is their life cycle?	The larvae migrate through the liver, lungs, and trachea on their way to the small intestine.

About a month after being swallowed, they reach sexual maturity and start reproducing.

Are there any signs to look for?	Potbelly
	Thinness
	Dry hair coat
	Vomiting
	Diarrhea
	Coughing (as the larvae migrate through the lungs and breathing tubes)
	Note: Adult animals can develop an immunity and show no signs of infection.
How are they diagnosed?	Check successive stool samples.
What is the treatment?	Medication is necessary.
	Note: Medication kills only the adults in the intestine, not the larvae migrating through the body, so two or more wormings are necessary to kill all the parasites.
Can they be prevented?	Keep your cat's environment sanitary.
	Remove feces from your yard.
	Wash concrete runs often.
	Control mice and cockroaches.
	Keep your cat indoors.
	Have your veterinarian check at least two or three successive stool samples of a new pet and worm your pet, if necessary.

Strongyloides

Who gets them?	Cats (rarely) and dogs
	Note: This parasite can penetrate the skin of humans and cause intestinal problems.
What do they look like?	They are too small to be seen with the naked eye.
How are they spread?	The free-living parasites burrow through the skin.
What is their life cycle?	They migrate through the internal organs on their way to the small intestine.
	Strongyloides attach to the wall of the small intestine and, when sexually mature, shed larvae in the feces.

Are there any signs to look for?	Loss of appetite
	Pneumonia
	Bloody diarrhea
	Weight loss
	Weakness
	Skin infections can also occur from skin invasion.
	Note: Younger pets have the more serious signs.
How are they diagnosed?	Check successive stool samples for the larvae.
	Note: When getting a stool sample, be sure not to include any soil, which has free-living worms that look like strongyloides but don't cause disease.
What is the treatment?	A drug called *thiabendazole* is effective.
Can they be prevented?	Keep environment sanitary
	Remove feces from your yard
	Wash concrete runs often, with salt or sodium borate (borax), if possible, which may be helpful in killing the eggs and larvae.
	Note: These chemicals can damage or kill grass and other vegetation.

Tapeworms

Who gets them?	Cats and dogs
	Note: There have been a few reported cases of children getting tapeworms from swallowing infected fleas.
What do they look like?	Live tapeworm segments are off-white and flat and move in a back-and-forth motion.
	They may be seen attached to the hair around the anus, in the stool, or on bedding.
	The dried-out segments look like rice granules or sesame seeds.
How are they spread?	The larvae are introduced by eating infected insects (fleas) or mammals (rats and mice, rabbits, or raw fish, beef, or pork).
What is their life cycle?	The tapeworm matures in the intestine.

	When sexually mature, the segments, loaded with eggs, detach and pass out the anus.
Are there any signs to look for?	Weight loss
	Occasional diarrhea
How are they diagnosed?	Check successive stool samples.
	Note: Examination of a segment can reveal the *source* of infection.
Can they be prevented?	Control flea infestation.
	Keep your cat away from rodents.
	Do not feed your pet raw meat or fish.

TRAINING YOUR CAT

In all the time humans have spent on making a civilized world, the cat has been able to bridge the civilized, uncivilized, and "other" worlds with grace and beauty. The cat, some feel, lives among energy fields that we are just beginning to investigate. For instance, a cat's time sense, such as lying by the door in anticipation of its owner's arrival, its psi-trailing (the ability to find its way home for hundreds of miles), and its empathic responses, such as lying near you when you are depressed, are incredible phenomena.

If you can understand your cat's ancient behavior and language, it will make your life together richer and more pleasurable. In addition, it will make the process of training a happy experience. You may find books like *Understanding Your Cat,* by Dr. Michael W. Fox, and *Catlore* and *Catwatching,* by Desmond Morris, helpful in getting to know your cat.

Your Cat's Language

A cat uses facial expressions and its tail as well as its voice for communication. Therefore, be observant and watch for these indicators:

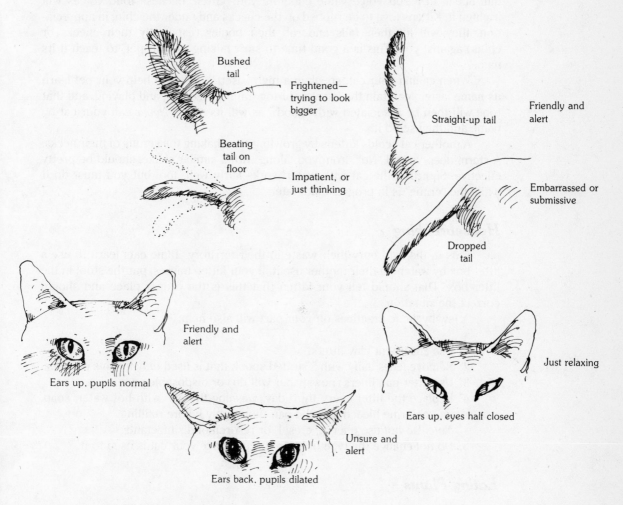

Bushed tail

Frightened—trying to look bigger

Beating tail on floor

Impatient, or just thinking

Straight-up tail

Friendly and alert

Embarrassed or submissive

Dropped tail

Friendly and alert

Ears up, pupils normal

Just relaxing

Ears up, eyes half closed

Unsure and alert

Ears back, pupils dilated

Recognizing these signs will give you an advantage.

In training, it's important to keep your cat's nature in mind. Specifically, a cat is more tuned to high-pitched sounds (remember the cockroach "talk") and to certain behaviors from its mother that should therefore be incorporated into your training procedures.

Touch is your cat's way of demonstrating and receiving love. Give your kittens a lot of cuddling and stroking, and let others do the same. Cats prefer to be stroked *with,* not against, the hair coat, by the way—start at the neck and stroke to the tail. Speak in a soft voice while cuddling your kitten, because loud voices will frighten it. Kittens love to be rubbed on the cheeks and under the chin; in appreciation, they will lift their tails and rub their bodies (especially their cheeks or chins) against you. This is a good time to start talking to your pet, to teach it its name.

When calling your cat, speak in a high falsetto. This will help your pet learn its name faster. Maintain the falsetto during training, feeding, and playing, and that tone will then be associated with "good," as will its name. *Never* call your cat by name and then scold it.

A mother cat scolds kittens by growling and shaking the scruffs of their necks. A stern, deep-voiced "No!" from you, along with a similar shake, should be pretty effective. Squirting the cat with water works fairly well, too, but you must do it while the "crime" is in progress, not later.

Housebreaking

Cats in the wild bury their waste in their territory. Tame cats learn to use a litter box by watching their mother use it. If your kitten misses, put the stool in the litter box. That should tell your kitten that this is the proper place and should correct the situation.

A few hygienic practices on *your* part will also help:

1. Use absorbent clay litters.
2. Remove feces daily with a slotted spoon that is used *only* for this purpose.
3. Use litter-pan liners (newspaper will do) or disposable pans.
4. Replace the litter every third day, washing the pan with hot water, soap, and chlorine bleach; dry the pan thoroughly before refilling.
   Note: Do *not* use phenol, cresol, or resorcinol disinfectants.
5. Do *not* change the type of litter you use once your cat is used to it.

Eating Plants

Wild cats eat both meat and vegetation, so the instinct to nibble on leaves is there. Eating your houseplants, however, can be dangerous to the cat as well as nerve-wracking to you. Fortunately, grass is a safe substitute. An indoor cat can be let out on a leash to eat its fill—as long as there is no weed killer around. Otherwise, plant some grass seed or wild bird seed in a low pot. And don't forget catnip!

"Hunting"—The Ultimate Game

Naturally, the hunting urge is very strong in even the youngest kitten. This instinct and its appropriate behaviors (stalking, crouching, chasing, pouncing, and killing) are reinforced in infancy by the kitten's mother. Both visual and auditory stimuli will excite your cat. A ball of noisy, crinkly, and shiny tinfoil makes an excellent toy for your kitten. If you attach a piece of string, you can flip the ball into the air, making a flying prey. Then watch your pet's graceful attempts to catch it! Remember to put toys like this safely out of reach when playtime is over: cats can swallow string and thread, causing serious intestinal obstructions.

Some other ideas for toys are empty boxes and paper bags, empty thread spools, and commercial catnip toys. Make sure that the toys do not shred and that they are too large to swallow.

GROOMING

Regular grooming of your cat consists of hair treatment, bathing, nail trimming, and ear cleaning.

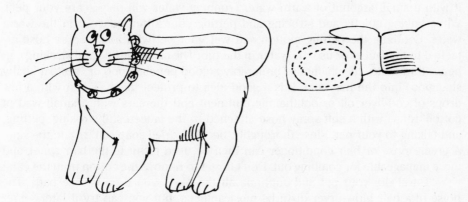

Hair Treatment

Different coats need different strokes: the combing or brushing needs vary according to the length and coat type. Longer coats need bristle, wire, or card brushes, and pet combs with rounded teeth that avoid irritating the skin. Brush short-haired cats weekly with a grooming glove. This will decrease the chance of hair balls (page 86).

Long-haired cats often have matted hair (from infrequent brushing and combing) behind their ears and under their legs. This should be pulled gently apart and combed out.

Many breeds of cats need regular clipping and stripping. You can learn to do it at home or find a professional groomer, who should be gentle and have a clean, odorless establishment. Ask your neighbors and friends for recommendations.

If you start the brushing and combing early (about twelve weeks of age) and stay gentle and patient, this will be an enjoyable and healthy experience for you and your pet.

Bathing

Cats need baths just as humans do, because tongues are *not* adequate cleansing tools. Since the oils come back in the hair and skin within twenty-four hours, bathing could be done as often as necessary, but once every month or two is adequate.

Start bathing your kitten at fourteen weeks of age (sooner if it gets very dirty—just avoid chilling it) so that it will be accustomed to regular baths. The *best* way to bathe is to make your pet comfortable and to make it a game. No noise and slow motions will ease your job. Before placing your pet in the sink or bathtub, fill it with a small amount of warm water (running water will only scare your pet). While talking quietly and stroking and petting your kitten, place it in the warm water. Continue the petting motion and wet your pet with a soft spray hose attached to the faucet or use the water in the tub. The same petting and stroking can be used to lather the shampoo (preferably a good pet shampoo or "no-tear" baby shampoo) into the hair coat. It is a good idea to protect the eyes first with a few drops of cod-liver oil or ophthalmic ointment and the ears with a small wad of cotton. Rinse with a soft spray hose attached to the faucet, still stroking, petting, and talking to your pet. Rinse thoroughly, because dried soap can irritate the skin. A creme rinse or hair conditioner can then be used to make the hair softer and more manageable for combing out. Don't forget to remove the cotton from the ears!

Towel dry your pet and continue all the ploys you used for the bath. The noise of a hair blow-dryer disturbs most animals, but you can try it later—*after* your pet is accustomed to baths. Make the whole experience pleasant and playful. A cat treat would definitely be in order after a successful bath. My cats are easy to bathe, although each needs special care. One has to walk around the water continually while we lather him; another must be rubbed on the cheek and talked to while being bathed.

If your cat doesn't take to bathing, try placing a window screen at an angle in the tub. The cat can cling to the screen, making bathing easier. Holding the cat by the scruff of the neck is also helpful.

Nail Trimming

Start trimming the nails at twelve weeks of age to accustom your pet to this important grooming practice. Long nails can get caught in carpeting, grow into the footpad, or cause your pet to stand improperly. The dewclaw (equivalent to the thumb) does not touch the ground and needs more frequent trimming.

You can trim your cat's claws with a "human" nail clipper, or with a Resco or a White nail clipper. Trim just in front of the pink area, or *dermis,* which contains nerves and blood vessels. If the nail is dark and the pink area cannot be seen easily, shine a bright penlight through the nail to see where the dermis begins. Otherwise, just trim the nail as it curves down.

A nail trimmed too short will bleed. Application of a styptic pencil or direct pressure with gauze or a clean cloth will stop the bleeding.

Ear Cleaning

Many owners neglect proper ear care and become aware of its importance only when their cat "smells funny." Then they look in the ear and discover an infection (see Ear Discharges, page 202).

The wax in the ears should be cleaned once a month (more often if your cat has a history of ear problems). Clean only that part of the ear canal that you can see; otherwise, you may damage the eardrum. Use a cotton swab soaked in mineral oil or alcohol. Wax protects the ear canal, so a small amount left behind is beneficial.

The hair in the ears should not be plucked unless there is so much hair that it impedes air circulation. If your doctor feels this is necessary, use your fingers to remove only the hairs that come out easily. Plucking can expose the hair follicle to bacteria, so be careful. Some doctors recommend an antibiotic ointment after plucking to prevent infection.

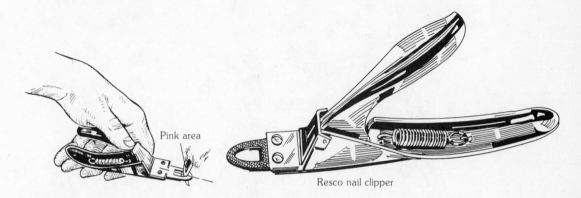

Pink area

Resco nail clipper

TRAVELING WITH YOUR CAT

Cats travel well if you plan ahead. If you start them traveling while they are still kittens, they'll grow into well-adjusted adult travelers.

First, get your pet accustomed to the carrier beforehand. (Sturdy carriers can be purchased at your veterinarian's office or at pet stores.) At home, play with your kitten and feed it in the carrier until your pet is used to being in it. Next, take frequent short trips in the car, with the kitten in the carrier. Soothing talk, loving strokes, and gentle playing will help give your pet confidence that nothing terrible will happen.

Be sure your cat always has an identification tag on its collar or harness when traveling. For extra assurance, your pet can also be safely tattooed with identification marks. In addition, your cat should be in good health, with all vaccinations up to date.

One more general rule: Try to make reservations at hotels or motels that allow pets.

By Car

Do *not* feed your cat for six hours before the trip, and if carsickness is usually a problem, remove access to drinking water two hours before departure. (If needed, Bonine or a medication prescribed by your veterinarian can be used to counteract motion sickness.) Always let your pet urinate and move its bowels before you start out. On long trips, plan for regularly scheduled exercise and water breaks. Feeding should be done at the final stop.

Take your cat's favorite food and bedding along. If feasible, take water from home as well, since the different mineral contents of water in new locations can give your pet diarrhea. Take along a litter box and litter, too.

Note: Do *not* keep a leash on your pet in the car. The leash can get caught on

door handles and other projections and cause serious injury. Do *not* leave your cat in the car in hot weather (see Heatstroke, page 134).

By Plane

When traveling by air, you should make preflight arrangements with the airline. Each company has different procedures, so call in advance to find out what you need to do. In any case, follow the feeding, water, and motion-sickness guidelines listed for travel by car. If traveling to a foreign country, you should contact the nation's nearest consular office to get any further instructions.

Generally, the airline will request (1) to see a health certificate for your cat; (2) that the cat travel in an approved carrier (available from the airline or from a pet store); (3) that both animal and carrier have proper identification tags, showing your name, address, and telephone number and your cat's name; and (4) that you check in at least one hour before departure. Some airlines will allow the carrier to travel with the passengers, under your seat.

BOARDING YOUR CAT

A good boarding cattery should be clean, relatively quiet, and well ventilated. The staff should treat boarders gently. Your veterinarian will be able to recommend a good place, if he or she does not have boarding facilities.

In general, you should call for reservations at least one or two weeks in advance (allow more time around holidays). Your cat must be healthy—all vaccinations up to date—and it should have an identification tag or tattoo. The staff should also ask for your veterinarian's name and telephone number and for a way to reach you in case of an emergency.

If, on your return, you find that your cat has diarrhea, you might request that the cattery feed your cat its regular, at-home diet the next time you board it there. Also, a mild tranquilizer might be helpful—but first discuss this with your veterinarian.

4

Going
to the
Veterinarian

Throughout your cat's life, veterinary attention—from vaccinations to laboratory tests, from radiology (X-rays) to surgery—will be needed. In this chapter, I discuss some of the encounters that your pet will have with the veterinarian. Guidelines are provided to help you choose a veterinarian to meet your cat's needs.

THE "G.P." AND SPECIALISTS

A local professional will probably be able to handle all your cat's health needs throughout its lifetime. This person will be your cat's family doctor or general practitioner, although sometimes he or she will have an advanced degree in a veterinary specialty, such as internal medicine. It takes four years of premedical or preveterinary education and four years of veterinary school for a person to become a veterinarian. Recently, internships and advanced degrees in over twenty specialties have become available to the twenty-six veterinary schools in the United States.

Solo Practice

The typical local veterinarian works very hard and is usually available when needed—like the physician in "the good old days"—although, of course, he or she takes time off for personal activities and veterinary meetings. However, if your local veterinarian is a "solo practitioner"—a veterinarian without partners—you may not always be able to see him or her. Upon reaching your veterinarian's answering service, you may be referred to another professional who is "on call" for the emergency group.

Group Practice

Veterinary group practice—a few doctors practicing in one building, or a central hospital with satellite outpatient clinics—has become a popular arrangement for veterinary care in the last few years. The sharing of night calls and weekend coverage, the reduction of office costs by shared expense, and the availability of consultation and of a more medically stimulating environment for the veterinarian all contribute to its increased popularity. The larger group practices may have a few specialists associated with them.

Referrals

Veterinary medicine is just like human medical care: sometimes the local doctor needs a specialist's expert help. If your local veterinarian feels that your cat has an especially serious or puzzling medical or surgical problem, you and your

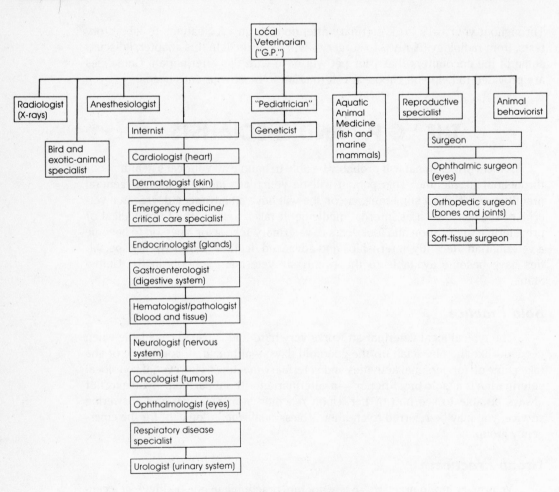

Veterinary Specialties

cat will be referred to a specialist in the area. Most specialists are found in group referral practices—for example, a cardiologist, an orthopedic surgeon, and a neurologist working together—or at veterinary schools. Most specialists complete three or more years of training after graduation from basic veterinary school. If your cat needs to see a specialist, your veterinarian will write a letter of introduction for you and provide a copy of your cat's complete medical and surgical history.

The types of veterinarians available for your cat's care can be grouped as shown on the accompanying page.

EVALUATING THE VETERINARIAN

Selecting a veterinarian deserves the same consideration as choosing your own family physician. Ask your neighbors, friends, local cat breeders and groomers, or even your own general practitioner for a recommendation.

The most important factor in the selection is your confidence in the veterinarian. To help you select and evaluate your veterinarian, consider the following points:

1. **Is the office clean and well equipped?**
2. **Is the doctor on an appointment system?**
    This reduces your waiting time considerably, makes the reception area less crowded, and makes your doctor less rushed.
3. **Can you take a tour of the clinic at a convenient time for the doctor or the staff?**
    Most veterinarians will be proud to show you their facilities.
4. **Does the veterinarian take an appropriate medical history?**
    All veterinarians have been trained to organize background information in a logical, concise, and accurate way. This is called "taking the medical history," and it is extremely important to good veterinary care. A history is divided into the major problem(s), the present illness, a review of the systems, and the medical history. Emergencies (such as injuries), simple problems, and well-pet exams (vaccinations) may not require many questions by the doctor.

The Major Medical Problem(s)

Before your visit, write down all the problems that your cat is having so that you won't leave out an important detail. The major medical problem should be expressed as the *title* of your story:

"Ralph has been urinating more than usual and drinking a lot more water."

67

Identify each problem without unnecessary details and let the doctor pick up from there.

The Current Illness

Your veterinarian will want to establish the progression of the current illness. This means that you must observe your pet very carefully at home so that you can provide all the relevant information. Again, organize your thoughts so that you can provide all the important facts:

"Three days ago, Ralph began drinking a lot more water. In fact, I had to fill a five-ounce bowl three times during the day. Now she [yes, I do see female pets with "male" names] is drinking six bowls of water daily. Her appetite is unsatisfied, though, and she keeps begging for food. She asks to go out to urinate every half hour, even during the night. She also began wetting on the kitchen floor. I didn't see any blood in the urine. I took her temperature when all this started, and it was normal."

Other information that may be useful is any medication that your pet took before and during the current illness. Bring the medications (or their names) with you. If X-rays or laboratory tests had been performed for past illnesses or for the current illness at another veterinarian's office, have the results phoned or sent to your current veterinarian. If your cat is allergic to any medication, make sure the doctor knows this.

The Review of Systems

Your veterinarian will ask you specific questions related to the skin, heart, lungs, stomach, intestines, urinary system, muscles, bones, nervous system, eyes, ears, nose, and throat. These questions will help your doctor determine which systems are involved in the current illness.

The Medical History

In many cases, previous illnesses, injuries, surgical procedures, or medications are related to the current illness. Be sure that you keep *complete* records. "She had little blue pills" does not tell your doctor anything, so be sure all medications are *named* when dispensed, and write the name in your cat's home health record. Dates of illnesses (both those treated and those not requiring a visit), dates of and reasons for hospitalization (with a *complete* list of all lab tests, X-rays, and drugs administered), and surgical procedures (including the anesthesia used) should be recorded. You would be surprised how many times this information is relevant to the illness. (See the sample home health chart, Your Cat's Records, at the front of this book.)

5. Does your veterinarian do a complete physical examination?

Your cat deserves a *complete* physical examination even during well-pet visits, such as for vaccinations. Many early problems can be picked up at these semi-annual or annual visits. A thorough medical history and physical examination will probably suggest the diagnosis to most competent veterinarians.

Each doctor has his or her own order in the physical exam. Some start by taking the temperature; others may examine the head or hair coat. A good physical exam can be very rewarding. Please do not talk to your doctor at this time unless a question is asked of you, since complete concentration is required.

The veterinarian will follow the same basic physical outlined in Chapter 2. Palpation will determine pain, size, shape, or consistency of the tissues and organs. Sharp taps with the fingers on the abdomen or chest wall will tell your doctor the hollowness or solidness of the body part examined. For example, an area that should sound hollow but sounds solid may indicate a mass that does not belong there. Using a stethoscope for *auscultation* allows the sounds of body functions (heartbeats, and lung and intestinal sounds) to be amplified. A visual inspection of your pet's gait, posture, hair coat, gum color, and other visible parts is also a feature of a complete physical. An *otoscope* will be used to look in your pet's ear canal; an *ophthalmoscope* will magnify the eye and its inner structure. An examination of your pet's retina (the back of the inner eye) is part of a thorough physical exam because the presence of certain systemic or local diseases can be discovered by checking the retina.

Certain diseases of the skin, mouth, ears, or internal organs have characteristic odors (for example, a sweet breath may indicate diabetes), so your veterinarian's sense of smell will also be brought into play. *Note:* A rectal exam is *not* a routine part of a cat's physical.

6. Does your veterinarian encourage you to ask questions?

All your questions should be answered in a clear, concise way and in language that you understand—not in medical jargon. Diagrams or simple line drawings are helpful, too.

7. Is your veterinarian gentle with your pet?

Sometimes a little calm talk or a few strokes are all that is needed to make the exam easier.

8. Does your veterinarian have any pets of his or her own?

9. Is your veterinarian careful with a biting or scratching pet?

Your veterinarian should explain that your pet will be gently but firmly restrained so that nobody gets hurt. Most doctors will have a veterinary assistant or use a towel or muzzle.

10. If you are a new pet owner, does the veterinarian give you litera-ture on good health maintenance and training, and does he or she explain it to you?

11. Will your doctor refer you to a veterinary specialist if needed?
    A good veterinarian knows his or her limitations.

12. Is your veterinarian a member of an emergency group, or is there another doctor on call when your veterinarian is not available?

13. Are all rates and fees explained to you?
    If your doctor does not take the initiative, be sure to ask what the fees will be for vaccinations, lab tests, radiographs, surgery, hospitalization, and treatment. Sometimes it is impossible to give you an exact figure, but high and low estimates are feasible, unless your pet's condition is so unpredictable that the treatment may change. If your pet will be hospi-talized for a few days, you could ask your doctor to keep you informed daily of your pet's accumulated tab. Knowing the daily financial picture, as well as the health picture, can be helpful. Many veterinary hospitals are nearly as well equipped as human hospitals, and the care is also equivalent—sometimes even better! Now there is national pet-care in-surance to take the sting out of paying those bills (see Pet Health Insur-ance, page 9).

14. Does your veterinarian use laboratory tests and radiographs (X-rays) discriminately, to confirm a diagnosis?
    Your doctor should explain to you in simple language why each test or series of radiographs is being done:

    "I'm going to catheterize Ralph—that is, place a sterile tube into the bladder. She'll be tranquilized, so it won't be uncomfortable. The urine collected will be checked to see if she has a bladder infection. A culture will be taken to isolate, identify, and count the bacteria. The appropriate antibiotic for killing the bacteria will be deter-mined by exposing the bacteria to various antibiotics in an anti-biotic sensitivity test. I'll take radiographs of the bladder to rule out bladder stones or bladder tumors."

15. Does your veterinarian hospitalize only for serious problems?
    Many pets' problems don't need hospitalization, and, in fact, pets seem to fare better in the home environment. Being treated by their owners, in close cooperation with the veterinarian, is comforting to pets. Most treatment and lab tests can be done on an outpatient basis. Besides, hospitalization can be expensive.

16. Is your veterinarian's hospital well equipped?
    This may be difficult for you to evaluate, but up-to-date veterinary hospitals do have modern radiograph equipment, surgical facilities, and laboratories.

If your answers are positive, you have a wonderful veterinarian. If you cannot give a positive answer to most of these questions, or if you are not comfortable with your veterinarian's diagnosis or treatment, seek another doctor or another opinion.

A happy veterinarian-owner relationship also requires a cooperative, aware, and concerned owner. You can have the best veterinarian in the whole world; but if you do not follow instructions, or do not understand the instructions, your relationship—and your pet's health—can deteriorate rapidly. Because you live intimately with your pet and know its habits and routine, you can often pick up very early and subtle changes that may go unnoticed by your doctor. The concerned and aware owner will use this book to best advantage by checking the Decision Charts and other chapters whenever necessary.

When a visit is necessary, bring paper and pen and write down (or have your veterinarian write down) *all* important instructions. Trying to remember everything is usually a waste of your time and money and may cause your pet's medical problem to persist, return, or get worse. In many cases, this situation leads to the denouncement, "That vet is no good!" If you have questions about a medication (why it was prescribed, what side effects it has, how long it should be given, etc.) or about a treatment or surgical procedure (why it is important, how it may help, what limitations it has, etc.), ask your veterinarian to *make* the information understandable. Lack of communication—not poor professional care—is the most frequent problem in the veterinarian-owner relationship.

For example, do *not* "double-up" on the medication at night if you were too rushed in the morning to give your cat its medicine. Excess doses can be worse than none at all. Let your doctor demonstrate the best method for administering the medicine if you feel that you will have problems. And do *not* stop the medication just because Ralph seems better. Follow your doctor's instructions. Stopping medication too early can cause an even more serious problem. If your pet experiences side effects from the medication, phone your veterinarian. A change in dosage or in the interval between doses—or a new drug altogether—may be recommended. If your doctor wants a follow-up exam, follow up!

One final word: Thank your doctor when he or she does a good job and is interested in your pet's health. Everyone, including your veterinarian, likes to be appreciated.

EMERGENCY CLINICS

Both the quality of emergency clinics and the range of services that they provide vary widely. You can use the guide Evaluating the Veterinarian (page 67) to help you get good emergency care. The best facility would be one that has a doctor with special training in emergency medicine/critical care, the on-call availability of specialists, and a support staff of veterinary technicians.

Owners who cannot find a veterinarian at night, or who do not know where else to go, are increasingly coming to emergency clinics. Thus, the typical facility is now filled with nonemergency cases. The various problems are all mixed together: trivial illnesses that could have been treated with the aid of this book, routine problems more easily and economically handled in your veterinarian's office, specialized problems that should have been dealt with at a time when hospital facilities were fully available, and true emergencies.

There are major disadvantages to using an emergency clinic as your sole medical contact. There is little or no provision for continued care. You may be seen by a different veterinarian each time. The emergency clinic doctor will attend to the chief problem but will seldom have sufficient time to deal with underlying problems. Special studies are arranged with difficulty. When a true emergency occurs, pets with less urgent problems are shunted aside. You cannot estimate how long you will have to wait. Because they support equipment required to handle true emergencies, emergency room fees are higher than those for standard office visits.

By using the procedures outlined in this book, you can use the well-equipped, well-run emergency clinic appropriately.

LABORATORY TESTS

Tests are often needed to confirm a diagnosis or to determine the best mode or the effectiveness of treatment. Some of the most common tests that may be requested are stool sample, skin scrapings (for skin parasites or fungus), complete blood count, blood chemistry, urinalysis, bacteriology, and tissue biopsy.

Stool Sample

Since cats like to examine their surroundings by licking both the ground and their peers' private areas, and since they walk barefooted and eat things they shouldn't (such as rodents), a stool sample should be checked once or twice a year. Most doctors will recommend that you bring it with you at vaccination time. A little is all that is needed, and it's okay if the sample has kitty litter on it. If you are gathering an outdoor sample, try not to include any soil, because it contains some worms (harmless "soil" strongyloides) that may confuse the examiner.

Skin Scrapings

Confirming a fungus infection (see Ringworm, page 190) involves transferring a skin scraping of the lesion to a container that contains "fungus food." Confirmation may take one to two weeks. As the fungus grows and uses the "food," the media in the container changes color from yellow to red. If there is a suspicion of a fungus infection, treatment will begin at the time of the scraping.

Complete Blood Count

If firefighters are in a smoking building, you assume that there is a fire and that it will soon be under control. If there are smoke and flames and no firefighters, the building may burn to the ground. Your cat's body has a remarkable "fire department" that consists of specialized cells, floating through miles and miles of blood vessels. Some carry oxygen (red blood cells), giving the blood its red color. Others can be mobilized to defend areas of tissue injury (from bacteria, trauma, chemicals, or heat, for instance) and inflammation by "eating up" the particles that invaded your pet's body (white blood cells). These "firefighters" consist of *erythrocytes* (red) and *leukocytes* (white). The white blood cells are divided into *neutrophils, lymphocytes, monocytes, eosinophils,* and *basophils.* The bone marrow produces all red blood cells and the neutrophils, eosinophils, and basophils. Lymphocytes and monocytes are produced in the lymph nodes, the spleen, the tonsils, and the lymphoid cells of the intestine.

The number and type of "firefighters" may help your doctor determine the type of disease present. For example, the panleukopenia virus can stop a cat's bone marrow from making neutrophils. The blood count for neutrophils and the total white blood count will then be very low. Therefore, a kitten or unvaccinated cat with the signs of panleukopenia (page 152), with a very low total white blood count, and with few neutrophils probably has the disease. The cat's "firefighters" are not available, and its "building" (its body) is in grave danger. Parasites that attack the red blood cells, such as *hemobartonella,* can be identified by staining a blood smear and then looking for the parasite in the red blood cells.

The neck (*jugular*) and front leg (*cephalic*) veins are the two most common sites for *venipuncture* (literally, puncturing the vein) to obtain blood for tests. Gentle restraint and a sterile needle and syringe are used, and most pets tolerate the procedure very well. However, fat or hyperactive cats and those with rolling or unusual veins may make it difficult to get a blood sample on the first try. Every veterinarian and technician has dealt with "problem veins." Reactions from the owner such as, "You mean you have to stick poor Ralph *again*?" will just add more stress to the job—so quiet, please!

Blood Chemistry

The health of your cat's body depends on the health of all its parts, and an unhealthy organ will eventually affect the other organs. In order to confirm a diagnosis or to monitor your pet's return to health or its setbacks, various enzymes and products of metabolism found in the blood should be measured. An increase or decrease in their levels can be used to identify and monitor the organ (or organs) that is sick, and the proper treatment can begin. A blood test alone is *not* a substitute for a physical examination, but veterinary recognition of the importance of blood chemistries has made this commonplace for good veterinary care.

Most veterinarians use a reliable commercial laboratory that provides accurate results at a reasonable price or perform tests in their own clinics, since the results from commercial labs may not be available for twenty-four to forty-eight hours. Pets that are very ill also need immediate results. Even so, the tests require time. In fact, your veterinarian may have to institute basic treatment before the final analysis is known. (In serious cases, life-support care, such as antibiotics, fluids, oxygen, and any other treatment thought necessary, *will* be started before all the test results have come back.) If you call the office the day after your cat has been examined to find out what exactly is wrong, your doctor still may not be sure of the complete picture.

The commercial laboratories may run as many as fifteen or twenty different tests on your cat's blood sample. This is called a *biochemical profile.* A few of the most common blood chemistries and other tests in a profile are briefly explained in the next section.

Biochemical Profile

Blood Sugar (Glucose)
Your doctor will run this test if diabetes is suspected (see pages 156 and 162).

Blood Urea Nitrogen (BUN) and Creatinine
Urea and creatinine are end-products of metabolism that are normally eliminated by the kidney in the urine. If the kidneys are not functioning properly, these products will be increased in the blood. This will not tell your doctor the *cause* of the kidney problem, but just that the kidneys are involved. Special radiographs, urinalysis, and even a biopsy may be needed to define the disease process.

Amylase and Lipase
More cases of acute *pancreatitis* (inflammation of the pancreas) are being diagnosed and treated properly, thanks to the availability of these tests. If your pet has abdominal pain and sudden and severe vomiting and is very weak and depressed, these tests may be beneficial. The cells of an inflamed pancreas release the amylase and lipase enzymes into the bloodstream, so their number is markedly elevated.

Liver Profile Tests
The liver has so many functions that to see how it is functioning overall, a liver profile has to be done. The blood tests include *bilirubin, protein, SGPT, SGOT, cholesterol,* and *alkaline phosphatase.* Sometimes this still is not enough to tell

your doctor the *cause* of the liver problem, so other tests, such as a liver biopsy, may be necessary.

Feline T-Lymphocytic Virus Test (FTLV)

The feline T-lymphocytic virus (FTLV), discovered in 1987, is similar to the human AIDS virus and attacks the cat's immune system. A simple blood test is available and is recommended whenever a cat shows signs of chronic infection (mouth sores, weight loss, anemia, chronic intermittent diarrhea, skin sores, respiratory infection, or abortion).

Test a "new cat" *before* bringing it into a home that has established FTLV-free cats.

Feline Leukemia Virus Test

See page 47.

Thyroid Test

An important "new" disease in cats over seven years of age is hyperthyroidism. It is caused by a benign growth of the thyroid gland, which makes the "body engine" go faster. The most common signs are weight loss, increased appetite, hyperactivity, rapid heart rate (over 200 beats per minute at rest), increased water intake and urination, and occasional vomiting. Less common signs are diarrhea, panting, and muscle weakness.

A simple blood test for thyroid hormone (T_4) is used for diagnosis of this problem. The enlarged thyroid glands can usually be felt in the neck area.

Urinalysis

This is an extremely helpful test for diagnosing diseases of the urinary tract and other problems, such as *diabetes mellitus* and liver disease. Your doctor will check to see if your pet is concentrating its urine (specific gravity) and will study the chemical analysis for such abnormalities as sugar in the urine, which may indicate diabetes or a kidney defect. Microscopic examination of the urine can be used to spot cells that may indicate inflammation, infection, or degeneration anywhere along the urinary tract.

Bacteriology

Zone of inhibition

Bacterial infections are very common in bite-wounds (*abscesses*) and in problems involving the ear, eye, and urinary tract. Your doctor may suggest culture and sensitivity tests, which involve transferring a small amount of the infected material to a container filled with "food" in which the bacteria can flourish. Small paper disks, each containing a different antibiotic, are placed in the container at even intervals. The antibiotics that are effective against the bacteria will produce *zones of inhibition*—areas around the disks where no bacteria will grow. The bacteria will also be identified by their growth pattern and microscopic features. Using a general antibiotic may cure the infection, but performing culture and sensitivity tests—especially in chronic infections—is better practice and may be cheaper in the long run.

Tissue Biopsy

Removing a tissue section for microscopic examination is often an excellent way to make a proper diagnosis, determine if the disease process can be reversed, and suggest the best therapy. Of course, biopsy of the internal organs is more difficult and has more risks than biopsy of the skin, but in skilled hands and with the proper instruments, tissue can be studied from the kidney, liver, or any other organ. Often, a local anesthetic and the appropriate biopsy instrument are all that is needed to obtain the sample. Biopsy is a good tool for determining the chance for your cat's recovery and the type and cost of the best therapy.

Radiographs (X-rays)

Radiographs have become another important tool for diagnosis. The radiographic equipment in many veterinary hospitals is equivalent to that in human hospitals—and just as expensive. Modern X-ray equipment provides excellent "pictures" of the bones and internal organs and the spaces between them. The procedure of taking X-rays is painless and relatively harmless, but your pet may be sedated because any movement may cause blurring. Two or more views are needed to get a three-dimensional "picture" of the area under investigation.

To get the "picture," X-rays are directed through your cat's body. They travel very rapidly and then penetrate a plate containing film. X-rays pass through air easily, but solid masses, such as internal organs and bones, will stop some of them. Those that hit the film turn it black when it is developed. The areas on the film not touched by the rays remain white. So a chest X-ray has white areas (such as the heart, backbones, and ribs) and black areas (lung tissue, containing air). Your doctor will study the X-rays under a bright light, looking for changes in the normal shape, size, and density of the organs.

Electrocardiogram

An electrocardiogram (ECG) is a graphic measure of the electrical activity of the heart. It is an inexpensive, safe, and painless technique for determining if your pet has heart disease. It is also helpful for diagnosing and monitoring treatments of illnesses not originating in the heart, such as urinary obstructions and Addison's disease. To obtain the ECG, your pet is placed on its right side, and *leads* are attached to its legs and body using clips. Cats rarely need to be sedated. The various leads are recorded, and the heart rate and rhythm and changes in the heart size are evaluated.

Bone Marrow Aspiration or Biopsy

If the blood-forming cells need to be studied, bone marrow may be aspirated from the tibia (leg bone) or ilium (hip bone). Bone biopsies may be collected under local or general anesthesia.

NONINVASIVE DIAGNOSTIC TECHNIQUES

Some newer diagnostic aids that are noninvasive or minimally invasive are being used by veterinarians in private practice or referral centers. Among these procedures are fiberoptic endoscopy, ultrasound imaging, computerized axial tomography (CAT) scan, and magnetic resonance imaging (MRI).

Fiberoptic Endoscopy

The endoscope allows the veterinarian to examine your cat's internal structures and organs. Endoscopy is a fast, safe diagnostic procedure that allows direct observation.

A tube attached to a fiberoptic light source and lenses for magnification is inserted into the body. Small tweezers (forceps) can be attached to the end of the tube for taking tissue specimens for microscopic study and cultures.

Your doctor may find the endoscope helpful for detection of a suspected foreign body (hair ball, bone) in the esophagus, stomach, or colon; direct examination of the upper or lower gastrointestinal tract or of the breathing tubes (trachea and bronchi); reproductive evaluation by direct examination of the ovaries, vagina, and uterus.

A sedative or general anesthesia is required. The name of the specific procedure indicates what will be viewed with the scope: arthroscopy (joints), bronchoscopy (trachea and bronchi), colonoscopy (colon), cystoscopy (bladder, urethra, and ureters), gastroscopy (esophagus, stomach, and duodenum—first part of the small intestine), laparoscopy (the outer surface of the abdominal organs, such as the ovaries for infertility evaluation).

Ultrasound Imaging

Ultrasound, which does not use radiation to show the internal organs, is very safe. The equipment is very expensive, however, and a doctor must be specially trained to interpret the pictures. This specialist might be a radiologist or cardiologist (for ultrasound of the heart). Many times these specialists work at large referral centers or veterinary schools.

In ultrasound, high-speed sound waves (more than 20,000 per second) are transmitted from the tip of a device called a transducer. This tip also houses a microphone. The sound waves bounce off various organs differently, and these reflected waves are displayed on a televisionlike oscilloscope. Sedation may not be necessary, because ultrasound is a painless procedure. A lubricant and the transducer are placed on a shaved area of the skin over the area to be examined.

Ultrasound is extremely helpful in diagnosing and monitoring a pet with cardiomyopathy and other heart diseases. This procedure is called an *echocardiogram*. Ultrasound is also very helpful in viewing the gall bladder, liver, spleen, kidney, lymph nodes, pancreas, uterus, ovaries, and the chest. Sometimes during biopsies doctors use ultrasound to view the internal organs while directing the needle or forceps to the site. Evaluating the fetuses during pregnancy is another very useful procedure.

Computerized Axial Tomography (CAT) Scan

The limited accessibility and high cost of CAT-scan systems have restricted their use to veterinary medical schools and to those hospitals that will scan animals.

In CAT scans, a camera takes hundreds of X-ray pictures from various angles. These images are fed into a computer and analyzed.

CAT scans are especially useful in localizing and defining the size and extent of brain tumors (many are treatable, by the way, with surgery, radiation therapy, chemotherapy, or immunotherapy).

Magnetic Resonance Imaging (MRI)

Magnetic resonance imaging (MRI) does not use radiation. Instead, the patient is placed inside a giant hollow magnet. The magnet aligns the hydrogen atoms in the body tissue being studied (like a child's magnet aligns pins). A radio signal similar to that used by an FM radio "jiggles" and energizes the atoms. The radio signal is stopped, and the atoms realign themselves at different speeds. A computer measures this process and converts it into an almost realistic picture. MRI is particularly useful in getting images of the brain and locating abnormalities.

The equipment costs millions of dollars, so this will not be on your local veterinarian's shopping list for a while. However, large university veterinary schools may have access to the medical center's MRI.

SOME IMPORTANT NEW DISEASES

You may save your cat's life by reading this section.

Hyperthyroidism

This disease, caused by a malfunction of the thyroid gland, is becoming more common in cats over seven years of age. A thyroid blood test is necessary for diagnosis (see page 75).

Cardiomyopathy

There are two forms of cardiomyopathy: dilated (the heart wall becomes thin) and hypertrophic (the heart wall thickens). The former has recently been linked to some cats' need for larger amounts of taurine (an amino acid) or inefficient way of absorbing this nutrient from the gastrointestinal tract. The heart-muscle changes have been reversed by twice daily giving 250 milligrams of taurine, which is available in health-food stores. Recently, I treated a cat that had a very thin heart muscle, as detected with ultrasound (echocardiography). The cat dramatically improved on taurine, and two months later a follow-up echocardiogram showed a normal heart muscle.

The clinical signs of dilated cardiomyopathy are lethargy, decreased appetite, and breathing difficulties. The cat with the hypertrophic form may display fainting, seizures, coughing, breathing difficulties, lethargy, or strokelike signs—inability to move the back legs, for example.

An echocardiogram (ultrasound) is the best procedure for diagnosing and differentiating the cardiomyopathies, because an electrocardiogram may appear normal. All cats over seven years of age should be checked for hyperthyroidism.

To help prevent the dilated form, always use a well-known cat food that is supplemented with taurine. *Do not use generic cat foods!*

Heartworm Disease

See page 49.

Hypokalemic Polymyopathy Syndrome

A sudden onset of muscle weakness, an inability to lift the head, a reluctance or inability to stand or walk, and a crouched posture may occur in cats that develop a low blood potassium. Such problems characterize hypokalemic polymyopathy syndrome, commonly known as general muscle disease. If treated promptly with potassium (blood potassium must be monitored), affected cats make a full, remarkable recovery.

It seems that a small percentage of cats excrete excessive amounts of potassium in the urine and are susceptible to this syndrome.

Cat-food manufacturers, especially those producing the low-magnesium diets, are now supplementing their products with extra potassium.

Feline Liver Disease

The signs of feline liver disease are common to many other diseases: appetite loss, vomiting, diarrhea, fever, weight loss, dehydration, seizures, or, occasionally, increased water intake and urination.

Your doctor will examine the back of your cat's eyes, because feline infections such as peritonitis and toxoplasmosis may affect the eyes as well as the liver. Blood tests, including the feline leukemia and FTLV tests, coagulation (blood-clotting) studies, urinalysis, and possibly an ultrasound procedure will be done. A liver biopsy is necessary in most cases to find out the *type* of liver disease, to give you a prognosis (a sense of how well your cat will do), and to indicate what the appropriate medication will be.

Feline liver disease is being recognized more frequently. It may be either primary—involving only the liver—or secondary—associated with other *systemic* diseases such as hyperthyroidism (page 75), diabetes mellitus, heart failure, infections, or toxins.

Feline T-Lymphocytic Virus (FTLV)

As noted earlier, FTLV, an AIDS-like virus, was discovered in cats in 1987. It suppresses the immune system and results in an increased susceptibility to a wide variety of infections.

What are the clinical signs? An AIDS-like syndrome is the most common form of the disease: progressively worsening gum inflammation, periodontal disease, sinus infections, weight loss, anemia, chronic intermittent diarrhea, neurologic signs, and chronic poor healing or recurrent infections of the skin and ears. The "pre-AIDS" signs—enlarged lymph nodes, persistent low-grade fever, and a very low white count—usually precede the other clinical signs.

I recommend that you have any new cat tested for FTLV and for the feline leukemia virus *before* you bring it home. Also, if you already have one or more cats, have each one tested *before* you bring a new cat home. The diagnosis involves a blood test. FTLV is highly infectious to cats but is spread only by intimate and prolonged contact.

FTLV-positive cats that do not show any signs of illness (asymptomatic) have a good chance at survival as long as they remain asymptomatic. Keep the FTLV-positive cat indoors so that the virus will not be spread to other cats.

It is hoped that a vaccine will be available soon.

Because this virus was discovered so recently, it is still, as of this writing, known by several names: the feline T-lymphotropic lentivirus, the AIDS-like virus, and "feline AIDS" are some ways your veterinarian may refer to it.

Note: FTLV is *not* related to AIDS. There is no way for a human to pick up AIDS or FTLV from a cat.

Your Cat's Home Pharmacy

Home medical care of your cat's minor illnesses and injuries may require medication—*sometimes.* Sometimes, because many of your pet's medical problems, such as a minor abrasion, a sprain, or occasional vomiting or diarrhea, resolve themselves without medication. Feline bodies have a remarkable capability for healing themselves, but we are a drug-oriented society: we feel that an injection of this or a tablet of that will do the job. In reality, a little time and knowledge are often all that is needed, and they may well be the most effective (and the cheapest!) treatment. This fact should not be abused, however. If the Decision Charts recommend seeing a veterinarian or trying drug or nondrug treatments, such as cleaning and soaking a wound or encouraging fluid intake, follow the instructions.

Veterinarians are occasionally confronted with an injury or minor illness that has healed itself even when the owner did not use the medication or follow the instructions. The owner calls a week later to say that the ear infection is completely healed or the diarrhea has disappeared. This does *not* mean that you should not follow your doctor's instructions!

BASIC NECESSITIES

The following is a list of medications that are good to have on hand, as well as the ailments they treat. Items in bold print are essentials; the other preparations are not so vital. *Remember:* Keep all medicines out of the reach of children.

The when and why of using medications, including dosage and side effects, are discussed later.

Constipation

Laxatives should *not* be used on a regular basis unless recommended by your veterinarian. Safe laxatives are made from *psyllium* (see below). Alternative laxatives are milk of magnesia or mineral oil. If an enema is needed, use warm water (best) or a Fleet enema.

Bulk Laxatives

Products such as Metamucil and Mucilose are refined from the psyllium seed. The substance from this seed is not absorbed by the digestive tract; it only passes through. Thus, it is a natural product and one with essentially no contraindications and no side effects. It provides bulk by drawing water into the stool. *Note:* If you think your cat has an intestinal obstruction or impacted feces, do *not* use a laxative.

Dosage:
½ to 1 teaspoon mixed in the food once or twice daily. Be sure to mix water into the food and supply drinking water at all times.

Medication	Ailment
*Milk of magnesia Bulk laxatives Mineral oil Fleet enema	Constipation
Guaifenesin (glyceryl guaiacolate)	Coughs
Kaopectate	Diarrhea
Antibiotic ophthalmic ointments	Eye irritations
Tinactin	Fungus
Petroleum jelly Commercial hair-ball medicine	Hair balls
*Bonine	Motion sickness
nothing safe	Pain and fever

Hydrogen peroxide (3 percent)
Activated charcoal
Milk of magnesia
	Poisoning
	  • To induce vomiting
	  • To absorb poison
	  • To speed passage through
	    the digestive tract

A and D Ointment **Antibiotic ointment** Betadine Domeboro solution **Hydrogen peroxide (3 percent)**	Skin irritations
Tomato juice Cranberry juice Vitamin C	Urinary infections
Kaopectate *Maalox *Mylanta **Pepto-Bismol**	Vomiting and stomach upsets

*Do *not* give to kittens without your veterinarian's approval.

Milk of Magnesia

The active ingredient, *magnesium,* causes fluid to be retained within the bowel and in the feces. It is also helpful in speeding passage of any poisons through the digestive tract.

Dosage:
1 teaspoon per five pounds of body weight. (One dose should do the job.)

Side Effects:

Milk of magnesia is nonabsorbable, but it does contain magnesium and some salt and should *not* be used if your pet has kidney or heart disease.

Mineral Oil

This is the cheapest and most effective laxative, but it can be dangerous if administered improperly or given for a long period of time. Mineral oil should *never* be given directly in the mouth because it is bland and may enter the breathing tubes and lungs before your pet can cough. Mineral oil in the lungs will cause a severe pneumonia. Instead, mix it in the food. If mineral oil is given for a long period of time, it can cause deficiencies of the fat soluble vitamins, A, D, E, and K.

Dosage:

1 teaspoon per ten pounds of body weight, mixed in the food once daily, for two days at the maximum.

Side Effects:

Pneumonia or vitamin deficiency if administered improperly.

Fleet Enema

If your pet has *obstipation* (impacted or hard feces in the lower intestine and rectum), you should see your doctor. If you must give the enema, use the Fleet pediatric enema. This may lubricate and soften the hard feces (see Constipation, page 223). Use only the mineral oil enema, not the phosphate type.

Dosage:

The lubricated nozzle is inserted into the rectum, and one ounce of the solution is gently administered. Another enema can be given half an hour later, if necessary.

Side Effects:

Note: Severe complications can result if used when fever, nausea, vomiting, or abdominal pain is present. Do *not* use in cats that are dehydrated or have known kidney disease.

Coughs

The only safe cough medicine I recommend for use without veterinary consultation is an expectorant. The expectorant liquefies the secretions and allows the body's defenses to get rid of the bad material. Cough suppressants should *not* be used without your doctor's advice, because they contain such narcotics as codeine. Over-the-counter cough suppressants may contain dextromethorphan, a close chemical relative.

Glyceryl Guaiacolate (guaifenesin)

If your cat has a dry, hacking cough, a lubricant soothes the inflamed area. If your pet has a cough with mucus, glyceryl guaiacolate liquefies the mucus secretions so that they may be coughed free. It does not suppress the cough reflex, but rather encourages the natural defense mechanisms of the body.

Read the label: Do *not* use Robitussin or 2-G with the additives PE (for the decongestant *phenylephrine*), CF or DM (for the cough suppressant *dextromethorphan*), or AC (for codeine). Use Robitussin or 2-G with only glyceryl guaiacolate (guaifenesin) in 3.5 percent alcohol.

Dosage:
¼ teaspoon every four hours.

Side Effects:
No serious side effects, but check with your doctor if the cough persists or the Decision Chart so indicates.

Diarrhea

Kaopectate is a very safe medication for cats. Do *not* use paregoric—it may be toxic to your cat. See your veterinarian if diarrhea persists or if the Decision Chart so indicates.

Kaopectate

Kaopectate contains *kaolin* and *pectin,* which coat the intestinal tract and help to form a solid stool.

Dosage:
2 teaspoons per ten pounds of body weight every four hours.

Eye Irritations

For short-term use, apply an ophthalmic ointment such as Neosporin or Neopolycin to your cat's eye three or four times daily. These ointments contain three antibiotics: *polymyxin, bacitracin,* and *neomycin.*

Fungus

Tinactin

If your pet has only one ringworm lesion, you can use this cream. It is available over the counter in drugstores.

Dosage:

Apply the cream to the skin lesion with a Q-tip twice daily. *Note:* Do *not* touch the lesion with your finger.

Side Effects:

If the skin becomes more irritated, stop the medication and see your veterinarian. *Note:* Do *not* get the medication in the eye.

Hair Balls

Brushing and combing your cat frequently will help prevent hair balls (swallowed hair from self-grooming). If your cat still vomits hair balls, a lubricant such as white petroleum jelly may help. A commercial hair-ball medicine (Kat-a-lax, Laxatone) from your veterinarian or pet store can also be used.

White Petroleum Jelly

Dosage:

½ teaspoon per ten pounds of body weight. Apply it to the cat's nose and it will be licked off. This can be given once weekly. The jelly melts in the stomach to an oil that lubricates the hair ball for easier passage in your cat's bowels.

Side Effects:

Keep in mind that white petroleum jelly has the potential to decrease the absorption of fat soluble vitamins (A, D, E, and K) if given in large doses or for a prolonged time.

Motion Sickness

First, try all the preparations for preventing motion sickness given on page 62.

Bonine

If you are unsuccessful, an antihistamine called Bonine (*meclizine hydrochloride*) can be used. It is effective against the apprehension, salivation, and vomiting or diarrhea that some pets experience when traveling. If Bonine is not successful

in eliminating the motion sickness, your veterinarian can provide you with tranquilizers or antihistamines that are effective.

Dosage:
12.5 milligrams given on an empty stomach one hour before traveling. The
dose can be repeated in twenty-four hours.

Side Effects:
Your pet may experience drowsiness. *Note:* Do *not* give Bonine to a pregnant
cat—it may cause birth defects.

Pain and Fever

Do *not* give aspirin or Tylenol to cats without your veterinarian's recommendation. Cats have problems detoxifying and excreting these substances.

Poisoning

To Induce Vomiting: Hydrogen Peroxide

If your cat swallows a poison that can be expelled by vomiting, a 3 percent
solution of hydrogen peroxide works very well. Do *not* induce vomiting if the poison swallowed is a petroleum-based compound or a strong acid or strong alkali
(see Swallowed Poisons, page 136). Be sure that the hydrogen peroxide purchased
is not a higher strength (such as for bleaching hair).

Dosage:
1 teaspoon every ten minutes until your cat vomits. You can repeat this two
or three times, if necessary. If this treatment is unsuccessful, 1 or 2 teaspoons of
salt or a mustard-and-warm-water solution put on the back of the tongue should
induce vomiting.

To Absorb Poison: Activated Charcoal

After vomiting, a few teaspoons of activated charcoal mixed in milk or water
can be given to absorb the poison if the specific antidote is not known. Activated
charcoal can be purchased in drugstores.

To Speed Passage Through the Digestive Tract: Milk of Magnesia
Dosage:
1 teaspoon per five pounds of body weight once daily.

Skin Irritations

Sterilizing Agents and Antiseptics

Soap and water is the best way to clean a wound. Hydrogen peroxide (3 percent strength) foams and cleanses wounds very well, and is inexpensive. Betadine, a nonstinging iodine preparation, kills germs and is a good agent to use on the skin, but it is expensive. To soothe the skin temporarily, calamine lotion can be applied, but it loses its effectiveness when it dries out. It must be washed off and reapplied frequently. *Note:* Do *not* get it in the eyes.

Dosage:
Cleanse the wounds three times daily. Trim the hair around the wound, if necessary.

Domeboro Solution

This is a soothing wet dressing for relief of skin inflammation. It has antiseptic properties and reduces itching.

Dosage:
Dissolve one teaspoon or tablet in a pint of warm water. Bathe or apply wet dressings of the solution to the affected skin for fifteen minutes. You can repeat this three or four times daily.

Ointments

A and D Ointment soothes irritated skin and can be applied three or four times daily to affected areas. The ointments containing antibiotics (Neosporin, Neopolycin, and Mycitracin) can be applied to affected skin three times daily.

Urinary Infections

Acidifiers help control bacterial infections of the lower urinary tract and help prevent a recurrence of crystal or stone formation in the tract.

Vitamin C and Juices

Tomato juice and cranberry juice are excellent urinary acidifiers—if your pet will drink them. You can measure their effectiveness by testing urine with litmus paper. If blue litmus paper turns red, the urine is acidic.

Dosage:

¼ to 1 cup of cranberry juice or tomato juice per day should be adequate. 100 milligrams of vitamin C three times daily.

Vomiting and Stomach Upsets

Kaopectate, Maalox, Mylanta, Pepto-Bismol

All of these products soothe the stomach lining.

Dosage:

2 teaspoons of Kaopectate per ten pounds of body weight every four hours. ½ teaspoon of Maalox or Mylanta per ten pounds of body weight very eight hours. ½ teaspoon of Pepto-Bismol per ten pounds of body weight every four hours.

Side Effects:

Maalox and Mylanta may loosen the stools a little. If your pet has a history of heart or kidney disease, consult your veterinarian before using either of these.

THE FIRST AID KIT

This is a *must*. Keep the kit in a convenient location but out of the reach of small children. A fishing-tackle box works very well, by the way.

Adhesive tape, 1 inch wide

Gauze bandages, 1-inch rolls

Absorbent cotton

Sterile gauze pads, 3 × 3 inches

Cotton-tipped swabs (Q-tips)

Rubbing alcohol

Rectal thermometer

Teaspoon

Tweezers

Sharp scissors with rounded ends

Medications (those in bold print on page 83 are the basic requirements)

GIVING PILLS TO YOUR CAT

Caution: Giving pills to cats with neck pain or to vicious cats can be dangerous.

- Place the palm of your hand over your cat's muzzle. With the thumb on one side and your fingers on the other, press hard against and under the upper teeth.
- Tilt the head up slightly. This usually causes the lower jaw to relax and drop a little.
- Using the middle finger of your other hand, push the lower jaw open.
- With your thumb and index finger, place the pill in the center of the tongue near its base.
- Close the mouth quickly and tap your pet's nose with your finger. This will cause the cat to lick and then swallow.
- Fractious cats can be held by the back of the neck. Open the lower jaw with a pencil (always use the eraser end). Toss the pill in the back of the throat and gently tap it down with the pencil.

A plastic pill gun (purchased from your veterinarian or pet shop) is very handy and can save your fingers from getting hung up on your cat's teeth. A flexible tip holds the tablet or capsule within the barrel until deposited in your cat's mouth. A sharp push on the barrel delivers the pill to the back of the throat.

GIVING LIQUIDS TO YOUR CAT

- Hold your cat's head at a 45° angle.
- Make a pouch in the corner of the lip fold by pulling the cheek outward.
- Using a spoon or eye dropper, slowly pour the liquid into the pouch.
- If your cat does not swallow the liquid automatically, jiggle the pouch slightly or tap on the nose with your finger; this will cause it to swallow. Be sure to keep the head at a 45° angle until the liquid is swallowed.

Note: Placing your cat in the bathtub will help avert a mess.

PART II

Caring for Your Cat

HOW TO USE THIS SECTION

This section describes most of the common problems of cats, many of which can be treated at home, without visiting your veterinarian. The system of Decision Charts should help you become confident in diagnosing the problem and using the right treatment for happy results. Prevention is also discussed. Remember the old adage: "An ounce of prevention is worth a pound of cure."

Finding the Right Decision Chart

If you suspect an illness, determine the chief sign—for example, coughing—and look it up in the contents or in the index. Then turn to the correct page. If your cat has more than one problem simultaneously, you may have to use more than one Decision Chart. For instance, if your pet has a cough and runny eyes, check the chart for each problem. If one recommends home treatment and the other advises a visit to your veterinarian, *see your doctor.*

Using the Decision Chart

It is very important to read all the general information on the particular problem first. In many cases, the chart may advise you to see the doctor immediately, but emergency treatment may also be needed before you get to the doctor's office. After reading the information, start at the top of the Decision Chart (do *not* skip around) and answer each question.

If home treatment is indicated, follow all instructions exactly, or the treatment will not be effective. If your cat is not improving, even with good care, *see your veterinarian.*

If the chart indicates veterinary consultation, it does not necessarily mean that the illness is serious. It may mean that more vigorous treatment or further examination and lab tests are needed. "See veterinarian NOW" means *immediate attention is needed.* "See veterinarian within 24 hours" is self-explanatory. "Make appointment with veterinarian" means a visit should be made in the next few days.

The procedures discussed on the next few pages will give you step-by-step guidance on how to handle any emergency. Read the entire section and practice the procedures to become familiar with them *before* you have to use them. Your veterinarian will be happy to help you with any you don't fully understand. I hope you'll never have to use these procedures, but your doctor will be very proud of you for being a prepared and helpful partner if an emergency does occur.

This chapter and Chapter 7, Accidents and Injuries, will help you recognize an emergency situation. Your job is to preserve your cat's life and to prevent further injury until veterinary care is available. *Note:* There are some other emergencies listed in Chapter 8, Common Problems and Diseases, so scan that chapter as well and become familiar with those situations. In addition, certain problems require emergency treatment from you before going to the doctor's office, so read the descriptive sections carefully *before* an emergency develops.

CHAPTER
6

Emergency Procedures

APPROACHING AN INJURED CAT

The friendliest animal, if injured, may try to bite because of fear and pain, so approach the cat slowly, talking in a quiet and reassuring voice. Call the cat by name, if you know it. Stop your approach when you are about a foot from the animal. Bend down slowly to the pet's level, still talking calmly. Gradually extend your closed hand, knuckles upward, toward the cat. If no aggression is seen, pet it first with your closed hand. If the animal displays aggression, try reassuring talk for a minute longer. If this is not successful, use restraint (see below).

Next, you should check for vital signs. Be sure the airway is clear and the cat is breathing. If not, give artificial respiration (page 98). Check the heartbeat and pulse (page 17), control any bleeding (page 124), look for signs of poisoning (page 136), treat for shock (page 100), and check for fractures (page 102).

RESTRAINING AN INJURED CAT

Remember: The least restraint is the best restraint. Cats fight leashes and may choke to death. A blanket or coat placed over the cat is very safe as long as the animal's breathing is not labored; this works well also with unfriendly cats. Holding the cat by the back of the neck for control is also effective.

Note: Do *not* muzzle a cat. It can be very difficult to do, and it can be dangerous to you and to the cat. Besides, it usually is not necessary.

GIVING ARTIFICIAL RESPIRATION

If there are signs of a breathing problem, such as blue gums, labored breathing, or a staring expression, or if the cat has collapsed, you will need to administer artificial respiration. Before beginning, however, check the pulse (page 17). If you cannot feel it, apply cardiopulmonary resuscitation (next page).

Place the cat on its belly or side. If there is no back or neck injury, extend the head and open the pet's mouth to look for obstructions. Clean the mouth of any blood or mucus with your fingers, then close it. Recheck the pulse.

Now: Inhale; put your mouth over the cat's muzzle, forming an airtight seal; exhale. Remove your mouth and allow the cat's chest to deflate. Repeat this process ten to fifteen times per minute, and continue it until you arrive at the veterinarian's office or veterinary hospital. Be sure to recheck the pulse often while performing artificial respiration. Treat also for shock (page 100).

GIVING CARDIOPULMONARY RESUSCITATION

If your cat is not breathing and has no heartbeat and pulse, you have an immediate life-threatening situation. If brain tissue is deprived of oxygen for more than four or five minutes, permanent damage or death will occur. Administering cardiopulmonary resuscitation (CPR) may keep the brain tissue from dying. A combination of heart massage and artificial respiration, CPR forces blood out of the heart by simulating the heart's pumping action. To be effective, it must be done rhythmically and in combination with artificial respiration. Veterinary aid is needed quickly as well, so send someone for help while you begin the treatment.

In human medicine, heart attacks (*myocardial infarctions*), choking, and strokes are common CPR emergencies. These are rare in veterinary medicine, however, so there are only a few instances where CPR is needed. Electrocution, near-drowning, and collapse from congestive heart failure may require CPR. If your cat is unconscious, has no pulse or heartbeat, or is gasping for breath, or if its pupils are dilating, you need to administer CPR. *Note:* If there is massive external or internal bleeding, CPR will *not* be effective because there is not enough fluid in the blood vessels to carry the oxygen.

Respiration

Place your pet on its side. Clean the mouth of blood and mucus. Inhale air, put your mouth over the cat's muzzle, forming an airtight seal, and exhale. Give your pet a new breath every three seconds (twenty per minute), while massaging the heart.

Massage

Place the heel of one hand over the cat's chest, just in back of its elbow, and your other palm on top of that hand. Pump firmly and quickly, doing it once every second (sixty per minute). Hold each thrust for a count of two and release for a count of one. Be careful not be break any ribs or to injure any rib fractures further. Have someone else feel for a femoral pulse (see page 17) as you massage. Discontinue the massage when the heartbeat is restored, but continue the artificial respiration until your cat breathes on its own.

APPLYING A TOURNIQUET

Seek veterinary aid immediately. A tourniquet should be used only if direct pressure is unsuccessful in stopping the bleeding. *Never* place a tourniquet over a fracture or a joint.

You can use a handkerchief, a cloth belt, or a piece of cloth as a tourniquet. Adjust it about one inch above the wound by tying a loose loop around the limb. Place a short, strong stick in the loop and twist the tourniquet until the blood stops flowing.

Loosen the tourniquet every ten minutes to allow some circulation. *Note:* Do *not* loosen it in the case of a snakebite (see page 142). Treat the animal for shock (see below) as well.

TREATING SHOCK

Shock is caused by severe insult to your cat's body—heavy bleeding, trauma, fluid loss (from vomiting, diarrhea, or burns), infection, heart failure, or breathing problems. It is a syndrome in which the heart and blood vessels are unable to deliver the nutrients and oxygen to the cells and are equally unable to remove the cells' toxic waste products. If not treated promptly, the shock process may be impossible to reverse and your cat can die.

The major signs of shock are

1. Pale or muddy gums
2. A weak and rapid pulse (see page 17)
3. Capillary refilling takes longer than two seconds (see page 17)
4. Rapid breathing (over forty breaths per minute)
5. A low rectal temperature (below 100°F), with skin and legs cool to the touch

Shock requires prompt veterinary attention. For immediate aid you should be sure the cat's airway is clear so it can breathe. If not, administer artificial respiration (page 98), check the heartbeat and pulse (page 17), and control any bleeding (page 124). If necessary, apply CPR (page 98).

Maintain body heat (with a blanket or coat) and very gently transport the cat to the veterinary hospital. If your pet is unconscious, keep its head lower than the rest of the body. If possible, phone the hospital so that the staff can prepare for your animal.

Large quantities of intravenous fluids, *corticosteroids,** and oxygen given in time can save your pet's life. In shock, the capillaries are like a dry riverbed. The intravenous fluids flood the capillaries and renew the vigorous blood flow that nourishes the dried-out cells.

Do *not* change the injured pet's position rapidly. A fast lift or rotation can cause shock to move into the irreversible stage.

If the cat is in electrical shock from chewing on wires, there is an added precaution: do *not* touch the cat if it is still in contact with the current! Unplug the electrical cord from the outlet and then check the cat's pulse and heartbeat and continue treating as for shock. You may also need to treat for burns in the mouth (page 128).

RESCUING FROM WATER

Most cats are excellent swimmers, but even the strongest swimmer can drown if it becomes exhausted or falls through thin ice. If your cat begins to drown in a lake or pool, the first thing you should do is send for help. Then try to reach your cat from land with your hand. If you must swim out, try to take a float with you. Grab your cat by the tail or the back of the neck, or let it grab the float with its front legs. Hold on to the cat and swim to shore.

Once you are both safely ashore, hold your cat upside down by the hind legs (hold at the hocks) and give a few sharp shakes to drain excess water from the lungs. Remove any weeds or other hindrances from the mouth. Lay the cat on its side and give artificial respiration (page 98). Check for a pulse (page 17). If there is no pulse or heartbeat, apply CPR (page 99).

You can help to revive the cat by holding spirits of ammonia under its nose. When the cat becomes conscious, wrap it in a blanket or coat to keep it warm. If you rescued your cat from ice water, treat it for frostbite and hypothermia (page 126).

---

*Corticosteroids are hormones produced by the adrenal gland that have many functions, including helping cells fight destructive agents. They are also produced synthetically by pharmaceutical companies for use in human as well as veterinary medicine.

APPLYING A SPLINT

If you suspect that your cat has fractured its leg, a temporary splint is needed to prevent jagged bone edges from injuring the neighboring blood vessels, tissues, and nerves. *Note:* For stability, a splint should include the joints immediately above and below the fracture. An improperly applied splint is worse than no splint at all.

Place a clean cloth around the limb for padding. Fasten a rolled (U-shaped) magazine, newspaper, or cardboard to the leg with tape.

Many times, the shape of the leg and the cat's resistance to handling when injured will make it impossible to apply a temporary splint. In this case, gently support the limb with a towel, blanket, or board on the trip to your veterinarian's office.

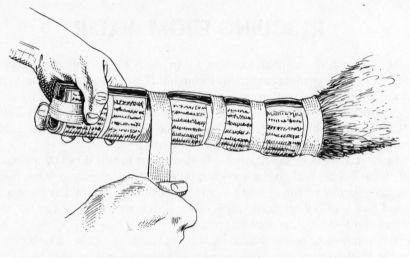

BANDAGING

Bandages are used to stop bleeding, to keep dirt and bacteria out of the wound, to keep the edges of the cut together, to support the injured area, and to keep your cat from scratching or excessively licking the wound. Bandages should not be so tight that circulation or breathing is compromised. *Caution:* If the wound isn't clean when you cover it with a bandage, you may hide a developing infection from early discovery, so get the cut clean and keep it clean.

A pressure bandage is any bandage applied with pressure. You can hold the bandage firmly with your hand or tie it in place. A Band-Aid is another pressure bandage, but it is limited to fairly small cuts and wounds.

Some cat owners leave bandages on too long. They should be changed frequently, every day or two and whenever they become .wet. The skin has to "breathe," and you have to be sure that the wound is not getting infected—don't wait until you can smell it. For painless removal, apply nail-polish remover liberally to the back of the adhesive tape for five minutes. This will dissolve the adhesive and release both skin and hair. *Note:* Do *not* let your bandaged cat outside.

You should have the following supplies in your first aid kit:

Gauze bandages, 1″ wide
Padding, either a cotton roll or a clean cloth
Adhesive tape, 1″ wide

Bandaging a Paw, Limb, or Tail

To make a bandage for a paw, limb, or tail, wrap the wound firmly with gauze pads, a gauze roll, or a clean cloth or handkerchief, using a spiral pattern. Place a few strips of tape crosswise at the end of the bandage.

Starting at the toes (or tip of the tail), wrap the adhesive tape in overlapping bands securely over the first layer. Be sure to include hair on both sides so the bandage will not slip. To avoid having the lower leg, paw, or tail tip swell, the bandage must include all of the extremity.

Bandaging the Chest or Abdomen

Place a gauze pad or clean cloth over the wound. A *many-tailed* bandage is made by tearing both narrow ends of a large, rectangular piece of clean cloth lengthwise into one-inch-wide strips—but only one-third of the way down. It will fit amply around the chest or abdomen. The strips are tied over your cat's back.

TRANSPORTING AN INJURED CAT

The easiest and gentlest way to carry a cat is in a cat carrier, which is such a good investment! First of all, it will prevent your cat from jumping through the steering wheel or on top of your head while you're driving, and sending *you* to the hospital! Your cat will also be calmer in the veterinarian's reception and exam room—a definite plus for the veterinarian-owner relationship.

If a cat carrier is not available, the one-hand carry is comfortable for your cat and affords secure restraint. The cat's back legs and body rest between your inner forearm and your body. The front legs are held between the fingers of the same arm. Your cat's head can be cradled in your other hand.

If you pinch your cat's front or hind paw and the animal does not react in pain, it may have a spinal injury—paralysis of both hind legs and possibly stiffness or paralysis of the front legs are possible. In this case, very gently slide your cat onto a blanket or board. Even a slight movement of the spine could cause irreversible damage. Check the pulse (page 17) and stanch any bleeding (page 124).

If your cat is seriously ill or injured, it is very important not to make the situation worse. If your pet is in shock (page 100), a fast lift or rotation can cause irreversible harm. Injuries to the spinal cord, chest, abdomen, or limbs can be made worse by inconsiderate handling. A cat carrier, blanket, coat, air mattress, or even a window screen can be used to transport the seriously injured or ill cat.

CHAPTER

7

Accidents and Injuries

CUTS AND WOUNDS

Bleeding—even small amounts—frightens many pet owners, but the blood's remarkable clotting mechanism stops most bleeding in five minutes. When a small blood vessel is injured, it *constricts* (narrows) to allow less blood to escape. *Platelets,* which are blood cells, arrive at the scene to plug the hole, and chemicals released by the platelets combine with factors in the blood to produce fiberlike strands called *fibrin,* which complete the blood clot and stop the bleeding.

Sometimes the injury to the blood vessel is too large for the clotting mechanism to be effective. Apply direct pressure to the wound for five or ten minutes and allow the clotting mechanism to work; that's usually all that is needed. Use the cleanest material available—gauze pads, sheets, towels, or clothing. A pressure bandage (page 102) can be applied for sustained pressure. If these measures are unsuccessful, a tourniquet (page 100) is needed.

Cut Footpad

The footpad has a lot of blood vessels and can therefore bleed profusely when cut. Since your pet walks barefoot, carelessly discarded beer-can pop-tops, jagged broken bottles, and other disposable conveniences are constant hazards. Generally, cats are very good about sidestepping such things, so this should be a rare injury. However, it's good to be prepared.

Skin wound (bleeding from blood vessel)

Constriction (narrowing) of blood vessel

Mobilization of platelets in blood vessel

Fibrin combines with platelets to complete the blood clot

Home Treatment

Clean the wound with soap and water after the bleeding stops. Hydrogen peroxide (3 percent) can also be used. Do *not* rub the wound hard, or the clot may loosen and the bleeding will recur. Gently remove any hair, dirt, or other foreign material from the area.

Wound

Serum and blood cells fill in and bring "building blocks"

Wound contraction

Wounds heal by skin contraction and by the presence of serum and blood cells at the site. Even gaping wounds will heal in time by this process if kept clean. There probably is some truth to the statement that cats lick their wounds to keep them clean and to enhance healing.

Direct pressure with a gauze pad or clean cloth should stop the bleeding of a cut footpad. If you cannot get to a veterinarian, check the wound for dirt or other debris and then bandage it firmly. If it starts bleeding again, flush the wound gently with 3 percent hydrogen peroxide and rebandage it.

Shallow footpad wounds do not have to be sutured. Your pet may have a sore paw and a limp for a few weeks, but nightly flushings with clean water and hydrogen peroxide will help heal the wound. If the wound becomes infected, go see your doctor.

What to Expect at the Veterinarian's Office

You should see your doctor if the wound is very deep, very large (longer than one-half inch), or very dirty, or has become infected. In these cases, your veterinarian will probably recommend surgery. A narcotic or tranquilizer and a local anesthetic (or general anesthesia) will be used so that your pet will not feel any pain. The wound will be explored for hair, dirt, and other foreign particles and flushed with sterile water mixed with antibiotics to prevent or eliminate infection. It will be sutured to decrease the healing time and to prevent dirt from reentering. If your cat chews its wounds, or if it is overactive, tranquilizers and/or a special protective collar may be prescribed during the healing period. Your veterinarian will also determine whether antibiotics are necessary.

Deep footpad wounds need to be sutured. Your doctor may also suggest antibiotics if the wound was extremely dirty. Cats are quite resistant to tetanus, but if the wound occurred around stables, your veterinarian may recommend a tetanus shot.

Removing Stitches • Your veterinarian will tell you when the stitches are to be removed. Unless your doctor wants to recheck your pet, you can do the job yourself. Gently grasp a loose end of the knot with tweezers. Using a pair of small, sharp scissors, cut the stitch as close to the skin as possible and pull it out. Cutting close to the skin reduces the chance of contamination and infection.

Stitch to be removed
Cut here
Skin (healed)

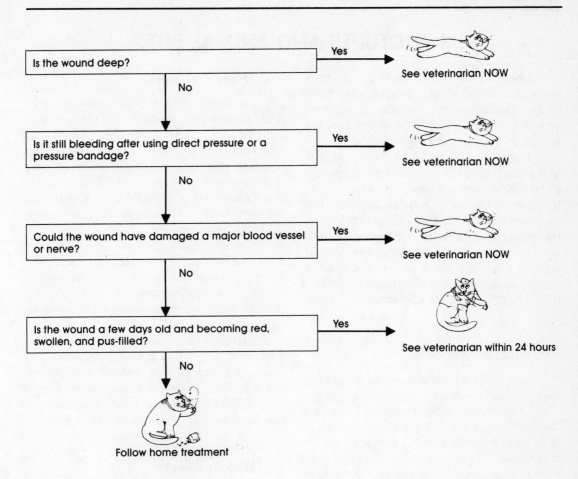

Is the wound deep? → **Yes** → See veterinarian NOW

No ↓

Is it still bleeding after using direct pressure or a pressure bandage? → **Yes** → See veterinarian NOW

No ↓

Could the wound have damaged a major blood vessel or nerve? → **Yes** → See veterinarian NOW

No ↓

Is the wound a few days old and becoming red, swollen, and pus-filled? → **Yes** → See veterinarian within 24 hours

No ↓

Follow home treatment

PUNCTURES AND ANIMAL BITES

One of the saddest things to see is a helpless cat admitted to our hospital after being shot or knifed. Puncture wounds can cause severe bleeding and injury to the internal organs. Veterinary aid is needed immediately.

If your pet was bitten by another animal, that animal should be quarantined for ten days to be sure it does not have rabies (page 154). If you know the owner and can ascertain that the animal has a current rabies vaccination, the quarantine can be done at home. If you do not know the owner or if the animal is wild, such as a bat, fox, raccoon, or skunk, quarantine is maintained at a veterinary hospital, a public health facility, or a local pound.

Embedded Fishhook

Cats really are curious, even about things that may hurt them, such as fishhooks. All too often, a cat sniffing around a fishing camp or a cluttered garage can well get a fishhook caught in its lip or nose. Restraining the cat (page 97) is necessary if you are going to remove the hook at home. Remember, just as a fish cannot escape a fishhook once it is embedded, neither can a cat. Therefore, the barb must be pushed through the skin and cut with pliers. The rest of the fishhook can then be removed.

Amputated Tail

If your cat's tail is caught in a slammed car or house door or run over by a car, arrange to see the veterinarian immediately after you apply emergency measures (see Home Treatment).

Home Treatment

EMERGENCY Check the entry and exit areas of puncture wounds. If necessary, give artificial respiration (page 98). Check the heartbeat and pulse (page 17) and control any bleeding (page 124). An amputated tail may require a tourniquet (page 100). Treat also for shock (page 100). Bullet and knife wounds can fracture bones, so a temporary splint (page 102) may be necessary.

The most common result of animal bites is not rabies but simple bacterial infections. The skin is normally a strong barrier against bacteria, but if penetrated, bacteria, hair, and dirt can enter and cause a serious infection or an abscess (page 192) days later.

Clip the hair around the wound with scissors; then clean the wound with soap and water and alcohol and remove any debris. Cover it with a gauze bandage or clean cloth. If the origin of the bite is unknown, quarantine may be necessary. Check with your doctor.

What to Expect at the Veterinarian's Office

Your veterinarian will be concerned about three things: (1) controlling the bleeding (if this hasn't been done); (2) cleaning the wound and possibly suturing it to avoid infection; and (3) in the case of an animal bite, identifying and confining the other animal.

Your pet may have to be given a tranquilizer and a local or general anesthetic in order to be cleaned and sutured. Antibiotics may be given to avoid infection, especially for dirty fishhook punctures. A rabies vaccination will be given if it is overdue.

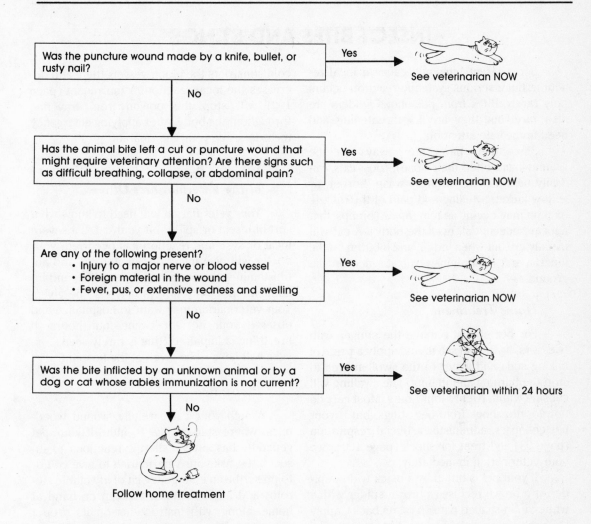

Was the puncture wound made by a knife, bullet, or rusty nail?

Yes → See veterinarian NOW

No ↓

Has the animal bite left a cut or puncture wound that might require veterinary attention? Are there signs such as difficult breathing, collapse, or abdominal pain?

Yes → See veterinarian NOW

No ↓

Are any of the following present?
• Injury to a major nerve or blood vessel
• Foreign material in the wound
• Fever, pus, or extensive redness and swelling

Yes → See veterinarian NOW

No ↓

Was the bite inflicted by an unknown animal or by a dog or cat whose rabies immunization is not current?

Yes → See veterinarian within 24 hours

No ↓

Follow home treatment

If there is dislocation of a tail bone but your cat can move its tail, your veterinarian will probably suggest that no treatment is necessary. However, large gaping wounds with no dislocation will require suturing. Sometimes the nerves, tissue, and bones are damaged beyond repair. Complete amputation of the tail will be recommended in this case.

INSECT BITES AND STINGS

Some insect bites will cause a local reaction, but a serious systemic reaction occurs only rarely. Bites from poisonous spiders are also rare, but they are life-threatening and need immediate attention.

Since their paws are always on the ground—and often their noses, too—cats can easily be stung by an angry wasp, hornet, or yellow jacket. Swelling and pain of the muzzle or paw may occur, as may *hives* (bumps that appear suddenly all over the body). A cat will usually cry out when bitten, and if bitten on the muzzle, will continuously rub its face on the ground.

Home Treatment

For bee stings, remove the stinger with tweezers, if you can see it, and apply a paste of baking soda and water to the swollen area to stop the burning and itching. The swelling will subside within twenty-four hours. Most cats do not go into shock from bee stings, but if your pet collapses, administer artificial respiration (page 98) and treat for shock (page 100). See your veterinarian immediately.

If your pet is bitten by a black widow spider or a brown recluse (a brown spider with a white violin-shaped pattern on its back), apply ice packs immediately to the bitten area. The cold constricts the blood vessels there and decreases the local reaction. A tourniquet (page 100) will stop the poison from traveling throughout the body. After applying emergency measures, see your veterinarian.

What to Expect at the Veterinarian's Office

Your veterinarian will need to know what sort of insect or spider bit your cat. If a severe local or systemic reaction has occurred, your doctor will give injections of steroids and antihistamines to counteract the swelling and inflammation. Pain relievers may also be given. Your veterinarian may want to hospitalize and observe your pet for twenty-four hours. If breathing is impaired (this is rarely seen), oxygen will have to be given at the hospital.

Prevention

Watch your cat carefully around woodpiles, where spiders like to hide. If your pet generally has severe allergic reactions to insect bites, ask your veterinarian to give you or to prescribe an emergency kit of injectable steroids and antihistamines to keep on hand at home, along with instructions on its proper use.

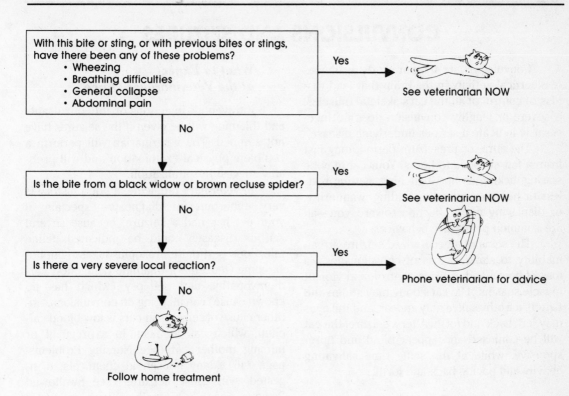

With this bite or sting, or with previous bites or stings, have there been any of these problems?
- Wheezing
- Breathing difficulties
- General collapse
- Abdominal pain

Yes → See veterinarian NOW

No ↓

Is the bite from a black widow or brown recluse spider?

Yes → See veterinarian NOW

No ↓

Is there a very severe local reaction?

Yes → Phone veterinarian for advice

No ↓

Follow home treatment

CONVULSIONS AND SEIZURES

Convulsions are temporary disturbances of electrical activity in the brain that lead to a loss of control of all the cat's skeletal muscles. A severe or lengthy convulsion does not necessarily indicate a serious underlying disease.

The aura, or preseizure period, may last from a few seconds to hours. Your cat may be staring, licking its lips, twitching, getting restless or nervous, salivating, hiding, wandering, or displaying more affection toward you—all are common preseizure behaviors.

The signs of a generalized seizure are an inability to stand, a loss of consciousness, a loss of bowel and/or urine control, and violent muscle spasms. The cat's body may stiffen and twitch, a frothy saliva may appear, and the eyes may jerk back and forth. After a seizure, the cat will be confused and appear blind and unresponsive, while at the same time salivating heavily and pacing back and forth.

Home Treatment

EMERGENCY Try to hold the cat down gently with a blanket. If you can't do so, clear the area of objects that may injure your pet. Stay calm—watching a seizure can be a frightening experience, but most seizures are not life-threatening. Your pet may have a few seizures in a row. If there is a high fever—greater than 106°F—an ice-water bath will help lower the fever. Ice packs placed on the inner thighs and under the front legs are also helpful. See Fever (page 149) for other suggestions.

After the convulsion, calmly and quietly pet your cat and reassure it with your presence. Keep lights and noise to a minimum, because the brain is very sensitive. Seek veterinary aid as soon as you can.

What to Expect at the Veterinarian's Office

Intravenous injections of anticonvulsants and thiamine will be given if the seizures have not stopped. The veterinarian will perform a complete physical examination and will probably suggest hospitalization.

In veterinary medicine, a good history is very important for diagnosis—especially if your pet has had a seizure, because several serious diseases could be indicated: feline infectious peritonitis, toxoplasmosis, lymphosarcoma (leukemia), thiamine deficiency, cardiomyopathy, and epilepsy (which has no known cause) can all bring on convulsions. Another cause of seizures in cats is low blood calcium, which can be seen in a pregnant or nursing mother cat (see Nursing Problems, page 246). Many household chemicals, if ingested, will cause seizures (see Swallowed Poisons, page 136). Finally, if your cat had a head injury followed by unconsciousness within the last two years, this could also be a factor.

Tests may be necessary to diagnose the cause of the seizures. Your veterinarian may recommend several of the following:

1. Blood count (infection, lead poisoning)
2. BUN and creatinine (kidney disease)
3. Urinalysis (kidney, liver disease)
4. Blood sugar test (low blood sugar, *hypoglycemia*)
5. Blood calcium test
6. Liver function blood tests (liver disease)
7. FIP, FLV, FTLV, and toxoplasmosis tests
8. Electrocardiogram

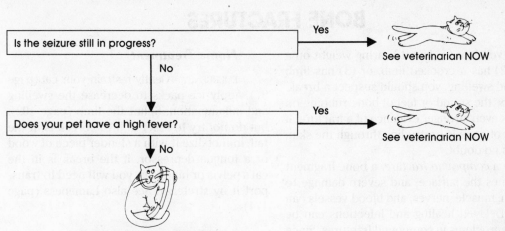

Is the seizure still in progress? — **Yes** → See veterinarian NOW

No

Does your pet have a high fever? — **Yes** → See veterinarian NOW

No

Phone veterinarian for advice

If spinal taps, specialized X-rays, CAT scans, and electroencephalograms are required, they are usually done at referral hospitals or universities.

Medication can control convulsions, but it may be necessary to try various doses and even combinations of drugs, so you must be patient. No medication is needed if your cat has only one seizure and the cause is not determined. Occasionally, your veterinarian may not be able to regulate the animal. You should then be referred to a veterinary neurologist (see page 66).

Prevention

Keep toxins containing lead, organophosphates, chlorinated hydrocarbons, and strychnine away from your cat.

Do not feed your cat raw fish. It contains thiaminase, an enzyme that breaks down thiamine (vitamin B_1). Thiamine is needed for normal nervous system functioning.

Keep antifreeze away from your cat. A few drops can cause seizures, kidney damage, and death.

BONE FRACTURES

If your cat (1) is not bearing weight on a limb, (2) has a crooked limb, or (3) has limb pain and swelling, you should suspect a break. *Crepitus,* the sound or feel of bone rubbing on bone, is even stronger evidence of a fracture. If a piece of bone is protruding through the skin, there is no doubt.

In a *compound fracture,* a bone fragment penetrates the surface, and severe damage to the skin, muscle, nerves, and blood vessels can result. Delayed healing and infections can be serious problems in compound fractures. Since bone is not very resistant to infection, cover a compound fracture immediately with gauze or a clean cloth and get veterinary assistance.

Limb fractures are not life-threatening, but they should be temporarily splinted so that the jagged bone edges do not injure any neighboring tissues and nerves. Remember: A splint should include the joints immediately above and below the fracture.

Fractures of the spine from trauma are extreme emergencies, especially if your cat is hit by a car. You may see a paralysis of the hind legs and a stiffness (outstretching) of the front legs after trauma.

Home Treatment

EMERGENCY   Gently restrain your cat (page 97). Apply ice packs to decrease the swelling and inflammation. Splint the limb (page 102), but do *not* try to reset it. If the break is in the tail, immobilize it with a slender piece of wood or a tongue depressor. If the break is in the cat's pelvis or hind legs, you will need to transport it by stretcher. See also Lameness (page 174).

What to Expect at the Veterinarian's Office

Your veterinarian will check all other systems to be sure that they were not injured. A radiograph (X-ray) is needed to verify the fracture and to determine the best method of repair. Some fractures will heal with external stabilization (splints or casts) alone, while others need internal fixation (metal pins, plates, or wires). Discuss the chances of healing and the cost of each technique with your veterinarian. Today, no cat has to be put to sleep because it has a fracture—a three-legged cat is still more agile than a two-legged person!

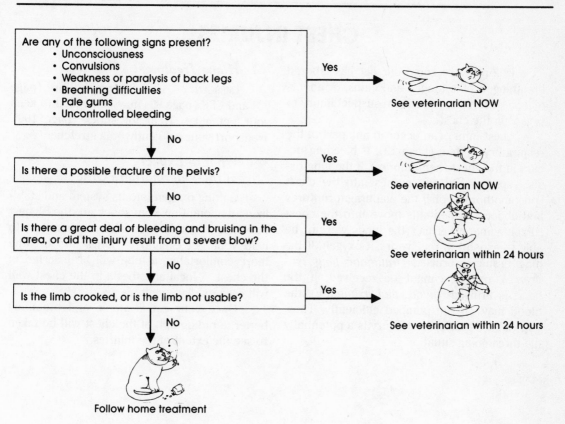

Are any of the following signs present?
- Unconsciousness
- Convulsions
- Weakness or paralysis of back legs
- Breathing difficulties
- Pale gums
- Uncontrolled bleeding

Yes → See veterinarian NOW

No ↓

Is there a possible fracture of the pelvis?

Yes → See veterinarian NOW

No ↓

Is there a great deal of bleeding and bruising in the area, or did the injury result from a severe blow?

Yes → See veterinarian within 24 hours

No ↓

Is the limb crooked, or is the limb not usable?

Yes → See veterinarian within 24 hours

No ↓

Follow home treatment

CHEST INJURIES

If, for any reason, your cat has labored breathing, a blue tongue and gums, or abnormal chest sounds, you should suspect injury to organs in the chest.

Chest injury can occur in any part of the respiratory system (page 19). If bleeding occurs in the chest (hemothorax), if the lung tissue ruptures and air escapes into the chest (pneumothorax), or if the diaphragm ruptures and abdominal contents move into the chest (diaphragmatic hernia), the lungs will not be able to expand to receive fresh oxygen. If the lung tissue is bruised (*traumatic lung syndrome*), oxygen cannot be received. If the heart is bruised (*myocardial irritability*), the blood may not be pumped efficiently. Thus, you can see that a chest injury is a potentially life-threatening situation.

Home Treatment

EMERGENCY Artificial respiration (page 98) and CPR (page 99) may be needed to keep your pet alive. Treat for shock (page 100). Transport your cat gently on a stretcher.

What to Expect at the Veterinarian's Office

Getting oxygen into its system and stabilizing its condition from shock are the highest priorities. If air or blood has to removed to help your pet expand its lungs and breathe more comfortably, a tube will be inserted in the chest. A local anesthesia in the chest wall will ease its placement.

Once your cat is stable and breathing better, a radiograph of the chest will be taken to see the extent of the injuries.

Are any of the following signs present?
- Labored breathing
- Blue tongue and gums
- Abnormal chest sounds

Yes

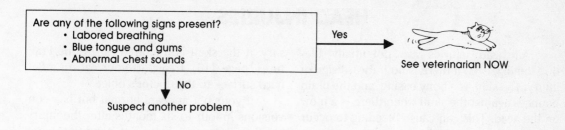

See veterinarian NOW

No

Suspect another problem

HEAD INJURIES

All head injuries are potentially life-threatening, even if there is no outward sign of injury. The skull is a bony casing, and the brain bounces against the skull when there is a blow on the head. This can cause bleeding to occur within and around the brain, and the accumulation of blood can compress the brain.

If your pet is or becomes unconscious, immediate veterinary attention is necessary. Other signs that the brain has been affected are

1. Uneven pupil size (caused by pressure on the brain from bleeding)
2. Pale gums
3. A slow pulse (less than 60)
4. Limb paralysis or stiffness
5. Convulsions

If your cat is unconscious, extend its head and neck and pull the tongue forward. Clean the blood and fluids from the mouth, and transport the animal on a flat, hard surface to the veterinarian or veterinary hospital.

The most frequent cause of serious head injury is being hit by a car. Kittens will also occasionally sustain head injury from being hit by falling objects. Adult cats are fortunate in having large muscles that cover their skulls and cushion some blows to the head. In serious accidents, do *not* overlook possible chest, abdomen, or limb injury, as well.

Home Treatment

EMERGENCY Observe your cat carefully: check the pupils, pulse, and gums frequently, and treat for shock. Control any bleeding with direct pressure, using a clean cloth. Remove all blood, mucus, and debris from the mouth and give artificial respiration (page 98), if neces-

sary. If the skull is fractured (see Bone Fractures, page 116), transport your cat on a flat, hard surface to the doctor's office.

If your pet appears normal but has convulsions in four to six months after the injury, check with your doctor. This condition is occasionally seen and requires no medication; the convulsions usually disappear in a few months. This is thought to be a temporary abnormal electrical brain discharge, provoked by the injury, which resolves itself. Of course, if the seizures get worse, further tests will be needed.

What to Expect at the Veterinarian's Office

Your veterinarian will need a good history of the accident that happened. Your pet's head, eyes, ears, nose, throat, and neck will be examined. The back of the eyes will be examined with an ophthalmoscope to check for pressure on the brain and for evidence of hemorrhage. A complete neurological exam, including checking of the reflexes, will be done. The chest and abdomen will be examined for injury or internal bleeding. The limbs and pelvis will be checked for fractures or dislocations.

Since bleeding within the skull can be suspected from a thorough physical examination and not by X-rays in general practice, skull X-rays are helpful only if a fracture is present. CAT scans, a very good diagnostic procedure, are available at major veterinary centers.

Oxygen and medication (steroids) may be used to reduce brain swelling, but your veterinarian will not give tranquilizers or other medication that may obscure the observation of your pet's improving or deteriorating brain

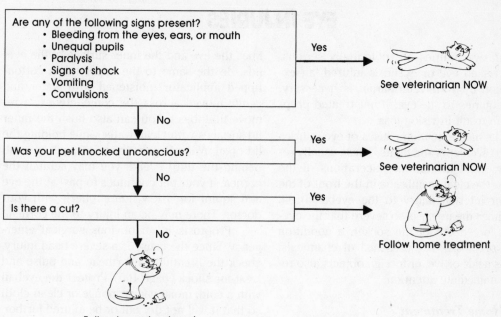

Are any of the following signs present?
- Bleeding from the eyes, ears, or mouth
- Unequal pupils
- Paralysis
- Signs of shock
- Vomiting
- Convulsions

Yes → See veterinarian NOW

No ↓

Was your pet knocked unconscious?

Yes → See veterinarian NOW

No ↓

Is there a cut?

Yes → Follow home treatment

No ↓

Follow home treatment

injury. If your cat was unconscious at any time, ask your veterinarian to make sure someone competent will be monitoring your pet through the night; an increasing number of hospitals are equipped for *intensive* twenty-four-hour care. (If not, ask if you could monitor the cat at home.) Registration in a university veterinary hospital or an emergency hospital may be requested if one is nearby and if your doctor feels that it would be helpful.

Neurosurgical intervention may be advised in selected cases. This is handled best by a neurosurgical specialist.

Prevention

Of course, a cat inside a house is unlikely to be hit by a car.

EYE INJURIES

All eye injuries are potentially serious. Whenever an eye or eyelid is injured, an examination by your veterinarian is necessary. Minor injuries to the eye, if not treated properly, can result in vision loss.

The most common causes of eye injuries are auto accidents and fights. These usually result in eyelid lacerations, lacerations of the cornea (the clear membrane in the front of the eye), or internal injury to the eyeball itself. Sometimes the injury is so severe that the eyeball is forced out of the socket, a condition called *proptosis*. The presence of chemicals, such as acids or lye, or foreign objects also requires immediate attention.

Home Treatment

EMERGENCY Chemicals splashed in the eye need to be flushed out *immediately,* using lots of clean water. This must be done as soon as possible to avoid permanent damage to the cornea. Flush five to ten minutes; afterward, apply a clean cloth or gauze bandage to protect the eye from further injury. See your doctor immediately.

Eyelid lacerations can bleed profusely. Applying direct pressure with a gauze pad or clean cloth to the lid for five minutes should control the bleeding. If the laceration is on the eyeball, cover it with gauze or a clean cloth, but do *not* apply pressure.

If a foreign object is under one of the eyelids, your pet will paw at the eye and squint. Of course, these signs are also seen in other conditions, but take a look under the lid—you may see a piece of sand or a loose eyelash. Use a bright light when looking for a foreign body in the eye. Pull the lower lid down with your thumb and inspect the pink conjunctiva that lines the eye and the inner surface of the eyelids; do the same to the upper lid. A cotton-tipped applicator moistened with water and *gently* moved across the conjunctiva can remove the object. You can also flush the inner lid surfaces with clean water while holding the lid open. *Note:* Do *not* try to inspect or swab behind the third eyelid; you may scratch the cornea. If your pet continues to paw at the eye and squint for a few hours, check with your doctor. There may be an injury to the cornea.

Proptosis is an obvious surgical emergency. Since the cause is a severe head injury, check the breathing, heartbeat, and pulse and treat for shock (page 100). Protect the eyeball with a cold, moist gauze sponge or clean cloth so that it will not dry out or be injured further. Control any bleeding with direct pressure. Immediate veterinary help is needed.

What to Expect at the Veterinarian's Office

Your doctor will perform a complete physical if generalized injury from an auto accident has occurred. An ophthalmoscope will be used to inspect all the structures within the eyeball, including under the lids.

A local anesthetic will make it easier to check behind the third eyelid if a foreign body is suspected. If a foreign body is found, a moistened cotton swab or eyewash solution will remove it. An antibiotic ointment is sometimes applied.

A harmless fluorescent dye will be administered, and the eye will then be examined with an ultraviolet light. Whenever the cornea is injured, the dye will confirm the extent of the damage. This procedure is painless. If there is damage to the cornea, antibiotic drops or oint-

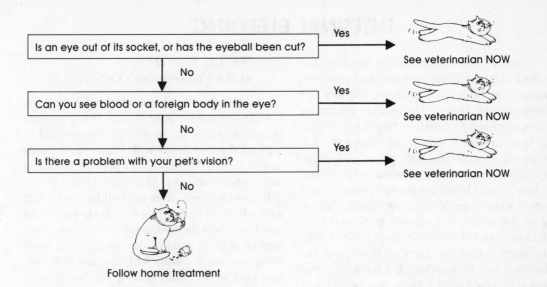

Is an eye out of its socket, or has the eyeball been cut? — Yes → See veterinarian NOW

No ↓

Can you see blood or a foreign body in the eye? — Yes → See veterinarian NOW

No ↓

Is there a problem with your pet's vision? — Yes → See veterinarian NOW

No ↓

Follow home treatment

ment will be used to protect this delicate membrane from infection. If an *iritis* (an irritation of the colored part of the eye) is present, drops to dilate the pupil are needed. Steroids are used to decrease the inflammation in minor injuries to the cornea (*corneal abrasions*).

In a case of proptosis, your doctor will recommend replacement of the eyeball in the socket *if* the accident just occurred and the globe is not severely damaged. If the vessels and nerves were not injured, vision may be saved.

Severe injury to the eyeball may necessitate removing the eye, or *enucleation*. Cats with one eye or no vision get around remarkably well and are very happy. So do not suggest "putting my cat to sleep" if an eye has to be removed.

Prevention

Keep your cat away when you are working with corrosive materials. Of course, keeping your cat indoors will also avert fights and auto accidents.

INTERNAL BLEEDING

Massive internal bleeding reduces the amount of fluid carrying oxygen and nutrients through the body. If the organs do not get enough oxygen, they die. Immediate veterinary help is needed if profuse bleeding is noted from any body orifice or if your cat shows the following signs: weakness, pale gums, abdominal pain, breathing difficulty, or weak pulse. If your cat was injured by an automobile, assume that there is some internal bleeding. Internal bleeding of the stomach is usually indicated by a bright or dark red color to the cat's vomit. If its excrement is dark and tarry or bright red, the intestines may be bleeding. If a red foamy material is coughed up, the lungs may be affected. Some poisons can cause internal bleeding. There are also many bleeding disorders that affect cats.

Home Treatment

EMERGENCY   Lay the cat down and cover it lightly. *Note:* Do *not* struggle with it. Transport the animal gently, because its body's ability to carry oxygen is decreased.

What to Expect at the Veterinarian's Office

If possible, call your veterinarian so he or she can prepare for your arrival. The first, most important steps are to provide oxygen and to replace the lost fluids with intravenous fluids and/or blood. Antibiotics to prevent infection and corticosteroids to maintain cellular health will also be given. Your pet will be kept warm with a heating pad or blankets. Its urine output and blood will be monitored to measure progress or deterioration of the condition. If these measures are not sufficient, surgical intervention may be necessary to stop the bleeding.

The anticoagulant rodent poisons are a common cause of bleeding in pets. The treatment for the anticoagulant poisons is vitamin K_1. *It must be given for as long as the anticoagulant is present in the body at toxic levels.* This is especially important with the very potent "second-generation" rat poisons brodifacoum and bromadiolone. A cat that swallowed these may have to be treated for three or four weeks.

Are any of the following signs present?
- Profuse bleeding from any body opening
- Weakness
- Pale gums
- Abdominal pain
- Breathing difficulties
- Weak pulse

Yes

See veterinarian NOW

No

Follow home treatment

HYPOTHERMIA AND FROSTBITE

A cat's fur is generally enough protection against extreme cold, but any long exposure to low temperatures and wind (for example, if the cat is injured and unable to reach shelter) can produce a severe lowering of your cat's body temperature (*hypothermia*). Shivering, stumbling, exhaustion, drowsiness, and a low body temperature (80°F to 90°F) may be present.

Frostbite is also rare in cats; however, your cat's ear tips and tail may be frozen on very cold days. Their positions on your pet predispose them to the full fury of chilly winds and icy temperatures. Frostbitten ear tips may appear pale (diminished blood supply) or red, swollen, hot, and painful to the touch. The hair may fall out and the skin peel.

Home Treatment

EMERGENCY For hypothermia, place the cat in a warm room. Warm-water baths, hot-water bottles, and an electric heating blanket (carefully used) will increase the body temperature. (Be patient; it increases slowly.) You can measure progress by rectal temperature (page 31) and by the cat's response (it will be more alert). Give warm liquids if your cat is conscious.

If your cat is frostbitten, warm the frozen areas with your hands or with moist, warm (*not* hot) towels. *Note:* Do *not* rub or squeeze. Ointments or pressure dressings should *not* be used because they may further injure the tissue. If your pet feels discomfort or pain, or if the skin seems to be becoming infected, see your doctor.

What to Expect at the Veterinarian's Office

If home treatment is unsuccessful, your veterinarian will treat for shock, continue the rewarming methods, and monitor the cat's heart and kidney function.

If any tissue is severely damaged by frostbite, antibiotics will be needed to avoid infection. Pain relievers may be suggested as well. Hasty surgery to repair or amputate the damaged tissue is usually not necessary. If the tissue is kept clean and antibiotics are given, healing usually occurs in a week.

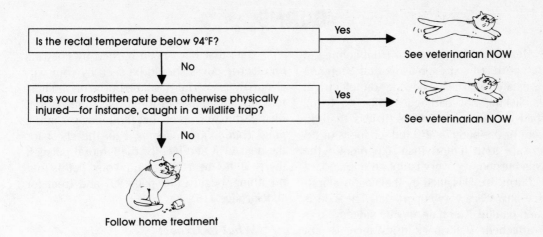

| Is the rectal temperature below 94°F? | Yes → See veterinarian NOW |

No ↓

| Has your frostbitten pet been otherwise physically injured—for instance, caught in a wildlife trap? | Yes → See veterinarian NOW |

No ↓

Follow home treatment

BURNS

Most burns in cats occur from coming in contact with hot water, grease, or tar; stepping on a heated burner; chewing on electrical wires; licking hot barbecue grills; or being trapped in burning buildings. If less than 15 percent of the body is affected, chances of recovery are good. If more than 50 percent of the body is burned, recovery is not anticipated.

Burns are classified by their depth. First-degree burns are very superficial. The skin is red and painful. The hair may be singed but is still attached. Veterinary assistance is not needed, and healing is rapid.

Second-degree burns are more extensive: severe swelling is present; the skin is red and painful and will slough; healing is slower. In addition, there may be a significant fluid loss from the burn. See your veterinarian.

Third-degree burns are very serious and need emergency veterinary care. The hair falls out, and the skin may be either black or pearly white. Since the entire skin layer has been destroyed, infection and fluid loss are great dangers. The burn is painless, however, because the nerves in the area have been destroyed. Healing is very slow unless a skin graft is performed.

Home Treatment

EMERGENCY Clip hair away from a first-degree burn with scissors, then flush the area with cold water. Gently dry it with clean or sterile gauze. You can also apply cold compresses. *Note:* Do *not* use ointments. Deep second- or third-degree burns should be seen by your veterinarian immediately. Simply cover the affected area with a clean cloth (*not* cotton), treat for shock (page 100), and go to your doctor. *Note:* Do *not* apply water, antiseptics, or ointments.

128

Cats that have been burned by chewing on electric cords should be seen by your veterinarian, also. There will be burns on the lips, tongue, and gums, but the threat to life is that the heart may stop or that fluid may get in the lungs (*pulmonary edema*). Feel the chest for the heartbeat and feel for the femoral pulse. If there is no heartbeat, and your pet is not breathing, begin CPR (page 99) and treat for shock (page 116).

What to Expect at the Veterinarian's Office

Your veterinarian will determine the severity of the burns. Clipping, cleaning, and giving antibiotics may be all that is needed. More serious burns may require intravenous fluids, steroids, antibiotics, and pain relievers. Hospitalization is also necessary for these cases, because close nursing care is required to save your pet's life. If the burns are extensive and your cat survives, skin grafts may be necessary.

A kitten that has bitten through an electric cord may have burns just in the mouth that require antibiotics to prevent infection and anti-inflammatory drugs to reduce swelling. If the current has injured the heart or lungs, intensive treatment for shock, including oxygen, may be needed to save its life.

Prevention

Don't allow your cat to lie below the stove when you are cooking, because a pot of boiling water or oil can easily be tipped over. If your pet insists on lying near the stove because it can't resist the wonderful smells, use the back burners whenever possible. Do *not* let your cat lie on the stove when the burners are hot. Many cats are heat-seekers and can burn

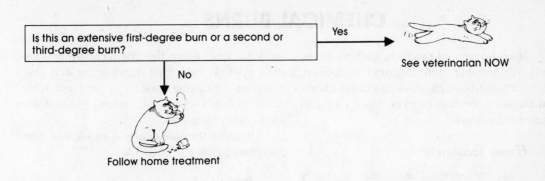

Is this an extensive first-degree burn or a second or third-degree burn?

Yes → See veterinarian NOW

No ↓

Follow home treatment

themselves severely on the stove. At the dinner table, never pass hot food over your pet's head. Many hot foods have been spilled on a pet waiting for a free handout.

Whenever a kitten in the teething stage (three to eight months) is left in a room unobserved for a long period of time, unplug the electric appliances that are not being used.

CHEMICAL BURNS

Many household products such as detergents (dishwasher and laundry) and oven, drain, or toilet-bowl cleaners can cause chemical burns of the skin or eyes. Mace can also cause severe burns.

Home Treatment

Wash the affected area with a steady stream of fresh water—preferably with a hose or hose attachment in the sink or bathtub. Do not touch the substance yourself, and do not spread it further over your cat's body.

Dacriose, a sterile eyewash, can also be used to wash away the chemical from your cat's eyes. A rinse (one quart water and one teaspoon of baking soda) can be used with *acids* (toilet-bowl cleaner, mace) but not alkalis (drain cleaners).

If any of the chemical was swallowed, see Swallowed Poisons (page 136).

What to Expect at the Veterinarian's Office

For alkali burns, thirty minutes of rinsing may be necessary. Severe chemical burns may require hourly administrations of medication.

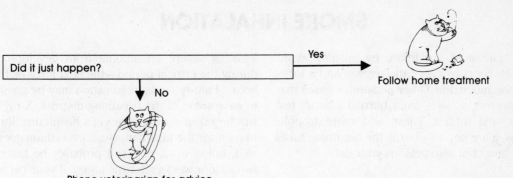

Did it just happen?

No → Phone veterinarian for advice

Yes → Follow home treatment

SMOKE INHALATION

Fire does not injure by burning alone: smoke contains very little oxygen and a lot of carbon monoxide. Other poisonous gases may be present as well, from burned plastic, textiles, and rubber. These add more trouble. Thus, a fire not only burns the breathing tubes and lungs but also poisons your cat.

Home Treatment

EMERGENCY   Remove your cat to fresh air. Check its breathing and use artificial respiration (page 98). Treat your cat for shock (page 100), then seek veterinary aid.

What to Expect at the Veterinarian's Office

If your cat is conscious, and there is no blood-tinged sputum being coughed up and no fluid in the lungs, humidified oxygen and steroids may be given to try to prevent such problems as severe pneumonia from developing during the critical period—the next forty-eight hours. Pain-relieving medication may be given to ease some of the breathing distress. X-rays will be taken during your cat's hospitalization to monitor the lung damage. If everything goes well, follow-up X-rays will probably be taken two to four weeks after the injury. If your cat is unconscious, is coughing up blood-tinged sputum, or has pneumonia, the outlook is more serious.

Prevention

Smoke alarms should be installed, and any other fire-prevention measures should be taken. Your local humane shelter or fire department can provide you with a decal for your door that will notify the fire department of the number of pets to look for and their usual location in your home in case of fire.

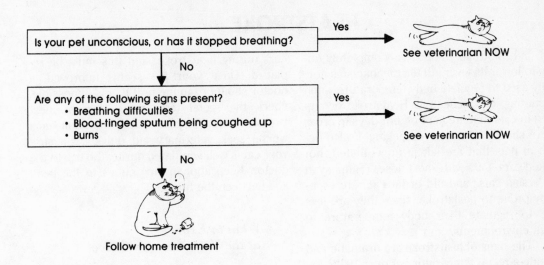

Is your pet unconscious, or has it stopped breathing? — **Yes** → See veterinarian NOW

No

Are any of the following signs present?
- Breathing difficulties
- Blood-tinged sputum being coughed up
- Burns

Yes → See veterinarian NOW

No

Follow home treatment

HEATSTROKE

In heatstroke, the body is completely unable to lower its fever. All the mechanisms normally used to regulate body temperature, such as panting, are ineffectual. Heatstroke occurs often in cats that are kept on hot days in areas where shade and water are lacking. It also occurs in pets that are left in unventilated, hot parked cars. Cats with short noses (Himalayan or Persian cats) and old or fat cats are especially prone to heatstroke, since they are less able to regulate their body temperature in warm environments.

The signs of heatstroke are dramatic and include a rectal temperature of over 106°F, extreme panting, a fast-pounding pulse, weakness, a staring expression, and collapse.

Home Treatment

EMERGENCY A high body temperature must be lowered rapidly to avoid brain damage or death. As in the treatment for fever, a cold-water bath or shower must be given immediately. Ice applied to the head and between the thighs is beneficial. Being in an air-conditioned room also helps bring down the fever. If the body temperature has not dropped to 103°F in ten minutes, a cold-water enema may be necessary. See the section on Fever (page 149), for instructions on giving a cold-water enema. *Note:* After a cold-water enema, improvement *cannot* be measured by rectal temperature.

If your cat stops panting, seems more relaxed, and responds normally to your voice, you are doing well. Give your pet ice cubes or a small amount of water. Great fluid loss occurs during heatstroke, and this must be replaced. Once your pet seems improved, a doctor should examine it. If this is impossible, check the rectal temperature for the next twelve hours. If your cat's condition gets worse, seek veterinary aid quickly. Be sure your cat is well ventilated during the trip to the doctor. Keep applying ice cubes to the head and between the thighs.

What to Expect at the Veterinarian's Office

If your emergency treatment was successful, your veterinarian will examine your pet to make sure that there is no permanent brain or organ damage. If emergency treatment at home was not successful, it will be necessary to replace lost water and treat for shock (intravenous fluids and steroids). Cold-water baths and enemas will be continued. Oxygen will be given if needed, and your cat will be hospitalized so that it can be observed closely for twenty-four hours.

Prevention

Adequate ventilation, shade, and free access to water are necessary. Do *not* leave your cat in the car on a warm day. Carry water in the car for your pet. Remember, the sun changes direction. *Note:* If your pet is short-nosed, old, or fat, these precautions may not be enough. Try keeping it in a cool room with an adequate water supply.

Is your pet's rectal temperature over 103°F even after emergency procedures? Does it still pant and seem tense and unresponsive?

Yes ──▶

See veterinarian NOW

No

Follow home treatment

SWALLOWED POISONS

Cats, when curious, can get into a lot of trouble by swallowing products that are around the house or in the garbage.

Home Treatment

EMERGENCY   If your cat swallows a poison (see the Decision Chart), call your poison control center immediately and get veterinary aid. Take the poison container and a sample of the vomit to the veterinarian. If your cat stops breathing, give artificial respiration (page 98). If you cannot reach your veterinarian or poison control center, check for the poison on the following lists and give the prescribed treatment. If the poison cannot be identified, force your cat to swallow egg whites, milk of magnesia, and/or milk (see Giving Liquids to Your Cat, page 91).

Petroleum Products, Acids, and Alkalis

Dishwasher granules	Paint remover
Drain cleaner	Paint thinner
Floor polish	Shoe polish
Furniture polish	Toilet-bowl cleaner
Gasoline	Wax (floor or
Kerosene	furniture)
Lye	Wood preservative
Oven cleaner	

Signs of poisoning by these products are bloody vomit, diarrhea, shock, depression, coma, convulsions (sometimes), coughing, abdominal pain, and redness around the mouth. *Note:* Do *not* induce vomiting! Make your cat swallow milk, egg whites, or olive oil to decrease absorption of the poison. Treat also for shock (page 100).

Acids and alkalis can also burn the mouth and skin, so flush these areas with large amounts of water. Apply a sodium bicarbonate paste to acid burns. Apply vinegar to neutralize alkali burns.

Other Known Poisons

Acetone	Insecticides
Alcohol	Linoleum (lead salts)
Algae toxins	Matches
Amphetamines	(*Note:* Safety
Aspirin	matches are non-
Antifreeze	toxic.)
Arsenic	Medicines
Bleach	Mothballs
Carbon tetrachloride	Mushrooms, wild
Chlordane	Paint, lead-based
Cosmetics	Perfume
Crayons	Pine oil
DDT	Rat or mouse poison
Deodorants	Red squill
Detergents	Roach poison
Fabric softener	Shellac
Fireworks	Sleeping pills
Fluoroacetates	Snail bait
Garbage Toxins	Strychnine
Hair dye	Suntan lotions
Hexachlorophene	Thallium
(in certain soaps)	Warfarin
Indelible markers	Weed killer

Signs of poisoning by these products include severe vomiting, diarrhea, delirium, collapse, coma, and convulsions. If your cat is conscious, induce vomiting: mix equal amounts of hydrogen peroxide (3 percent strength) and water and administer one tablespoon of this fluid. A mustard and water solution also works well. Another way to induce vomiting is to put a few tablespoons of salt on the back of the

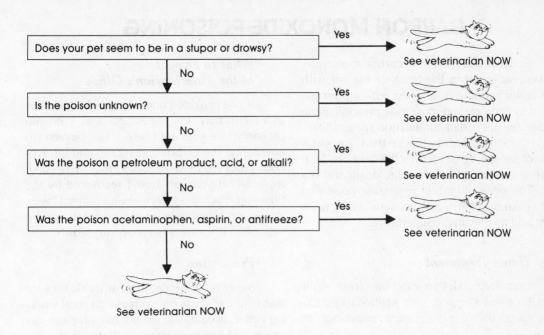

Does your pet seem to be in a stupor or drowsy? — Yes → See veterinarian NOW

No ↓

Is the poison unknown? — Yes → See veterinarian NOW

No ↓

Was the poison a petroleum product, acid, or alkali? — Yes → See veterinarian NOW

No ↓

Was the poison acetaminophen, aspirin, or antifreeze? — Yes → See veterinarian NOW

No ↓

See veterinarian NOW

cat's tongue; repeat this until vomiting occurs. Then treat for shock (page 100).

Do *not* give cats acetaminophen or aspirin. Acetaminophen (even one-half of a 325-milligram tablet) will cause breathing difficulties, liver and red blood cell damage, and head swelling. Prompt treatment by your veterinarian with supportive care, Mucomyst, and Tagamet can save your cat's life.

Wipe up any dripping antifreeze (ethylene glycol) when adding it to your car. Antifreeze is *highly toxic:* disorientation, seizures, and kidney failure can occur within thirty minutes after antifreeze is swallowed.

What to Expect at the Veterinarian's Office

If your cat is unconscious, oxygen and intravenous fluids will be given. Other life-preserving procedures, such as stomach pumping, may be necessary. Hospitalization will be required.

If your cat is conscious, treatment will depend upon what particular poison was swallowed and whether an antidote is known.

CARBON MONOXIDE POISONING

Exhaust fumes contain carbon monoxide. If your cat is put in the trunk of the car with the motor running or in a car with a poor exhaust system, carbon monoxide poisoning can occur. See also Smoke Inhalation (page 132).

Carbon monoxide blocks the transportation of life-giving oxygen to the body cells. If oxygen cannot get to the cells, death will occur. The signs of carbon monoxide poisoning are weakness, cherry-red gums, twitching muscles, and an elevated temperature.

Home Treatment

EMERGENCY   Get your cat into fresh air. If breathing has stopped, give artificial respiration (page 98). See veterinary assistance at once.

What to Expect at the Veterinarian's Office

If you provided immediate aid, no further treatment may be necessary, and you can probably take your cat home. If not, oxygen (to counteract the carbon monoxide) and intravenous fluids (to treat for shock) may be needed, especially if your pet hasn't recovered by the time you reach the veterinarian's office. Observation for a few days in the hospital may be suggested if your cat is recovering slowly.

Prevention

Never put your cat in a car trunk. Be sure that your car's exhaust system is in good working order. If camping, do *not* use propane gas stoves or heaters in an unventilated tent.

Has your pet stopped breathing?

Yes → See veterinarian NOW

No

Follow home treatment

POISONOUS PLANTS

Cats may be curious and chew up your house plants. Following are some common houseplants that are dangerous to your cat:

Christmas cherry: The berry is poisonous.

Dieffenbachia, also called dumb cane: The leaves can cause vomiting, diarrhea, swelling of the tongue, and even suffocation.

Dried arrangements: The seed pods and beans of tropical plants may be highly toxic.

Ivy: The leaves can cause breathing problems and stomach illness.

Mistletoe: The berries are highly toxic and can cause vomiting, diarrhea, and convulsions.

The following outdoor plants can also be hazardous if chewed and/or swallowed:

Castor bean	Lobelia
Daphne	Mistletoe
Foxglove	Monkshood
Horse chestnut	Nightshade
Jimson weed	Poison hemlock
Larkspur	Water hemlock
Laurels	Yew
Lily-of-the-valley	

Home Treatment

EMERGENCY If you discover that your cat has dined on a houseplant, call your poison control center immediately and get veterinary aid. If you don't know the name of the plant, take it along to the veterinarian's office. Give artificial respiration (page 98), if necessary. If you cannot reach a poison control center or your veterinarian, see Swallowed Poisons (page 136), and follow the treatment.

What to Expect at the Veterinarian's Office

If your cat is unconscious, oxygen and intravenous fluids will be given. The stomach may be pumped, as well. Hospitalization will probably be required, since other life-support procedures may be necessary.

If your cat is conscious, vomiting will be induced. Treatment will depend on the particular poison and whether the attempts to make your cat vomit have been successful.

Prevention

There is one step that you can take to prevent poisoning from houseplants: do *not* keep known poisonous plants in the house! If you just can't do without that beautiful plant that is potentially hazardous, the following may prevent its ingestion:

1. If your cat is kept strictly indoors, walking it outside (on a harness) each day and allowing it to chew the grass may cure the houseplant gourmand. *Note:* Be sure that your lawn has not been sprayed with weed killers.

2. If your cat cannot be walked, grow indoors some grasses that your cat may eat, such as wheat or oats. A bellyful of either of these may satisfy the "chewing-of-the-green" urge.

3. Most cats love catnip—they eat both fresh and dried leaves. You can grow your own. It is a perennial—it comes up year after year. Sit back and watch your cat's antics after a catnip snack. You'll see a lot of rolling and acts of bravado.

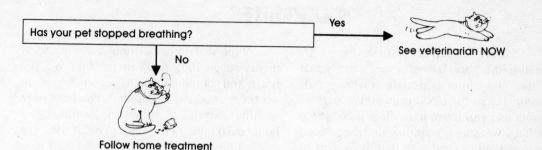

Has your pet stopped breathing? — Yes → See veterinarian NOW

No ↓

Follow home treatment

4. If you catch your cat nibbling plants, spray the cat with your plant mister at the time of the "crime" to convince your cat to stay away.
5. Mothballs or cayenne pepper in the soil may irritate your cat's "smeller." Cats don't like to be irritated and, therefore, may stop chewing the plants.

Note: Some mothballs contain *naphthalene,* which causes a hemolytic anemia if ingested by the pet.
6. Of course, keeping the hazardous plants out of reach is a very smart step and will usually work, unless your pet is determined to be "Supercat."

SNAKEBITES

Cats are not bitten by snakes very often because they are "street smart" and usually stay away from poisonous snakes. Snake venom attacks the blood cells and/or nervous system and can cause immediate pain, severe swelling, weakness, vomiting, diarrhea, bleeding from the nose and anus, paralysis, convulsions, and coma.

Home Treatment

EMERGENCY Identify the snake by checking the fang marks. A poisonous snake usually leaves just two marks (fangs) in the skin. A non-poisonous snake usually leaves U-shaped teeth marks, and the bite is not very painful.

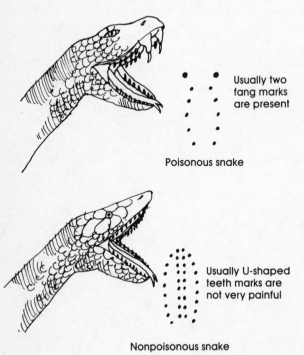

Usually two fang marks are present

Poisonous snake

Usually U-shaped teeth marks are not very painful

Nonpoisonous snake

If the snake was poisonous, apply a tourniquet (page 100) between the bite and the heart. You should be able to get one finger under the tourniquet, so that the wound can ooze slightly. Leave the tourniquet on for one to two hours maximum. Keep your cat quiet and lying down. Clip the hair over the wound with scissors. Apply alcohol to the wound and make a shallow linear (not X-shaped) cut over the fang marks using a flame-sterilized knife or razor. Use a suction cup to suck out the venom. You can use your mouth also—but only if there are no open sores in or around your mouth. Spit out the venom—do *not* swallow it. Repeat for fifteen minutes. Leaving the tourniquet on, wash the wound with soap and water and apply cold compresses. Clean the wound with alcohol.

If your cat is struggling too much, just apply a tourniquet and see the veterinarian as quickly as possible.

If the snake was nonpoisonous, apply cold compresses and clean the wound with soap, water, and alcohol.

What to Expect at the Veterinarian's Office

Hospitalization will be necessary. Additional suction of the wound will be done. Ice packs will be applied to decrease pain and tissue damage. *Antivenin,* if available, will be given to neutralize the venom. Shock treatment, antibiotics, fluids, steroids, and possibly oxygen may be needed.

Prevention

Keep your pet away from known snake-infested areas. Keep an antivenin kit handy.

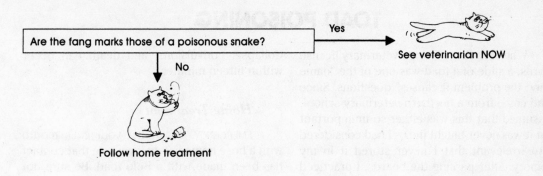

Are the fang marks those of a poisonous snake?

Yes → **See veterinarian NOW**

No

Follow home treatment

TOAD POISONING

When I took my Florida veterinary license boards, a slide of a toad was one of the "name it and the problem it causes" questions. Since I had come from a northern veterinary school, I assumed that this was either so unimportant that it was never taught me or I had considered it so irrelevant that I never stored it in my memory. After passing the boards, I practiced in Florida and found out quickly that there the Bufo toad is as common as oranges. It is found in other areas, too, but the Florida variety seems to be much more deadly.

Bufo toads are slow-moving creatures, and a cat may pick one up in its mouth. The wartlike salivary glands on the back of the toad's neck release a poison that, after being rapidly absorbed through the cat's mouth and stomach lining, causes heart irregularities. Within minutes, the cat will shake its head, salivate profusely, and become uncoordinated. The breathing and heart rates become rapid.

Collapse, convulsions, and death can occur within fifteen minutes.

Home Treatment

EMERGENCY Wash out your cat's mouth with a hose immediately if you see that contact has been made with a Bufo toad. Be sure not to tilt the head all the way in the air as you do so, or water may go down the cat's breathing tubes. See your veterinarian immediately.

What to Expect
at the Veterinarian's Office

Intravenous drugs will be administered to correct the heart irregularities. If you have already rinsed out the cat's mouth yourself and have managed to get the cat to the veterinarian quickly, your cat has the best chance for survival.

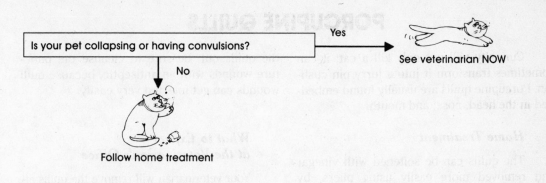

Is your pet collapsing or having convulsions?

No → Follow home treatment

Yes → See veterinarian NOW

PORCUPINE QUILLS

Curiosity will not only kill a cat; it can sometimes transform it into a furry pin cushion. Porcupine quills are usually found embedded in the head, nose, and mouth.

Home Treatment

The quills can be softened with vinegar and removed more easily using pliers, by slowly twisting out each quill. This is *extremely* painful, and it may be difficult to restrain your cat without sedation. If you get the quills out, be sure to cleanse the puncture wounds with an antiseptic, because quill wounds can get infected very easily.

What to Expect at the Veterinarian's Office

Your veterinarian will remove the quills after administering a tranquilizer or general anesthesia. The wounds will be thoroughly cleansed, and your cat will be given antibiotics.

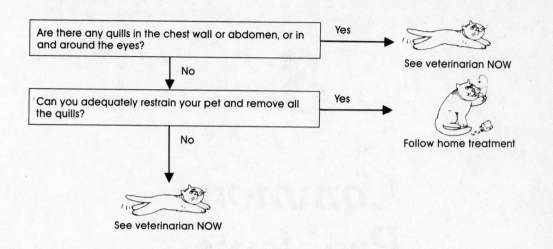

Are there any quills in the chest wall or abdomen, or in and around the eyes?

Yes → See veterinarian NOW

No ↓

Can you adequately restrain your pet and remove all the quills?

Yes → Follow home treatment

No ↓

See veterinarian NOW

Common Problems and Diseases

FEVER

In cats, a body temperature above 103°F is a fever, but an elevated temperature is not necessarily a sign of illness. Many healthy pets will have a variation in temperature of one or two degrees depending on the time of day, their emotional state and amount of activity, or the environment, such as a hot automobile. Muscle activity and food digestion are the most important ways cats produce heat to maintain body temperature. Some healthy animals that are nervous will shake so much (i.e., increase their muscle activity) at the doctor's office that a 104°F temperature may be recorded.

The most common causes for persistent fevers in cats are viral and bacterial infections. Examples are feline leukemia virus, FTLV (AIDS-like) virus, panleukopenia (viral), skin abscesses (bacterial), respiratory infections (viral and/or bacterial), toxoplasmosis, and feline infectious peritonitis. Other causes are heatstroke (environmental), *eclampsia* (low blood calcium), immune-mediated diseases (systemic lupus erythematosus), and cancer (lymphosarcoma or leukemia).

The hair coat of most cats insulates against heat loss or heat gain. If it is a hot day, the only way cats can lower their body temperature is by panting, since they do not have sweat glands (except on the foot pads). If they are left in a car on a hot day, the panting mechanism will not be able to lower the body temperature enough, and heatstroke may result.

Bacteria, viruses, and probably cancer cells cause fever by stimulating certain white blood cells to produce chemical substances called *pyrogens*. Pyrogens can be helpful in combating unwanted invaders. Therefore, fever is not always a bad sign—it may mean that your pet's body is responding to the challenge and fighting the infection.

There are a number of signs that will tell you when your cat has a true fever. Depression, a sad expression, and lack of appetite are common signs. Some cats seem cold and shiver; others feel hot and pant or seek cool places. You may also notice an increase in both the heart and respiratory rates.

Feline Infectious Peritonitis (FIP)

Feline infectious peritonitis (FIP) is a contagious viral disease of wild and domestic cats that does not infect humans. The disease has an insidious onset: the cat is lethargic, has progressive weight loss, a loss of appetite, and a fever that does not respond to antibiotic therapy. Fluid may accumulate in the abdomen and/or chest. The eyes, central nervous system, and abdominal organs may be ravaged by the inflammatory reaction. At this writing there is no cure, and supportive therapy will prolong life for only a short time. Euthanasia is the most merciful solution, should your cat develop FIP.

The FIP virus may cause no signs, only mild signs (sneezing, watery eyes, and a nose discharge), or the full-blown disease as just described. Researchers are currently trying to determine why all infected cats do not get the full-blown disease. Cats with only mild signs unfortunately become carriers and pass the virus to others. Your veterinarian can diagnose FIP with a thorough physical exam, analysis of abdominal or chest fluid, a positive FIP antibody test, and other laboratory data.

The FIP or the leukemia virus is suspected to cause the "kitten mortality complex," which includes the deaths of unborn fetuses, newborn kittens, and very young kittens. The Cornell Feline Research Laboratory (New York

State College of Veterinary Medicine, Cornell University, Ithaca, New York 14853) is studying FIP in the hope of developing an effective treatment and a vaccination. The support of cat lovers is needed. Please write to the laboratory for further information.

Home Treatment

Take your cat's temperature as you did during the home physical, using a rectal thermometer, which has a rounded, stubby tip. Shake down the thermometer and apply Vaseline or mineral oil to the bulb. Restrain your cat (page 97), lift its tail, and gently slide the thermometer into the anus. Leave it in for three minutes. It is helpful to wrap your cat in a blanket or sheet, leaving its tail end exposed, and hold it between your arm and body. This leaves at least one hand free to hold in the thermometer, which might break if the cat moves a lot. But remember that cats dislike restraint. Remove the thermometer and read the mercury level as you normally do. *Note:* Do *not* administer aspirin, which can cause a toxic reaction. And do *not* "starve" a fever, since the body needs more fuel (calories) than usual in this weakened state.

If the fever is over 105°F, see Heatstroke (page 134). A cold-water bath or shower must be given immediately to lower the body temperature before brain damage or death results. Ice applied to the head and inner thighs is also beneficial. If the body temperature has not dropped to 103°F in ten minutes, a cold-water enema may be necessary. Fill an enema bag with cold water and ice cubes. Lubricate the tip and insert it gently into the anus. Hold the bag high until your cat shows signs of discomfort, then let the water drain out. *Note:* After a cold-water enema, improvement *cannot* be measured by rectal temperature.

If your pet has a fever and is not vomiting, be sure that it eats and drinks. The caloric (energy) requirements increase when heat increases, because energy is used faster and must be replaced. There is also an increased need for fluids in the feverish body. If your pet will not drink voluntarily, see Giving Liquids to Your Cat (page 91). *Note:* Water should *not* be given if your pet is vomiting. In this case, let it lick ice cubes.

Cats that will not eat or drink and cannot be nursed by you should be seen by your doctor as soon as possible, especially if your pet's condition deteriorates.

What to Expect at the Veterinarian's Office

Again, a fever may be a *sign* of illness. If your pet has a fever along with other signs and is getting worse, do not hesitate to see your veterinarian. Your doctor will do a complete physical examination. Blood tests, urinalysis, and X-rays may be necessary to find the cause of the fever.

If an infection is suspected, antibiotics will be given. Intravenous or subcutaneous fluids may be administered if your pet has not been able to take in enough fluids to meet the body's daily needs. Fluid therapy is very important for pets that will not eat or drink. Feeding with a nasogastric tube may also be necessary if your pet is not eating.

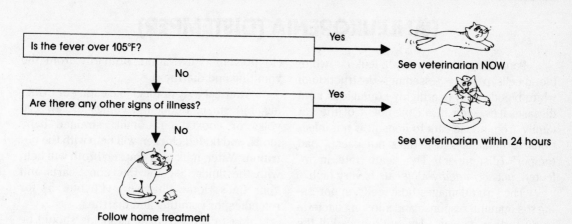

Is the fever over 105°F? — Yes → See veterinarian NOW

No ↓

Are there any other signs of illness? — Yes → See veterinarian within 24 hours

No ↓

Follow home treatment

PANLEUKOPENIA (DISTEMPER)

Panleukopenia (pan = all, leuko = white blood cells, penia = lessening—destruction of white blood cells) is a highly contagious viral disease. It is seen in all members of the cat family, from house cats to lions. It is not infectious to humans and it does not cause "bad temper" (distemper). The death rate in infected, *unvaccinated* young cats is very high.

The virus damages body cells, suppressing the immune response and allowing bacteria to do further damage. The antibiotics kill the bacteria, thus giving the body time to overwhelm the virus and repair the damage. If your cat can be kept alive for a week, the chance for recovery is good.

The virus has a predilection for intestinal cells and bone marrow. Its general signs are a high fever (104°F to 105°F), loss of appetite, weakness, vomiting, and diarrhea (sometimes bloody). Since these signs are so similar to those of other serious problems, such as leukemia, toxoplasmosis, some poisonings, and intestinal obstructions, an immediate visit to your veterinarian is essential.

The virus is spread by direct contact with the saliva, vomit, urine, or feces of an ill cat. The virus is very hardy, and most disinfectants are ineffective in destroying it. There is no drug that specifically kills the virus.

Home Treatment

Your doctor may ask you to be an active partner in helping your cat get well, because good nursing care is as important to recovery as the antibiotics and fluids that your veterinarian will administer. It is important to provide both adequate nutrition (to maintain body condition and to help fight infection) and fluids (to prevent dehydration, primarily from the vomiting and diarrhea).

Your cat may not feel like eating or drinking, but small, frequent feedings of raw egg yolks or cooked eggs, milk, strained baby foods, and boiled chicken will help with the nutrition. Water, milk, and chicken broth will help with the fluids. See the Decision Charts and Your Cat's Home Pharmacy (Chapter 5) for remedies for vomiting and diarrhea.

Most cats with panleukopenia should be treated, because the majority will survive. Good nursing care, good veterinary care, patience, love, and understanding can be very rewarding.

What to Expect at the Veterinarian's Office

Since the signs of panleukopenia are similar to those of other diseases, blood tests and X-rays may be necessary for diagnosis and for determining the proper treatment regimen. Of course, a complete physical examination will be done. Your doctor may suggest home care and possibly frequent veterinary visits as the best treatment plan. Antibiotics, fluids, antivomitins, antidiarrheals, vitamins, and sometimes blood transfusions are needed to help your cat recover.

Prevention

The kitten series of vaccinations should begin at seven to nine weeks of age, with the last one given at twelve to sixteen weeks of age. Yearly boosters are needed to keep up the antibody level and to keep the body's "memory system" on guard.

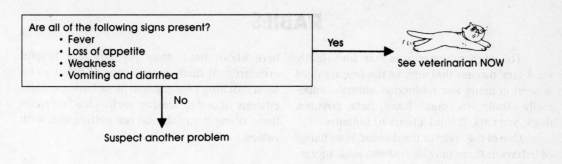

Are all of the following signs present?
- Fever
- Loss of appetite
- Weakness
- Vomiting and diarrhea

Yes → See veterinarian NOW

No ↓

Suspect another problem

RABIES

The word *rabies* evokes fear, and rightly so. A viral disease that attacks the brain, rabies is seen in many warm-blooded animals, especially skunks, raccoons, foxes, bats, coyotes, dogs, and cats. It *is* infectious to humans.

One of the signs of the disease is a change of behavior: there may be restlessness, aggressiveness or extreme shyness. In fact, wild animals may seem tame. Infected animals' pupils are dilated as well.

In the *furious stage,* the animal will bite at anything in its way. Loud noises or bright lights can stimulate the biting attacks. The animal also becomes uncoordinated. In this stage, the animal may die during convulsions, or it may go on to the *dumb stage.*

In the dumb stage, the paralysis of the throat causes voice changes, salivation, and an inability to eat or drink. The lower jaw will be paralyzed and unable to close, and the tongue and lower jaw will hang loose. Generalized paralysis, coma, and death follow.

The virus is spread by the bite of a rabid animal—the virus-laden saliva enters the wound. Airborne transmission in caves inhabited by bats has been reported. (Just a word here about bats—they are shy and helpful creatures. At dusk, many types of bats can be seen catching mosquitoes. Most bats are good citizens of our spaceship earth—leading quiet lives, doing their job and not getting sick with rabies.)

Home Treatment

No home care is effective. See your veterinarian *immediately* if the Decision Chart applies.

What to Expect at the Veterinarian's Office

An animal suspected of being rabid will be quarantined, and public health officials will be notified.

Prevention

Keep your cat's rabies vaccination up to date. The first vaccination is given between three and six months of age. A booster is given at one year and then annually thereafter.

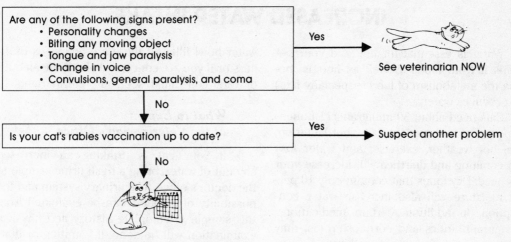

Are any of the following signs present?
- Personality changes
- Biting any moving object
- Tongue and jaw paralysis
- Change in voice
- Convulsions, general paralysis, and coma

Yes → See veterinarian NOW

No

Is your cat's rabies vaccination up to date?

Yes → Suspect another problem

No

Make appointment with veterinarian

INCREASED WATER INTAKE

Water is essential for life, and your pet obtains it from foods as well as liquids, because the metabolism of food (especially fats) also produces water.

Cats need about 30 milligrams (1 ounce) per pound of body weight daily, but lactation, fever, hot weather, exercise, and water loss from vomiting and diarrhea will increase your pet's need. Dry foods that contain only 10 percent moisture will also increase water consumption. In addition, certain medications, such as antibiotics and corticosteroids, may cause your cat to become very thirsty.

However, excessive thirst is seen as well in such serious illnesses as hyperthyroidism, pyometra (infected uterus), diabetes, and liver and kidney disease. Therefore, veterinary attention may be necessary.

Home Treatment

An increased water intake in an alert and active pet is of no concern. Keep your cat's water bowl filled. If there are any signs of illness or if you are concerned about the amount of water consumed, see your veterinarian.

What to Expect at the Veterinarian's Office

If your cat is drinking an increased amount of water, bring a fresh urine sample to the doctor's office. The urinary system and the possibility of diabetes can be evaluated from this sample. A complete history and physical examination will be done. If vomiting or diarrhea is thought to be the cause of the fluid loss and increased thirst, a stool sample and bowel X-rays will be taken. Blood tests may be needed to check the status of all the internal organs. Hyperthyroidism is becoming more common in cats over seven years of age. Thyroid blood tests will be checked.

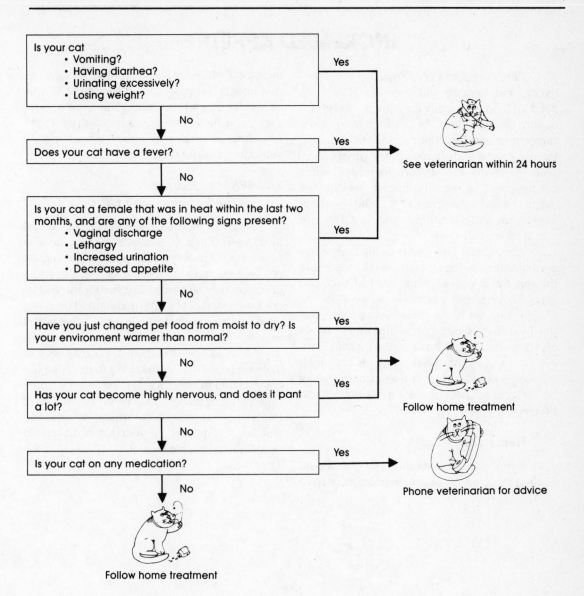

Is your cat
- Vomiting?
- Having diarrhea?
- Urinating excessively?
- Losing weight?

Yes → See veterinarian within 24 hours

No ↓

Does your cat have a fever?

Yes → See veterinarian within 24 hours

No ↓

Is your cat a female that was in heat within the last two months, and are any of the following signs present?
- Vaginal discharge
- Lethargy
- Increased urination
- Decreased appetite

Yes

No ↓

Have you just changed pet food from moist to dry? Is your environment warmer than normal?

Yes → Follow home treatment

No ↓

Has your cat become highly nervous, and does it pant a lot?

Yes → Follow home treatment

No ↓

Is your cat on any medication?

Yes → Phone veterinarian for advice

No ↓

Follow home treatment

INCREASED APPETITE

More exercise, a cold environment, pregnancy, and nursing will increase your cat's need for food, especially for calories and good-quality protein. However, an increased appetite could mean something more. For example, the early signs of diabetes or hyperthyroidism, seen frequently in cats, are increased water consumption, increased urination, weight loss despite a voracious appetite, and possibly depression and vomiting (these last two are late signs in diabetes).

Worms may also cause an increased appetite, although they could equally decrease the appetite or cause no change at all. Still, you should not rule out worms (see page 48).

If your pet has a voracious appetite, but the food just passes out as unformed stools and dramatic weight loss occurs, thyroid, pancreatic, liver, or intestinal problems (in which the food is not absorbed or used properly) may be the cause. These require veterinary attention, also.

Home Treatment

If you suspect that more exercise, a cold environment, pregnancy, or nursing may have increased your cat's caloric and protein requirements, no professional treatment will be necessary, in all probability. You should, however, read the section on nutrition (page 34). Any other dramatic appetite changes require veterinary consultation.

What to Expect at the Veterinarian's Office

Since an increased appetite can be caused by so many things, your doctor will take the time to get a good history and to perform a complete physical exam. Blood tests, a fecal exam, and a urinalysis may be needed. Prepare for the visit by not feeding your cat in the morning and by taking urine and stool samples to test for diabetes and worms, respectively.

A word about diabetes: Most owners of diabetic pets do a remarkable job in giving the daily insulin injections and checking the urine. Although the disease cannot be cured (as of this writing, at least), a controlled diabetic can still live a happy life. If your cat is diagnosed as a diabetic, please treat it.

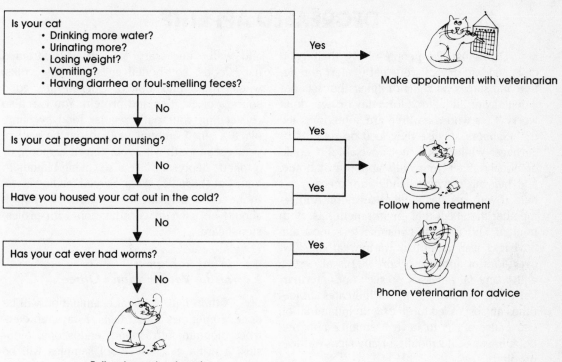

Is your cat
- Drinking more water?
- Urinating more?
- Losing weight?
- Vomiting?
- Having diarrhea or foul-smelling feces?

Yes → Make appointment with veterinarian

No ↓

Is your cat pregnant or nursing?

Yes

No ↓

Have you housed your cat out in the cold?

Yes → Follow home treatment

No ↓

Has your cat ever had worms?

Yes → Phone veterinarian for advice

No ↓

Follow home treatment

DECREASED APPETITE

Cats—just like people—have their good days and bad days. If your pet is alert and active and shows no signs of illness but has not eaten any or all its food for a day or two, don't worry. Cats who roam free are sometimes fed by neighbors, or else they feed on rodents or garbage. While this is not advisable, it could obviously affect your cat's appetite at home, and begging on your hands and knees won't help if your pet has eaten elsewhere. And remember the effect that environment has. Both humans and animals consume less food and have less of an appetite in warm weather. However, loss of appetite (*anorexia*) is also seen with many cat illnesses, so see your veterinarian if the Decision Chart so indicates. Sometimes an abscessed tooth or gum inflammation can cause a cat to have a smaller appetite. Look in your cat's mouth for any signs of these problems.

Home Treatment

If your cat is not eating and you cannot see your veterinarian, force feeding may be necessary to provide the calories, nutrients, and water necessary for survival. Strained baby foods, soft-boiled eggs, raw egg yolks, whole milk, and boiled chicken are good sources of calories and protein. You can also try feeding your pet's regular food by hand: place a small amount of food on the roof of your cat's mouth with your finger, a spoon, or a tongue depressor. See also Giving Liquids to Your Cat (page 91). *Note:* Forced feeding is *not* to be used instead of a veterinary visit. It should be used in coordination with professional care.

What to Expect at the Veterinarian's Office

A thorough physical examination will be done. Sometimes blood tests, X-rays, an electrocardiogram, ultrasound, endoscopy, biopsies, a urinalysis, and stool samples will be necessary to identify the problem and determine the best treatment.

Your cat may have to be hospitalized and supported with intravenous fluids and feeding with a nasogastric tube if it is not eating or drinking enough.

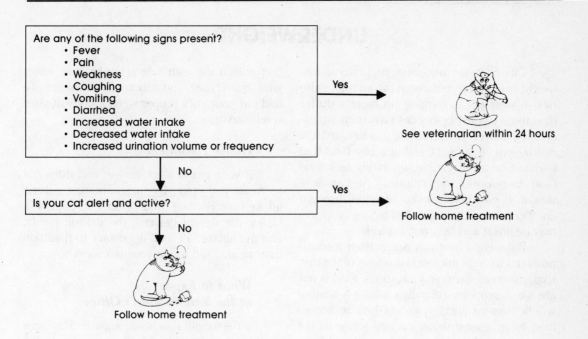

Are any of the following signs present?
- Fever
- Pain
- Weakness
- Coughing
- Vomiting
- Diarrhea
- Increased water intake
- Decreased water intake
- Increased urination volume or frequency

Yes → See veterinarian within 24 hours

No

Is your cat alert and active?

Yes → Follow home treatment

No

Follow home treatment

UNDERWEIGHT

Cats that are underweight or have lost weight usually are not receiving enough calories. If your pet is burning up more calories than usual (by living in a hot environment, exercising more, or becoming excited over a nearby female in heat), eating a new food that may not be as digestible, or eating less food (and therefore fewer calories), it can lose weight. If you have moved recently, brought another new pet home, or had a baby, your cat may be upset and may not eat well.

But weight loss can occur from medical problems as well. In certain diseases of the thyroid, pancreas, liver, and intestines, food is not absorbed properly (diarrhea and/or vomiting will be present also). A weight loss accompanied by increased urination and water intake may indicate the presence of hyperthyroidism, diabetes, or kidney disease. Heart disease (such as cardiomyopathy or heart-valve disease) can cause a weight loss called *cardiac cachexia,* in which the body does not get the proper nutrition because of poor circulation. Worms can steal the nutrition your cat's body needs. The list of medical problems that can cause weight loss is endless, so an examination by your veterinarian is essential.

There is nothing really wrong with being just a little underweight, however. Healthy pets that are on the lean side seem to have fewer joint, heart, lung, and pancreatic problems. To find out your cat's proper weight, consult your veterinarian.

Home Treatment

If your cat is alert, active, and does not seem ill, you could try increasing the caloric intake (see Feeding Your Adult Cat, page 40). Check the weight desired, the caloric needs, and the amount of food necessary to maintain that weight, and weigh your pet weekly.

What to Expect at the Veterinarian's Office

If the weight loss is accompanied by signs of illness, or if no weight gain is seen with the increased food intake, see your veterinarian. A complete history and physical examination will be done, and your cat's dietary and bowel patterns will be scrutinized. Blood tests, including the FLV and FTLV tests, a stool sample, a urinalysis, an electrocardiogram, an echocardiogram, endoscopy, biopsies, and X-rays may be necessary to find the underlying cause for the weight loss. *Note:* There is an increased incidence of hyperthyroidism in cats over seven years of age.

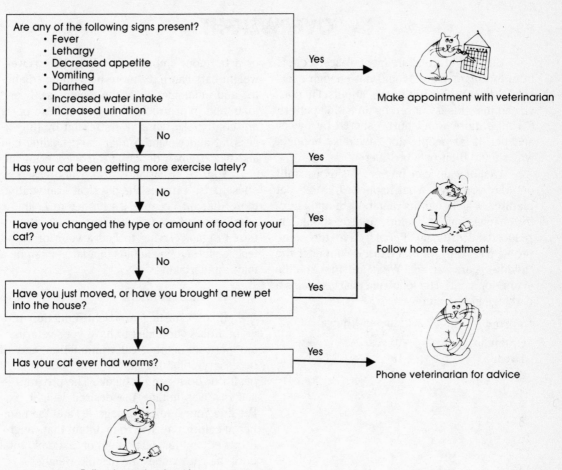

Are any of the following signs present?
- Fever
- Lethargy
- Decreased appetite
- Vomiting
- Diarrhea
- Increased water intake
- Increased urination

Yes → Make appointment with veterinarian

No

Has your cat been getting more exercise lately?

Yes

No

Have you changed the type or amount of food for your cat?

Yes → Follow home treatment

No

Have you just moved, or have you brought a new pet into the house?

Yes

No

Has your cat ever had worms?

Yes → Phone veterinarian for advice

No

Follow home treatment

OVERWEIGHT

Obesity in cats, in most cases, comes from too many calories and not enough exercise. Fat people seem to have fat pets. I'm convinced that this is caused by an eating pattern ("a little more won't hurt") shared by owner and pet. If fat people don't exercise enough, why should their pets be different?

Weight gain can be very insidious until one day you say, "What happened?" As a pet matures or gets old, its metabolism and activity change, and its caloric intake should be reduced accordingly. People have the same problem keeping off that extra weight after the "middle years" arrive. What are the "middle years" for a cat? The following chart explains a cat's age in human terms:

Cat Age	Human Equivalent
6 months	10 years
1 year	15
2 years	24
4	32
6	40
8	48
10	55
12	65
14	70
16	80

If there is an increase in caloric intake, a slowdown in metabolism (due to body-age changes), or a decrease in exercise (due to action on your part or to a lazy or aging pet), a weight gain will occur. *Hypothyroidism* (a lack of thyroid hormones) is rare in cats, and an *ovariohysterectomy* (removal of the ovaries, tubes, and uterus in a female) does not seem to cause a weight gain.

But sometimes owners misinterpret a weight gain or "large belly" as a fat problem when in reality a heart, liver, or kidney problem (with fluid accumulation in the abdomen) or a hormone imbalance is the cause. Overweight cats can have more pancreatic (diabetes and inflammation of the pancreas), heart, lung, and joint problems because these parts are continually being overstressed by the excess fat and weight. Surgery and healing can also be extremely difficult in an overweight cat.

Your veterinarian is *also* overstressed by obese pets. It makes the physical examination more difficult because it's harder to hear the heartbeat and lung sounds and to feel the internal organs. Trying to find a vein for blood tests or intravenous fluids in a fat pet can be a major undertaking.

Home Treatment

Before starting a weight-reduction program, it is a good idea to have your veterinarian perform a physical examination and, if necessary, blood tests to rule out related health or hormone problems. The program itself involves finding the desired weight (see Feeding Your Adult Cat, page 40) and the number of calories needed to maintain that weight. Feed your cat just 60 percent of that daily total until the cat reaches the desired weight.

For instance, if your cat weighs twelve pounds, and ten pounds is the desired weight, then 400 calories $\times$ 60% = 240 calories should be fed daily until your cat weighs ten pounds. Be patient: it may take three or four months. Once the goal is reached, you can slowly increase the calories to the calorie maintenance level (400 calories for ten pounds).

The cat's normal food or special prescription diets can be used for the weight-reduction program, but all family members must cooperate. No table food or treats are allowed, because these add considerable calories. Keep a weekly record of your cat's weight. If there is not a steady weight loss, contact your veteri-

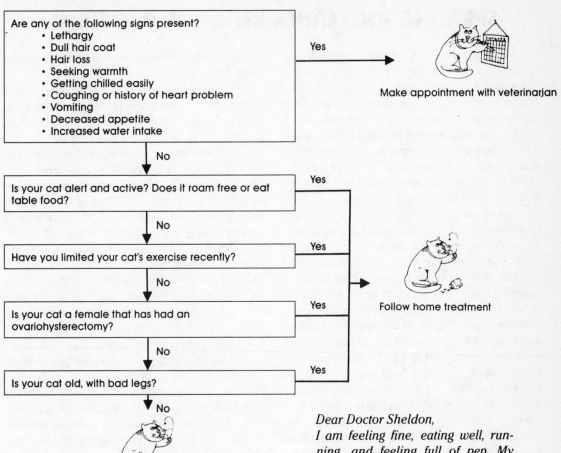

Are any of the following signs present?
- Lethargy
- Dull hair coat
- Hair loss
- Seeking warmth
- Getting chilled easily
- Coughing or history of heart problem
- Vomiting
- Decreased appetite
- Increased water intake

Yes → Make appointment with veterinarian

No ↓

Is your cat alert and active? Does it roam free or eat table food?

Yes →

No ↓

Have you limited your cat's exercise recently?

Yes →

No ↓

Is your cat a female that has had an ovariohysterectomy?

Yes →

No ↓

Is your cat old, with bad legs?

Yes → Follow home treatment

No ↓

Follow home treatment

narian. *Note:* If your pet roams free and is fed by neighbors, gets into trash, or hunts for rodents, forget about weight reduction.

Take a "before" and an "after" picture of your cat. Your veterinarian will be proud of you and your pet's accomplishment. A sincere owner who practices good preventive medicine for his or her pet is deeply respected by veterinarians. I want to share with you a postcard I received this summer from my patient Smokey Meisner, on vacation in the Poconos:

Dear Doctor Sheldon,
I am feeling fine, eating well, running, and feeling full of pep. My sugar color chart is staying between blue negative and +1. My owners are happy and enjoying their vacation because of how you help me. They appreciate you, and I love you!

Lick, lick, lick!
Smokey Meisner

Smokey had been terribly overweight but went on a diet and lost the excess weight. The Meisners brought me "before" and "after" pictures, and the difference is truly amazing. Smokey, I am sad to say, became a diabetic (a high risk with obesity) but is otherwise happy.

165

SPRAYING AND OTHER BEHAVIOR PROBLEMS

Cats have been a favorite companion of humankind for about five thousand years. Their grace, beauty, and regal bearing have charmed royalty and common folk alike. During this time, the cat was quite independent. It did not live in close quarters, did not share the social pressures common to modern times, and was not bred selectively. These factors singly or in combination are thought to contribute to an increase in behavior problems.

Both intact and neutered male cats (and to a lesser extent, females) may back up to vertical objects, such as furniture and drapes, raise and quiver the tail, and squirt a small amount of urine on the object. This is called *spraying. Note:* This is *not* to be confused with *urolithiasis* or *cystitis* (page 230). Spraying apparently makes the surroundings more familiar and comfortable to the cat by giving them the cat's own smell, and it lets others know that Morris, Jaws, or Ralph "was here." If the cat perceives a threat to its environment, such as a new addition to the household (another pet, a baby), a furniture change, or a new cat in the neighborhood, spraying may occur. In these cases, however, it will probably be temporary.

Home Treatment

Castrating the male cat before sexual maturity solves the spraying problem before it begins, but castration after maturity is still highly effective (see page 250). If castration doesn't appeal, try placing mothballs or the cat's food bowl in the "spray zone." Cats don't go to the bathroom where they eat, and they detest the smell of mothballs. (*Note:* Do *not* use mothballs if small children are in the household. Also, some mothballs contain naphthalene, which causes a hemolytic anemia if the cat licks or chews them.) Hormones or a new home for the cat may be needed if the behavior persists.

Cats are very proper about their toilet habits: they cover their bowel movements in their territory (if their mothers taught them correctly, this is the litter box). A change of litter type, infrequent cleaning of the litter box, or any perceived environmental threats can disrupt this habit. First, try to correct the environmental change. Clean the area and place the feeding bowl, toys, or mothballs nearby. If flowerpot soil has become the new bathroom, a few mothballs placed in the soil or some cayenne pepper sprinkled on top should send your cat back to its litter box. Increasing the number of litter boxes, relocating them, and removing any box covers may be helpful. If your cat is having loose bowel movements outside of the litter box, see Diarrhea (page 220).

Thumb sucking or sucking on pacifiers or other objects is a favorite pastime of small children, especially when they are anxious, tired, hungry, or stressed. Similarly, cats—especially those that were orphaned or undernourished during the nursing period—may try to suck your blankets, sweaters, pants, or anything made from wool; your skin or hair; or its own body. At the same time, they will knead as they do when nursing. A firm "No!" and a shake by the scruff of the neck should be helpful in eliminating or reducing this behavior.

What to Expect at the Veterinarian's Office

If any behavior problems have not been modified by the Home Treatment, please consult your veterinarian. Many times a "behavior" problem is actually a *medical* problem such as urolithiasis, diabetes, or hyperthyroidism. Each cat is a unique personality, and discuss-

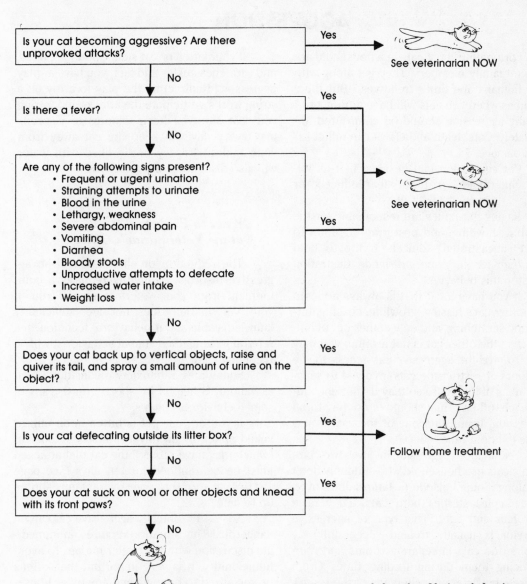

Is your cat becoming aggressive? Are there unprovoked attacks?

Yes → See veterinarian NOW

No ↓

Is there a fever?

Yes →

No ↓

Are any of the following signs present?
- Frequent or urgent urination
- Straining attempts to urinate
- Blood in the urine
- Lethargy, weakness
- Severe abdominal pain
- Vomiting
- Diarrhea
- Bloody stools
- Unproductive attempts to defecate
- Increased water intake
- Weight loss

Yes → See veterinarian NOW

No ↓

Does your cat back up to vertical objects, raise and quiver its tail, and spray a small amount of urine on the object?

Yes →

No ↓

Is your cat defecating outside its litter box?

Yes → Follow home treatment

No ↓

Does your cat suck on wool or other objects and knead with its front paws?

Yes →

No ↓

Follow home treatment

ing your cat and home situation with your veterinarian may be very helpful.

Recently, the University of Pennsylvania veterinary hospital established a referral clinic (sponsored by the National Institutes of Health) to handle problems that owners have with their animals. The staff includes a veterinary neurologist, an animal-behavior specialist, a social worker, and a psychiatrist. Animal behavior specialists are available at other veterinary schools as well.

AGGRESSION

Fortunately, most cats in a household are pleasant family members. They get along with their humans and other "relatives." But there are times when two cats will have a "dogfight," but any aggression should be confronted immediately. Cats' teeth and claws can inflict serious damage.

Cat aggression can be classified as follows: intermale, territorial, fear-induced, or play.

Raging hormones are responsible for the growling, howling, and posturing common to intact (uncastrated) tomcats trying to hold onto their territory and girlfriends. Castration will stop this behavior.

If you have a cat that is always a victim of another cat's hissing, growling, chasing, biting, and scratching, and only comes out of hiding when the other cat is not around, you may want to give the aggressive cat access to the outdoors or restrict the cats involved to separate areas of the house so they do not encounter each other. This should stop territorial aggression. If not, find one of the cats a new home (without other cats).

Fear-induced aggression involves two compatible cats in a household who suddenly don't get along. Some episode (a lamp falling over, for example) startles both cats. They raise their hair and fight. This type of aggressive behavior is usually treated successfully by keeping the cats in separate rooms and reintroducing them during feeding times (from separate bowls at opposite ends of the room). Playing with both cats in the room will also help them like each other again. Harnesses and leashes may be used when introducing the cats.

If your kitten or cat stalks, pounces, bites, and scratches ankles and feet, you have a "play aggressor." Redirecting the play to a toy on a string works. Anticipate the attacks and "string your cat along." Fifteen minutes of vigorous play every day will keep the cat away from your ankles. A spray bottle filled with water will also discourage the attacker.

What to Expect at the Veterinarian's Office

The reduction or elimination of an aggressive disorder frequently requires a commitment from your veterinarian and you. If your veterinarian does not feel sufficiently knowledgeable about behavioral techniques, a referral to a qualified animal behaviorist will be recommended.

Sometimes antianxiety medication (such as Valium) is helpful for short-term therapy of some behavior problems.

If you or your pet is bitten in an unprovoked attack by an unvaccinated outdoor cat (which may have rabies), the cat that attacked must be quarantined for ten days (see page 154). Make sure that your own tetanus shot is up to date.

Note: A chronically aggressive cat can be dangerous! This situation requires an immediate discussion with your veterinarian. To avoid future injury, it is very important that kittens be socialized to humans and any other household members (dogs, birds, etc.) during the critical socialization period—five to sixteen weeks of age. (Please read Training Your Cat, which begins on page 56.) Improper socializa-

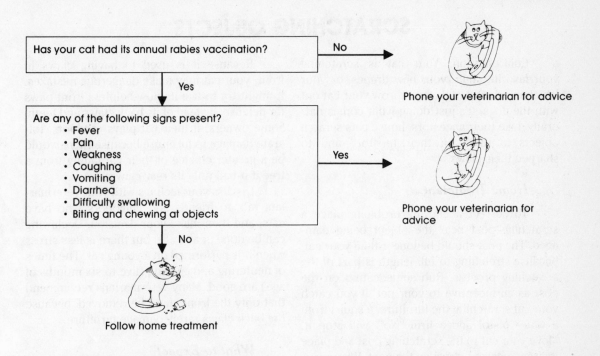

Has your cat had its annual rabies vaccination?

No → Phone your veterinarian for advice

Yes ↓

Are any of the following signs present?
- Fever
- Pain
- Weakness
- Coughing
- Vomiting
- Diarrhea
- Difficulty swallowing
- Biting and chewing at objects

Yes → Phone your veterinarian for advice

No ↓

Follow home treatment

tion is a major cause of future aggressive behavior, although there may also be an inherited basis. Kittens may go through a phase when they "hunt" your feet or ankles; this can be stopped by sharply saying "No!" or by diverting the kittens' attention to other playthings. A cat that is well socialized to humans is a very great pleasure.

SCRATCHING OBJECTS

Confrontation: Your cat is scratching your favorite chair, your new drapes, or your Ishfahan oriental rug! Don't throw your cat out with the dogs. It's just doing what comes naturally. Like their ancestors, house cats scratch objects to mark off their territory and to sharpen their claws.

Home Treatment

To correct a clawing problem, place a scratching post near the object being damaged. The post should be longer than your cat, because stretching to full length is part of the scratching process. Rub some catnip on the post as an incentive to your pet. If you catch your cat scratching the furniture, a squirt from a water pistol and a firm "No!" will stop it. Move your cat to the scratching post and place its front legs and claws on the post. When your cat uses the post, reward it with a food treat, a kind word, or gentle petting.

You can also try trimming your cat's nails weekly (see Grooming, page 59).

Declawing

If all else fails, consider having your cat's front claws surgically removed. Declawing is necessary only if your cat is using its claws on people or destroying your home furnishings by refusing to use a scratching post. A cat is not damaged physically or emotionally by declawing, but it may still think the front claws are present. For instance, your cat may go through the usual scratching motions (thought to be a way of removing worn nails) when it gets up in the morning.

Because it is used to having claws in front, your cat may make dangerous mistakes. It might try to use its now-helpless front paws for defense, instead of its back claws and teeth. Some owners, if their cat plays outdoors, tolerate damage to furniture because there would be a greater chance of their cat falling from a tree if it had only its rear claws.

Discuss your feelings with your veterinarian, talk to friends and neighbors who have cats, and then make your decision. Declawing can be done at any age, but there is less stress when it is performed on a young cat. The times of neutering and spaying (five to six months of age) are good. Many veterinarians recommend that only the front claws be removed, because the back claws rarely damage furniture.

What to Expect at the Veterinarian's Office

Declawing is a surgical procedure. A general anesthesia is used for the operation because the claws and the area from which they grow (basal germinal cells) are removed. Some doctors suture the digits afterward. The paws should be kept bandaged for two or three days after surgery.

Most cats recover remarkably well from this operation. A few cats are tender for a week or two after surgery; they may touch their paws lightly to the ground or occasionally hold one up. When the bandages are removed, I advise using shredded newspaper with just a few granules of kitty litter in the litter box for one week after surgery. This will reduce the chances of irritation or infection while the paws are healing.

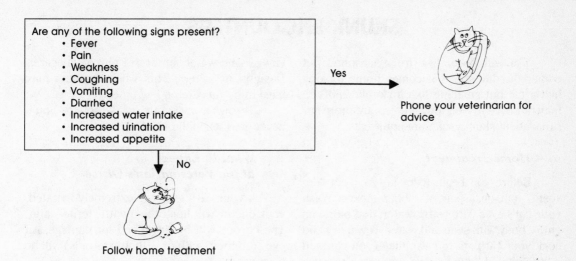

Are any of the following signs present?
- Fever
- Pain
- Weakness
- Coughing
- Vomiting
- Diarrhea
- Increased water intake
- Increased urination
- Increased appetite

Yes → Phone your veterinarian for advice

No

Follow home treatment

SKUNK ENCOUNTERS

You will become a truly seasoned pet owner the day your cat comes home looking like a cat but smelling like a skunk. And you may not have to wait long: kittens are more curious about skunks than are adult cats.

Home Treatment

Before you begin to make your cat "descent," put on a pair of rubber gloves. Wash your cat's eyes with warm water, and bathe its entire body with soap and water. Towel dry and soak your cat with tomato juice (you can add a little diluted lemon juice). You can also use a vinegar-and-water solution (1 pint of vinegar in 1 gallon of water). This whole process may have to be repeated a few times.

Throw away your cat's collar—you'll never get the smell out of it.

What to Expect at the Veterinarian's Office

If your cat's eyes are extremely irritated, your doctor will flush them with sterile water. The cornea will be examined for damage. An eye antibiotic (with or without steroids) will be dispensed.

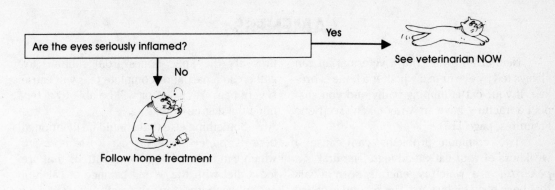

Are the eyes seriously inflamed?	Yes →

See veterinarian NOW

No ↓

Follow home treatment

LAMENESS

Neither an owner nor a veterinarian can always tell by eye or feel whether a bone is broken. If your cat is limping badly and you suspect a fracture, have an X-ray taken (see Bone Fractures, page 116).

Two common problems can cause a weakness of your cat's hind legs. The first is a *pelvic fracture,* which is generally seen in cats that have been hit by cars. The second is called *arterial thromboembolism.* This sudden blockage of the artery that supplies blood to both hind legs is being recognized more often in cats of all ages. The syndrome usually occurs suddenly: the cat exhibits severe pain and a weakness or paralysis of both hind legs, which are cool to the touch because no warm blood is reaching them. No femoral pulse (see page 19) can be felt. Clots can develop in the lung, brain, or other organs, and shock and death can occur suddenly. It occurs most frequently with a heart condition called *cardiomyopathy* that causes clots to be carried from the heart to distant blood vessels in the body.

Besides these two major causes, there are other reasons for lameness. Tar, paint, and thorns can stick to your cat's footpad and between the digits. When your cat tries to chew off these substances, its paws can get irritated. The irritation, in turn, makes your pet tender on the paw and then lame. This is a frequent occurrence. Many cats are brought to the doctor with a "broken leg," which is actually a lameness caused by an abscess (page 192).

Tissues that connect the bones of a joint and give it stability during movement are called *ligaments.* Sometimes these are stretched (*strained*), slightly torn (*sprained*), or completely torn. The most common ligament sprain or complete tear is seen in the knee of the cat. The *anterior cruciate ligament* prevents the knee bones from rubbing together, so a partial or complete tear will cause severe pain. Your doctor will be able to determine the degree of tearing.

Something else that should be mentioned here is *paper bone disease (osteoporosis),* which can be seen in growing kittens that are fed a diet with the wrong balance of calcium and phosphorus (an all-meat diet) and not enough vitamin D_3. In this case calcium is lost from the bones. The kitten is reluctant to walk, has pain in the legs, and may stand with its paws turned inward. Its bones are fragile and fracture easily.

Osteoarthritis (bony changes in the joint) is the result of joint instabilities that were not or cannot be corrected satisfactorily, of joint injuries, or of the aging process (one old fellow called it "older-itis"). After sleeping or lying down, your cat is stiff and feels pain that seems to disappear as it moves around.

Dislocation

Dislocations of the hip joint are occasionally seen in cats that have been hit by cars. The hip joint is a snug "ball-and-socket" arrangement. Trauma can tear the muscles and tendons over the hip and pop the ball out of the socket, causing a dislocation, or a *luxation,* of the hip joint. If the hip is dislocated, the cat may not be able to place the leg on the ground. Fractures of the pelvis may accompany traumatic injury to the hips.

Home Treatment

Activity restriction (home confinement) can be tried for a few days, if the chart so indicates. *Remember:* Cats *cannot* be given aspirin to decrease the pain and inflammation.

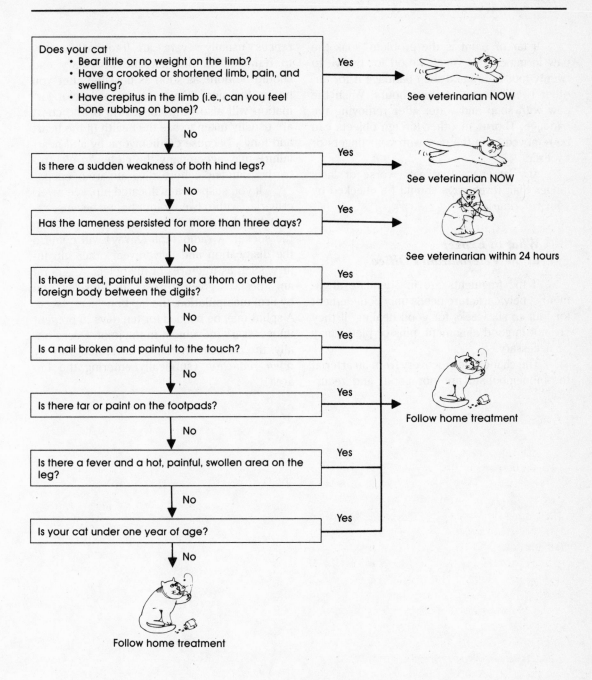

Does your cat
- Bear little or no weight on the limb?
- Have a crooked or shortened limb, pain, and swelling?
- Have crepitus in the limb (i.e., can you feel bone rubbing on bone)?

Yes → See veterinarian NOW

No ↓

Is there a sudden weakness of both hind legs?

Yes → See veterinarian NOW

No ↓

Has the lameness persisted for more than three days?

Yes → See veterinarian within 24 hours

No ↓

Is there a red, painful swelling or a thorn or other foreign body between the digits?

Yes →

No ↓

Is a nail broken and painful to the touch?

Yes →

No ↓

Is there tar or paint on the footpads?

Yes → Follow home treatment

No ↓

Is there a fever and a hot, painful, swollen area on the leg?

Yes →

No ↓

Is your cat under one year of age?

Yes →

No ↓

Follow home treatment

If tar or paint is the problem, soak the paw in mineral or vegetable oil for twelve to twenty-four hours and then bandage it for another twelve to twenty-four hours. Wash the paw with soap and water after removing the bandage. Thorns or other foreign objects can be removed from the paw with your fingers or tweezers.

Any lameness that gets worse or lasts longer than three days should be checked by your veterinarian.

What to Expect at the Veterinarian's Office

If the fragments are in adequate alignment, a pelvic fracture needs only confinement for four to six weeks for good healing. If they are not in good alignment, pins or plates may be necessary.

The chances for recovery from an arterial thromboembolism are not good, and recurrences (usually severe) are frequent. Surgery to remove the clot may be necessary and should be done as soon as possible after you notice the signs. Drugs to decrease clot formation will also be tried. X-rays of the chest are usually taken to see the health of the heart and lungs, because cardiomyopathy and heart failure may accompany the clots. An electrocardiogram and echocardiogram are needed.

If you suspect a dislocated hip, see a veterinarian within twenty-four hours, because recent hip dislocations are easier to replace in the socket. A radiograph (X-ray) will confirm the dislocation and may reveal other hip injury, such as fractures of the pelvis. A general anesthesia is given to relax the muscles, and by firm manipulation, the hip bone is replaced. A splint may be needed for ten days to prevent unnecessary movement in the joint. Occasionally, the dislocation can be corrected only by *open reduction* (surgically entering the hip area).

SKIN-PROBLEM CHART

Problem	Itching	Color	Skin Appearance	Major Location	Age Seen	Duration	Other Signs
Allergic inhalant dermatitis	Severe	Red to yellow, with pus	Crusty areas if infected	Generalized	Begins at one to three years of age	Usually seasonal, unless house is dusty	Bites paw, rubs face, sometimes sneezes
Flea-bite dermatitis	Moderate to severe	Red to yellow, with pus; moist	Some hair loss; crusty areas if infected	Base of tail, lower back, inner thighs, neck	Over six months	Warm weather, unless fleas are in house	
Contact dermatitis	Sudden and severe	Red or yellow, with pus; flat	Raised if infected	Neck (around flea collar), armpits, abdomen, between digits	Any age	Until controlled, unless plants are abundant (seasonal)	
Ticks	Moderate	Yellow to red	Scabs; yellow to red moist areas if infected	Ear flaps, between digits, head, neck, shoulders	Any age	Until controlled	
Rodent ulcer	None	Red	Thickened, ulcerated areas	Upper lip; less commonly, inside mouth, between digits, belly, and hind legs	Any age	Until controlled	
Feline acne	None	Gray to yellow, with pus	Pimples, blackheads, crusty areas	Chin	Any age	Until controlled	
Ringworm*	Occasional	Red	Hair loss; round, scaly, inflamed areas	Face, front legs, paws	Usually young	Until controlled	
Abscess	None	Red	Swollen, soft, hot areas; scabs	Anywhere—face, legs, tail base	Any age	Until controlled	Fever, appetite loss, lethargy, lameness if on leg
Food allergy	Moderate	Red to yellow, with pus	Scars, crusty areas if infected	Head	Any age	Until controlled	May also see diarrhea (colitis), with occasional blood or mucus

*Infectious to humans and other animals

ALLERGIES

Your cat's body has a remarkable immune system of antibodies. These protein substances produced by cells called lymphocytes destroy antigens that invade the body, such as viruses and bacteria. This system can become supersensitive to such foreign particles as flea saliva, pollen, house dust, and wool, however, and this supersensitivity can produce chemicals that cause an *allergy,* a severe inflammatory reaction.

Allergic inhalant dermatitis has not been as well documented in cats as it has in dogs. It is caused by a supersensitivity to certain particles in the air such as pollen from trees, ragweed, grass and other plants, house dust, feathers, and wool. The allergy follows a predictable history:

1. It is inherited, so if the parents had it, the offspring probably will, too.
2. It is seasonal—the signs appear about the same time every year.
3. The signs begin between six months and three years of age.
4. The signs include severe biting and scratching, paw licking, sneezing, face rubbing, and generalized redness.

Home Treatment

Home treatment is directed toward providing symptomatic relief and avoiding the foreign particle, or *allergen.* If the offending allergen is thought to be house dust, vacuuming daily and using Dust-seal (L. S. Green Associates, 162 W. 56th Street, New York City 10019) in the environment may help. If wool or feathers are thought to be the culprits, eliminating as many things composed of wool or feathers as possible is recommended.

Bathing your cat with a mild shampoo (such as baby shampoo) will soothe any skin inflammation and remove any allergens on the hair coat. Calamine lotion or Domeboro solution can be applied to the irritated skin. Hydrogen peroxide (3 percent) and antibiotic ointments are also helpful.

If the signs persist, see your veterinarian. Other skin diseases that may cause similar signs are flea-bite dermatitis (page 180) and contact dermatitis (page 182).

What to Expect at the Veterinarian's Office

Your veterinarian will take time to get a good history. He or she may be able to identify the allergen in your pet's environment.

If allergic inhalant dermatitis is the problem, two avenues of treatment are possible—steroids or hyposensitization. Most veterinarians, at this time, use a low dose of steroids to relieve the itching. *Note:* Steroids should *not* be given for long-term treatment because they have some very serious side effects.

The other type of treatment involves testing for the allergy. It can be a long and frustrating treatment, because the cats seem to keep developing allergies to new and different foreign particles. Allergy testing and hyposensitization are not used much in cat medicine at this time.

Food allergies presenting scabs on the head and, possibly, diarrhea may improve if for three weeks you put your cat on a daily diet of boiled chicken, brown rice, and a half-teaspoon of clam juice for taurine. If it works, talk to your doctor about a long-term diet.

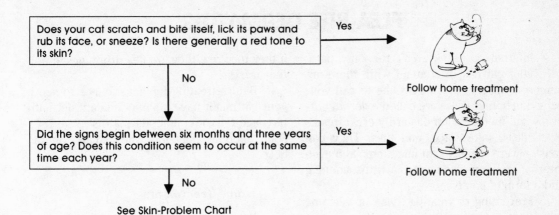

Does your cat scratch and bite itself, lick its paws and rub its face, or sneeze? Is there generally a red tone to its skin?

Yes → Follow home treatment

No ↓

Did the signs begin between six months and three years of age? Does this condition seem to occur at the same time each year?

Yes → Follow home treatment

No ↓

See Skin-Problem Chart

FLEA-BITE DERMATITIS

Internal parasites aren't the only parasites your cat has to contend with: there are numerous insects that would like to call your pet's skin home. These are called *external parasites* and include such dastardly creatures as ticks, fleas, mites, lice, and flies. They can cause severe itching, skin infections, and even internal problems such as tapeworms, anemia, and a form of paralysis.

Preventing or treating these unwelcome creatures requires use of insecticidal preparations. Understanding parasites' life cycles will give you an edge in this battle, and the following discussion should be beneficial. Ticks and mites are discussed separately (see pages 184–185).

Any cat older than six months of age can develop an allergy to flea saliva. Fleas are thin, wingless, brown insects that are extraordinary jumpers and move through the hair coat rapidly. The flea injects its saliva under the cat's skin as an aid in retrieving its meal (the cat's blood). The saliva acts as foreign material that can cause your pet to itch and bite itself profusely. Even people may be bitten by hungry fleas; their favorite human areas are ankles and waists, and the bites are very itchy.

Hair loss and skin infection are characteristic, especially on the lower back, neck, and inner thighs, favored flea feeding sites. The hair loss usually has a pattern: a triangular patch on the lower back and patches at the tail base, on the neck, and on the inner thighs. You may even see fleas jumping or moving in these areas, although often you won't see fleas on your cat. Flea droppings are the black specks (digested blood) found primarily on the hairs of the lower back. To test, place the droppings on white paper and moisten them with water.

If they turn red, they are flea droppings; if not, they are dirt.

Before treating for fleas, check to see if your cat might have allergic inhalant dermatitis (page 178) or contact dermatitis (page 182). Food allergies may just show scabs on the head.

Home Treatment

You must control fleas on all animals in the household and in the environment. A natural control agent that can be tried *before* your cat gets fleas is brewer's yeast. Mixing 0.1 gram per pound in the food daily seems to make some cats "distasteful" to fleas.

For flea control on all the animals in the household, you can use flea powders or dips, or flea collars. When using dips, read the directions carefully. Sponge your pet with the dip, avoiding the eyes, and repeat as the directions indicate. *Note:* Do *not* apply dips to open sores.

If you use a flea collar, use the recommended size for your cat. The flea collar must be aired for a few days before you place it around your pet's neck. If the skin underneath the flea collar becomes red and hair is lost, *remove* the collar. Some animals are sensitive to the chemical. *Note:* Do *not* combine flea collars with other insecticides. For example, don't dip your cat and then put a flea collar on it.

There has recently been some discussion about the wisdom of animals or their owners inhaling the vapors in the collars. If your pet sleeps on your bed, it might be prudent to remove the flea collar until the morning.

Since fleas spend most of their life cycle *off* your cat, controlling or treating the environment is most important to avoid that frus-

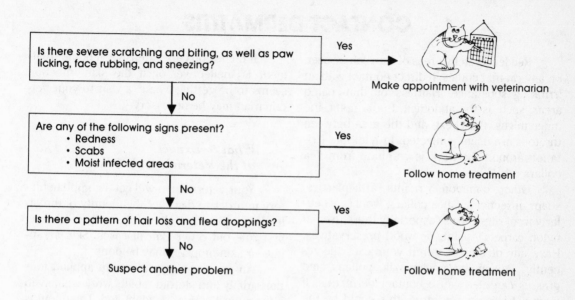

Is there severe scratching and biting, as well as paw licking, face rubbing, and sneezing? — **Yes** → Make appointment with veterinarian

No ↓

Are any of the following signs present?
- Redness
- Scabs
- Moist infected areas

— **Yes** → Follow home treatment

No ↓

Is there a pattern of hair loss and flea droppings? — **Yes** → Follow home treatment

No ↓

Suspect another problem

---

trating "Where are the fleas coming from? I sprayed my cat a month ago!" routine. Vacuum weekly for a few months, especially rugs, upholstery, cracks and crevices, and closets. Throw the vacuum bags away after vacuuming; otherwise, the fleas will hatch in your vacuum, closets, and so forth. Wash or throw away the cat's bedding. Finally, a commercial insecticide should be sprayed around your house periodically for a few months. If you think it might stain something, test by spraying only a small area first.

Your cat should be treated from the end of the winter through the first frost if you live in a varied climate.

What to Expect at the Veterinarian's Office

If you have tried everything and your cat is still scratching, see your veterinarian. He or she will make sure that none of the "rule-outs" are present. If a flea-bite allergy is suspected, corticosteroids, which can reduce or stop the itching, will be prescribed. If there are open sores, your doctor may give you antibiotics, a medicated shampoo, and a topical ointment to use. Be sure to discuss flea control for the pet *and* the house to avoid a recurrence of the problem.

CONTACT DERMATITIS

Reddened, itchy areas of skin can be seen on any cat that comes in direct contact with an irritating substance. Hairless or thin-coated areas, such as the abdomen, the armpits, the inner thighs, the chest, and the area between the toes are usually affected. In addition, irritation around the neck is common from flea collars.

Other common irritants are plastics, soaps, insecticides, flea collars, wool (particularly wool rugs), dyes (especially those used in nylon carpets), paint, or wood preservatives. Have any of these entered your cat's life recently? Poison ivy, poison oak, pollens, and grasses can also cause contact dermatitis. If your pet is on a new drug, this could be the source of the problem.

Home Treatment

First, try to identify the offending substance. If you think you have found the culprit, try to eliminate it from your cat's environment.

To relieve the itching, apply calamine lotion to the red areas three times daily. Cool compresses of Burrow's solution (Domeboro), applied for fifteen minutes every six hours, is an alternative. *Note:* Cats should *not* be given antihistamines without your veterinarian's okay.

If the lesions are extensive, if home treatment is ineffective, or if the skin infection seems to be getting worse, a visit to your veterinarian may be necessary.

What to Expect at the Veterinarian's Office

Your veterinarian will get a complete history in order to discover the identity of the offending substance. He or she will, of course, first rule out other skin diseases. Skin scrapings or skin biopsies may be done.

An antibiotic-steroid cream applied four times daily and steroid tablets work well, even if the culprit cannot be identified. Treatment is usually necessary for one to two weeks. Steroids should not be used for long periods of time, but if the condition recurs, steroids can be used for a short time again. Your doctor may advise medicated baths and cold applications of Burrow's solution.

Prevention

Air out a new flea collar for three days before using it, and buy the recommended size for your cat. If a neck irritation occurs, do not use a flea collar.

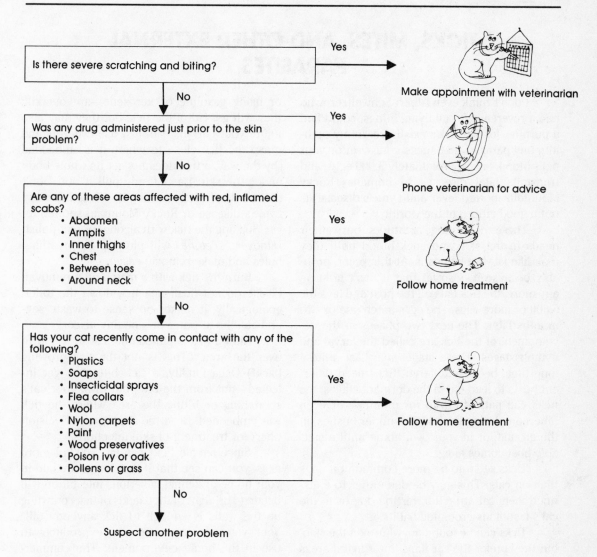

Is there severe scratching and biting? — **Yes** → Make appointment with veterinarian

No ↓

Was any drug administered just prior to the skin problem? — **Yes** → Phone veterinarian for advice

No ↓

Are any of these areas affected with red, inflamed scabs?
- Abdomen
- Armpits
- Inner thighs
- Chest
- Between toes
- Around neck

— **Yes** → Follow home treatment

No ↓

Has your cat recently come in contact with any of the following?
- Plastics
- Soaps
- Insecticidal sprays
- Flea collars
- Wool
- Nylon carpets
- Paint
- Wood preservatives
- Poison ivy or oak
- Pollens or grass

— **Yes** → Follow home treatment

No ↓

Suspect another problem

TICKS, MITES, AND OTHER EXTERNAL PARASITES

I don't think even Albert Schweitzer, who had a reverence for all living things, could find a purpose for the tick's existence. In my opinion, any parasite that sucks your own or your pet's blood, lays approximately 5,000 eggs, and transmits fatal diseases to humans (Rocky Mountain spotted fever and Lyme's disease) is not a good citizen of the world!

These disgusting creatures bury their heads in the skin and suck blood until they look like fat, brown beans. At this point, probably because it is so fat that it can't hold on any more, the tick falls off the host and lays the 5,000 or more eggs. The eggs hatch one or two months later. The next two phases in the development of the tick are called the larval and nymph stages. These stages may last quite a long time, because different ticks need different hosts to feed on. In the dormant stages, the ticks can patiently wait for months—or even hibernate during the winter—under bushes, in the ground, or in your own home until a suitable host comes along.

Ticks seem to be more common on dogs than on cats. This may be due either to a distinct chemical attraction for the dog or to the cat's fastidious grooming habits.

Ticks can be found anywhere on the skin, but they prefer the ear flaps, interdigital areas (between the toes), head, neck, and shoulder areas.

Home Treatment

Tick removal is surrounded by many myths and old wives' tales. Some of the popular methods—using a match to burn off the tick or using gasoline or kerosene—are overkill: they will get rid of the tick, but they may also injure your cat! Instead, just use tweezers and grasp the tick close to where it is embedded (by the way, a tick does *not* get its whole body under the skin!) and firmly pull it out. Don't pull a tick off with your fingers. Ticks can carry Lyme's disease or Rocky Mountain spotted fever. Soaking the tick with alcohol or nail-polish remover (*acetone*) will plug up its breathing holes and make removal easier.

Burn the tick with a match *after* removal. Please do not flush one tick down the toilet; ecologically, it makes no sense to waste several gallons of water on one tiny insect.

After a tick is pulled out, a scab will form over the area. (This is not the tick growing back!) Occasionally, a tick bite may get infected—not from the bite, but from your cat's scratching or biting the area where the tick was embedded. Read the appropriate Decision Chart for treatment of skin infections.

Since female ticks can lay 5,000 or more eggs, you can see that if those eggs are laid in your home or kennel, a serious infestation will occur. (The sight of thousands of ticks crawling up the walls is enough to tick anybody off!) Your veterinarian can dispense products to use in the home environment. The commercial products found under Flea-Bite Dermatitis (page 180) should also help keep the tick infestation under control.

An exterminator may be necessary to get rid of heavy tick infestations, because ticks can live for a long time in the cracks and crevices of floors, woodwork, and walls without having a blood meal.

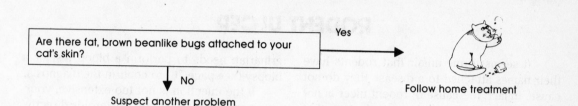

Are there fat, brown beanlike bugs attached to your cat's skin?

Yes → Follow home treatment

No ↓

Suspect another problem

"Chiggers" is the popular name for the red or harvest mite. In its larval stage, it is orange or red, the size of a pinhead, and parasitic on most mammals (dogs, cats, humans). The larvae hitch a ride on your leg or your pet's leg in the woods. Their bite causes severe redness and itching. Chiggers can be found anywhere on the body, but their favorite hangouts are the head, neck, ear canals and flaps, and abdomen. After getting a good blood meal, the larvae drop off and become nymphs. Later they develop into adult chiggers, which feed on plants. The adult chigger lays eggs that develop into larvae, which are the only parasitic form.

If only the ears are affected, use the same treatment for ear discharges (page 202). Your veterinarian will dispense a safe insecticidal preparation if a generalized infestation is present. An antibiotic-steroid cream will control the itching.

You can prevent chigger problems on your cat by using an insecticidal preparation during warm weather (the same as for fleas, page 184).

The white mite known as "walking dandruff" is large enough to see. This mite causes itching and can affect cats, humans, and dogs. The same insecticides administered for fleas, used for about three weeks, are effective.

The adult fly and its larvae (*maggots*) occasionally cause skin problems. Maggots develop from eggs that are laid by flies. If they are in wounds, remove them with tweezers. Clean the area with Phisohex and apply an antibiotic ointment to the wound.

Lice look like very small white oval specks and are seen best with a magnifying glass. They are spread by direct contact and cause severe itching. They spend their whole life cycle on the pet. Fortunately, lice are not seen very often on cats. A bath is an effective treatment. After drying, an insecticide can be used.

RODENT ULCER

It seems to me unfair that rodents have their names attached to a disease they do not cause. In fact, the cause of rodent ulcer is not known, although researchers conjecture that the cause is either a derangement in the immune system or a virus.

Rodent ulcer is a thickened, red, and ulcerated sore most commonly found on the upper lip. Other areas that may be affected are the inside of the mouth, the spaces between the digits, the skin of the belly, and the back of the hind legs. Red lesions and blisters on the nose, legs, or body or in the mouth may also be part of the "immune-mediated diseases," a new complex of diseases diagnosed by a biopsy and special immuno-fluorescent studies.

Home Treatment

See your veterinarian as soon as possible, because early treatment is extremely important.

What to Expect
at the Veterinarian's Office

Most diagnoses of rodent ulcer are made easily, by inspection. But sometimes the veterinarian needs to perform a blood test or a biopsy (see page 76) to confirm the diagnosis.

If the infection is not too extensive, your veterinarian will inject corticosteroids directly into the sore and/or prescribe corticosteroid tablets to be taken for about a month. Most rodent ulcers will disappear if treated early—at least, the first time. Unfortunately, the recurrence rate is 10 to 25 percent within six months. Other modes of treatment for recurring rodent ulcers are *megestrol acetate* (Ovaban), agents that stimulate the immune system, radiation therapy, and surgery. *Note:* Megestrol acetate (Ovaban) should *not* be used in intact (unspayed) females. Although it works well, it can have some side effects, such as increased appetite, water intake, urination, and weight gain. Cats treated with Ovaban may develop diabetes or hypothyroidism.

This disease requires patience from the veterinarian, the owner, and the cat because treatment is sometimes lengthy (in fact, a cat should be treated for at least a month with one agent before another drug is tried) and recurrences are not uncommon. But it is so satisfying to see the rodent ulcer respond to treatment and *never* come back.

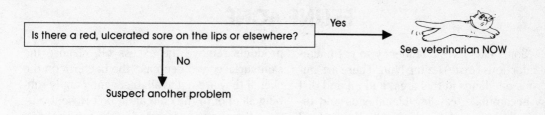

Is there a red, ulcerated sore on the lips or elsewhere? → **Yes** → See veterinarian NOW

No

↓

Suspect another problem

FELINE ACNE

Some cats have a tendency to get bacterial infections (*acne*) on the chin. There are numerous oil glands in this area, and oil and dirt may accumulate, causing blackheads and inflammation around the hair follicles and oil glands. This can progress, if not treated, to a deep skin infection.

The cause of feline acne is not known. Cleanliness may be a factor, because lazy chin cleaners seem to have more infections. A genetic predisposition is probably involved as well, because the condition is seen frequently in littermates and their parents.

Home Treatment

Wash daily with Phisohex or Phisoderm and rinse thoroughly. A human acne medication containing benzoyl peroxide, such as Oxy-5, seems to work well, too, but avoid contact with the eyes or mouth. Apply once daily for three days only. If undue skin irritation, flaking, or dryness develops, discontinue using the ointment and consult your veterinarian. These products remove the excess oil, cleanse the skin surface, and decrease the bacteria on the skin. If they are not available, gently apply rubbing alcohol to the chin and don't rinse it off.

Feline acne, if treated early, can heal in a week or two. Unfortunately, the condition recurs, but cleaning the chin daily might prevent recurrences. If the chin infection is severe or does not respond to home treatment, see your veterinarian. Occasionally, a ringworm lesion or demodex mite infection may be found on the chin.

What to Expect at the Veterinarian's Office

Your veterinarian will prescribe antibiotics (for two or three weeks in some cases) and will probably be proud of you for starting the cleansing program just described and will encourage you to continue. A scraping for demodex mites and a bacterial and fungus culture will be done in unresponsive cases.

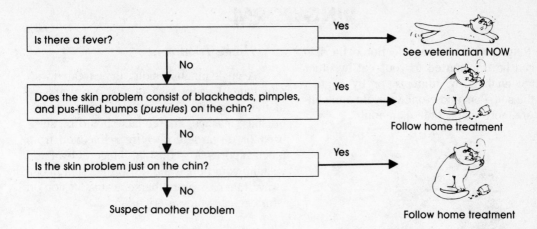

Is there a fever? → **Yes** → See veterinarian NOW

↓ **No**

Does the skin problem consist of blackheads, pimples, and pus-filled bumps (*pustules*) on the chin? → **Yes** → Follow home treatment

↓ **No**

Is the skin problem just on the chin? → **Yes** → Follow home treatment

↓ **No**

Suspect another problem

RINGWORM

Ringworm is a fungus infection of the skin that can be transmitted to your cat by other infected animals, by humans, or by contact with the soil. Pets under one year old and children are more suspectible than adults.

Ringworm lesion

The classic ringworm lesion is a rapidly spreading, circular, hairless, scaly area surrounded by an outer edge that is red. However, ringworm lesions do not always take on the classic form. Your doctor has further tests to verify this diagnosis.

Home Treatment

A single fungus lesion can be treated with *tolnaftate* (Tinactin), which you can purchase in the drugstore. The pet's bedding, combs, brushes, leashes, and collars should be sterilized or discarded, because reinfection from fungus spores is a constant danger. Clean and vacuum your house and throw the vacuum bag away. If there is more than one small lesion on your cat, see your veterinarian.

What to Expect at the Veterinarian's Office

Your doctor will use an ultraviolet light (one type of fungus will fluoresce green), a skin scraping, and/or a fungal culture to diagnose ringworm. The treatment of choice for ringworm is topical Tinactin or Conofite combined with *griseofulvin,* an oral medication, for at least one month. Since griseofulvin can depress the bone marrow in some cats, blood counts should be done before and during treatment.

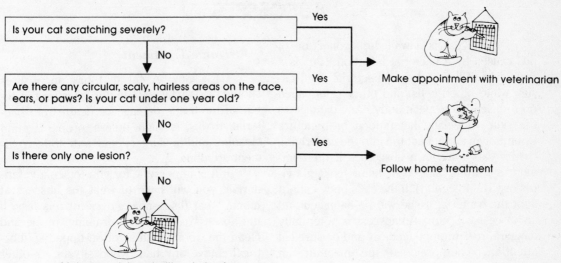

Is your cat scratching severely? — Yes → Make appointment with veterinarian

No ↓

Are there any circular, scaly, hairless areas on the face, ears, or paws? Is your cat under one year old? — Yes → Make appointment with veterinarian

No ↓

Is there only one lesion? — Yes → Follow home treatment

No ↓

Make appointment with veterinarian

ABSCESSES

An abscess is a walled-off collection of pus caused by a bacterial infection. (Pus is a collection of live and dead bacteria, dead tissue, white blood cells, and other cells called on to defend your pet's body.) Any damage to the skin, especially lacerations or puncture wounds, can admit bacteria into the underlying tissue. Cats may form abscesses if their immune system is "sick" (i.e., feline leukemia virus or FTLV infection). If the cat's body cannot fight the bacteria, tissue will be damaged and an abscess will form. An abscess is potentially dangerous: if prompt medical and/or surgical attention is not provided, the infection can spread to the chest, brain, heart, kidneys, or liver via the bloodstream.

An abscess is characterized by a warm swelling that is painful to the touch. Your cat may also be lethargic and have a fever. A common occurrence is having a cat brought to the office with a lameness and lethargy that have become worse over a few days. Pressing on each area of the limb, hip, or shoulder may elicit pain. The owner thinks the cat's leg is broken, but a swelling and a scab over a healed bite wound can be felt. The cat's rectal temperature can be 104°F to 105°F.

Home Treatment

EMERGENCY A cat that has an abscess should be seen by your doctor, because the potential for tissue damage or death from bacterial toxins is high unless proper wound cleaning and/or surgery and antibiotic treatment are done.

If it is impossible for you to see a veterinarian, you will have to treat the abscess at home. Wear disposable gloves for this task. If the abscess is open and draining, probe and clean the wound with a cotton-tipped applicator. Remove any hair, wood slivers, or other matter that may be in the wound. Pour a small amount of hydrogen peroxide (3 percent) into the wound, three times daily, or use an eye dropper or turkey baster. Press on the swelling to help the hydrogen peroxide flush the wound.

If the abscess has not burst, apply hot towels to the area to help bring it to a head. When you can feel a soft spot in the swelling, use a clean razor blade to nick the swelling. The pus should drain out easily. Probe and flush the wound as just explained. Try to get your cat on antibiotics as soon as possible.

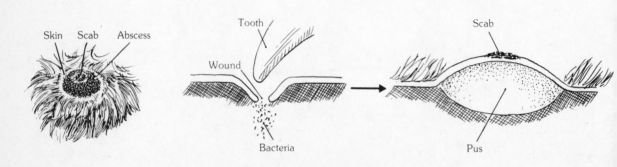

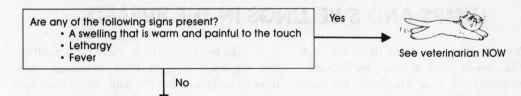

Are any of the following signs present?
- A swelling that is warm and painful to the touch
- Lethargy
- Fever

Yes → See veterinarian NOW

No ↓

Suspect another problem

What to Expect
at the Veterinarian's Office

Your doctor will probe the wound for dirt, debris, and foreign material and may flush the abscess with antibiotic, sterile saline, or hydrogen peroxide solutions or surgically *debride* the area (remove dead and infected tissue). A drain may be left in the wound to allow flushing of the wound for a few days. Antibiotics will be given for one week. A blood count, feline leukemia test, FTLV test, bacterial and fungal cultures, and skin biopsies may be done.

Prevention

Cleaning wounds promptly with soap and water or hydrogen peroxide and gently probing for hair, dirt, or foreign material will prevent many infections (see Cuts and Wounds, page 106).

Keep your cat indoors and have it vaccinated for feline leukemia. Test any "new" cats for feline leukemia and FTLV before introducing them to your established indoor house cats.

LUMPS AND SWELLINGS IN THE BREASTS

Breast tumors are seen in female cats older than seven years of age. The incidence may be greater in cats who have not been spayed (received an ovariohysterectomy) before their first heat (see Preventing Pregnancy, page 249). See your veterinarian.

A nursing female can develop an infection in one or more breasts (*mastitis*), which become red, hot, hard, and painful. This may be accompanied by fever and loss of appetite. The cat may lose interest in the kittens, who in turn become restless and weak because of the infected milk.

A mother cat can have engorged breasts after weaning, but they will not be red, hot, hard, or painful. In addition, the cat will remain alert and active and will still eat well.

The breasts may enlarge about two months after the heat period. If the cat is not pregnant, this is due to normal hormone changes. Milk can be produced, and other signs of false pregnancy (page 241) can occur.

Home Treatment

If the mother cat has mastitis, your doctor will prescribe antibiotics. *Note:* Do *not* let the kittens nurse, since the antibiotics in the milk could be toxic. This means hand feeding kittens under two or three weeks old. (See page 246 for directions.)

Also keep the kittens away if the mother has engorged breasts after weaning, since nursing will stimulate the milk production. Apply cold compresses to the breasts. Improvement should be seen in one to three days; if not, contact your doctor. No treatment is necessary for the slight breast swelling seen in females during the heat cycle.

What to Expect at the Veterinarian's Office

Breast tumors can range in size from smaller than a pea to masses involving the whole gland. They can also be benign (not cancerous) or malignant (cancerous), so see your doctor *early*—do *not* wait for the nodules to get larger. Your doctor will palpate the breast and the adjacent lymph nodes for evidence of malignancy. If the nodule is thought *not* to be a cyst, a radiograph of the chest will be taken to check for the possible spread (*metastasis*) of a malignant tumor. If the X-ray is normal, your doctor may recommend surgical removal of the nodule and a biopsy (microscopic examination of a tissue sample) of both it and the adjacent lymph nodes. If the nodule is malignant, further therapy will be considered (see Cancer, page 255).

Mastitis is usually treated successfully with antibiotics.

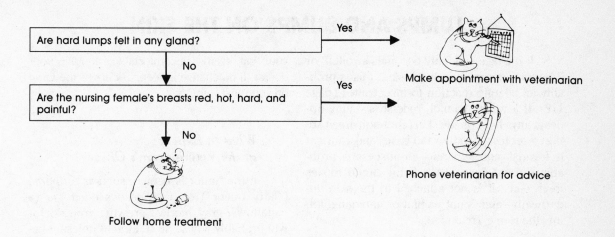

Are hard lumps felt in any gland? — Yes → Make appointment with veterinarian

No

Are the nursing female's breasts red, hot, hard, and painful? — Yes → Phone veterinarian for advice

No

Follow home treatment

LUMPS AND BUMPS ON THE SKIN

If the face suddenly becomes swollen, or if bumps appear all over the skin, this is probably an allergic reaction to insect bites (page 112). If a warm, painful, reddish swelling appears anywhere on the skin (common areas are the lower legs, head, or tail base) and your cat is feverish and lethargic, an abscess is probably present (page 192). If the bump moves freely—i.e., it is not attached to the skin underneath—and is not painful or enlarging, follow the Home Treatment.

Home Treatment

If none of the signs just described are seen, watch the lump. If its appearance changes or your cat seems uncomfortable, contact your doctor. If no change is seen, ask about the lump on your next visit.

What to Expect at the Veterinarian's Office

If the tumor is benign, such as a *lipoma* ("fatty tumor") or a *sebaceous adenoma* (a cauliflower-gray, hairless growth), your doctor will probably advise no treatment unless it becomes irritated. Any suspicious skin growths should be removed and biopsied. Skin tumors, if malignant, are the most curable cancers.

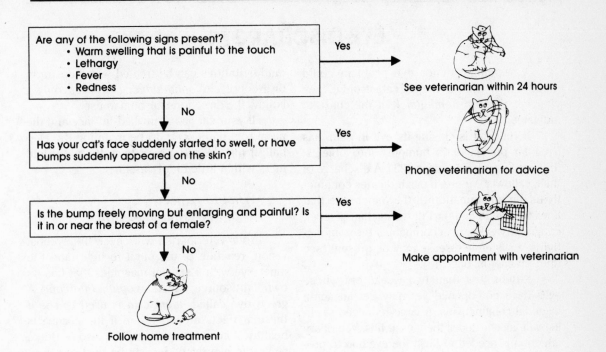

Are any of the following signs present?
- Warm swelling that is painful to the touch
- Lethargy
- Fever
- Redness

Yes → See veterinarian within 24 hours

No

Has your cat's face suddenly started to swell, or have bumps suddenly appeared on the skin?

Yes → Phone veterinarian for advice

No

Is the bump freely moving but enlarging and painful? Is it in or near the breast of a female?

Yes → Make appointment with veterinarian

No

Follow home treatment

EYE DISCHARGES

A seemingly minor eye problem could rapidly turn into a major catastrophe. See your veterinarian *immediately* if the chart so indicates.

If your cat is closing its eye in pain, has irregular pupils, or is bumping into objects, first see Eye Injuries (page 122). A discharge of thick yellowish or green pus indicates conjunctivitis, an inflammation of the membrane that lines the eyelid and part of the eyeball. If fever, cough, or weakness accompanies the conjunctivitis, a systemic disease may be present (see Rhinotracheitis, page 46).

Kittens less than two weeks old whose eyes have not opened yet may get an acute bacterial conjunctivitis. A large reddened swelling will appear under the closed lids. Veterinary attention is needed to flush the eye and to provide the proper medication. If you have to treat it yourself, gently pull the lids apart and flush the eye with clean water three times daily.

If your cat has a watery eye discharge, licks its paws, sneezes, and rubs its face on the floor, see Allergies (page 178). A constant watery discharge that does not seem to bother your pet is probably an abnormal overflowing of tears, called *epiphora.* It is hereditary in certain breeds—Persian cats, for one. The hair in the inner corner of the eye is always moist and stains a dark brown. It can be caused by misplaced eyelashes, blocked tear ducts, nasal fold hairs irritating the eye, or an eyelid defect.

Home Treatment

See your veterinarian today if the chart indicates that this is necessary. Otherwise, mild irritations can be treated with Neosporin or Neopolycin *ophthalmics* (for eyes only!). Follow the directions for human use.

If your cat has a "pushed-in" face and the nasal fold hairs seem to be irritating the eyeball, it may help to press down the nasal fold hairs with a little bit of Vaseline.

What to Expect at the Veterinarian's Office

Your veterinarian will check the eyelids, vision, reaction of the pupil to light, and the inner eye with a special magnifier that has its own light source, called an *ophthalmoscope.* A green dye called *fluorescein* is used to see if the tear ducts are open and if the cornea is healthy. A complete physical will also be done, since the eye infection may be part of a systemic disease.

Antibiotic eyedrops or ointments are frequently given for eye infections. Cortisone-type eye medicine should be prescribed very infrequently, since certain infections (such as herpes) may get worse with these medicines. If herpes is diagnosed, special eyedrops and other medicines will be needed.

Misplaced eyelashes or eyelid defects may have to be corrected surgically. Blocked tear ducts may need to be flushed out if the medication is not working.

Cats with recurrent respiratory infections should be tested for the feline leukemia and FTLV (AIDS-like) viruses, and for yeast infection (cryptococcosis).

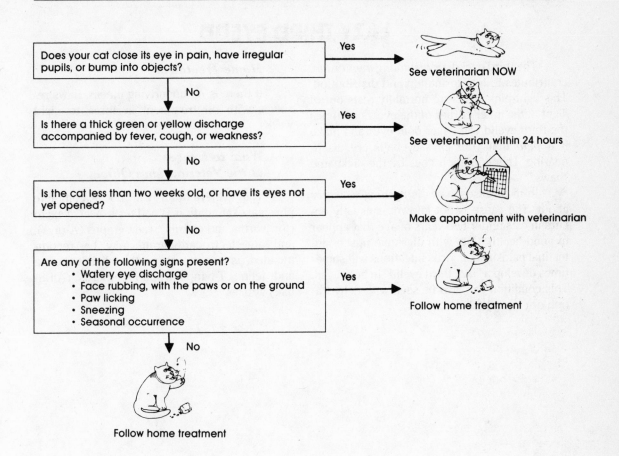

Does your cat close its eye in pain, have irregular pupils, or bump into objects? — **Yes** → See veterinarian NOW

No

Is there a thick green or yellow discharge accompanied by fever, cough, or weakness? — **Yes** → See veterinarian within 24 hours

No

Is the cat less than two weeks old, or have its eyes not yet opened? — **Yes** → Make appointment with veterinarian

No

Are any of the following signs present?
- Watery eye discharge
- Face rubbing, with the paws or on the ground
- Paw licking
- Sneezing
- Seasonal occurrence

Yes → Follow home treatment

No

Follow home treatment

LAZY THIRD EYELID

The third eyelid, or *nictitating membrane,* contributes to tear formation and distribution. This light-pink structure normally rests out of sight in the inner corner of the eye. Sometimes the third eyelid will cover *both* eyes and make it *appear* that your cat's eyeballs are disappearing. This condition goes by the nickname "haws."

In most cases, haws is nothing to worry about. The cause is not known. It usually occurs in cats under two years of age that appear in good health. Cats with digestive upsets, intestinal parasites, or virus infections will sometimes develop a "lazy third eyelid" in both eyes. This condition can also be seen with dehydration or (rarely) tetanus.

Home Treatment

If there is no underlying illness, haws resolves with no treatment in three to eight weeks.

What to Expect at the Veterinarian's Office

Your veterinarian will do a complete physical examination. Blood tests, a fecal exam (for worms and giardia), radiographs (X-rays), and an electrocardiogram may be recommended, as well as tests for the feline leukemia and feline T-lymphotropic lentivirus (AIDS-like) viruses.

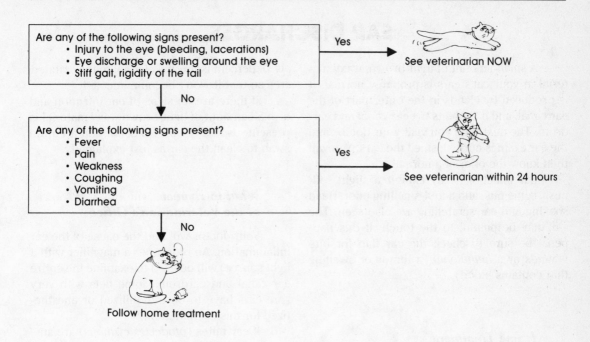

Are any of the following signs present?
- Injury to the eye (bleeding, lacerations)
- Eye discharge or swelling around the eye
- Stiff gait, rigidity of the tail

Yes → See veterinarian NOW

No ↓

Are any of the following signs present?
- Fever
- Pain
- Weakness
- Coughing
- Vomiting
- Diarrhea

Yes → See veterinarian within 24 hours

No ↓

Follow home treatment

EAR DISCHARGES

A small amount of light-brown, waxy material in your cat's ears is probably normal. It is produced by glands in the outer part of the ear canal, and it protects the ear canal and eardrum. The next time you visit your doctor and the ear exam is normal, smell the ears. You will then know the odor of a normal ear.

Ear infections may exhibit a slight redness, some pus, and a foul-smelling odor. Head shaking and ear scratching are also seen. The ear may be painful to the touch. If this happens, be sure to check the ear flap for bite wounds or a *hematoma* (a tumor or swelling that contains blood).

Home Treatment

Ear infections usually require the help of a veterinarian, since the cat's ear canal has a complex shape. If you are unable to see a veterinarian, clean the inner ear flap and the part of the canal that you can see with baby oil and a cotton swab. Use a few drops of baby oil in the ear canal and massage the ear to break up the wax and debris. Hold the ear flap straight up over your pet's head so you don't damage the ear drum and gently remove any wax and debris with the cotton swab.

Place a few drops of 70 percent isopropyl alcohol in the ear twice daily. Massage the ear canal to be sure that the alcohol makes it way to the bottom of the L-shaped ear canal. If there is no improvement in two or three days, see your doctor. If there is improvement, continue the treatment for ten days.

Thorns or ticks on the ear flap or at the opening of the ear canal can cause your cat to scratch its ear. Use tweezers to remove it. Apply 70 percent isopropyl alcohol to the irritated area so that it won't become infected.

If there are no signs of ear infection and a small amount of light-brown waxy material is present, use baby oil or alcohol and a cotton swab to clean the ear as just explained.

What to Expect at the Veterinarian's Office

Your doctor will find the cause of the ear inflammation. An otoscope (a magnifier with a light source) will be used to examine the entire ear canal and eardrum. Some pets with very sore ears have to be tranquilized or anesthetized for this examination.

If ear mites (*otodectes cyanotis*) are suspected, your doctor will examine the dry, black, waxy material under the microscope, looking for the eight-legged mites. If they are present, your veterinarian will dispense an insecticidal or oil preparation to put in the ears. Since the mites can hide under the debris, proper cleaning of the waxy material is essential for a cure. Also, since the mites may live on other parts of your pet's body and are contagious to other household pets, an insecticidal powder or spray should be used on all the animals.

Bacterial ear infections can be treated with antibiotic preparations. If the infection does not clear up or if it recurs, your doctor will do culture and sensitivity tests for bacteria, fungus, and yeast on the exuded matter so that the treatment will be more effective.

Some ear infections can be frustrating to treat. Feline leukemia and FTLV tests may be done. If the infection is chronic, your doctor may suggest an ear flush under anesthesia or

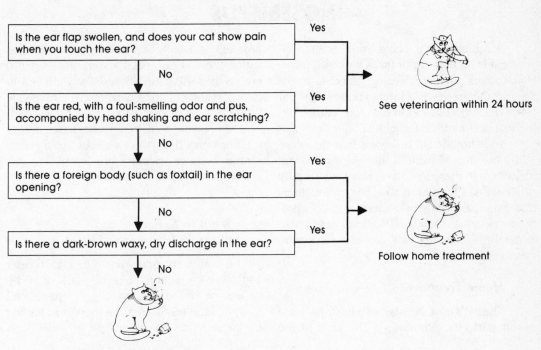

Is the ear flap swollen, and does your cat show pain when you touch the ear? — Yes →

No ↓

Is the ear red, with a foul-smelling odor and pus, accompanied by head shaking and ear scratching? — Yes →

See veterinarian within 24 hours

No ↓

Is there a foreign body (such as foxtail) in the ear opening? — Yes →

No ↓

Is there a dark-brown waxy, dry discharge in the ear? — Yes →

Follow home treatment

No ↓

Follow home treatment

surgery to keep the ear dry and enhance drainage. The success rate of surgery is very high.

Prevention

Keep an eye on the ear! Check your cat's ears weekly for early signs of trouble, such as slight redness. Clean the wax occasionally from the ear canal, but remember that a certain amount of wax is normal and protective. Place cotton in the ears before bathing because soap and excessive moisture may lead to inflammation.

NOSEBLEEDS

Nosebleeds can occur from trauma (if your cat is hit by a car or has a bad fall), infection, tumors, violent sneezing, bleeding disorders, or the presence of foreign bodies. The cat has a rich blood supply in the nose, and bleeding can occur with the slightest injury.

You should also be aware that there are many bleeding disorders that are now being identified. In these instances, there are usually other signs, such as red blotches on the gums and ears, pale gums, weakness, and collapse. Some poisons such as Warfarin can cause generalized bleeding that can include severe nosebleeds.

Home Treatment

The cat's nose consists of a bony part and a soft part (the *turbinates*). The area of the nose that is usually involved in nosebleeds lies within the soft portion. Cats are nose breathers, so they will naturally resist any attempt to clear the nose, especially when the air passage is blocked. Squeezing the nostril for a few minutes or applying cold compresses or ice across the nose may help. If nosebleeds are a recurrent problem or are becoming frequent, a veterinarian should be consulted.

What to Expect at the Veterinarian's Office

Blood tests, including blood-clot tests and tests for autoimmune diseases, may be necessary. Endoscopy, cytology, biopsies, and X-rays of the nasal area are helpful in finding the cause of the nosebleeds.

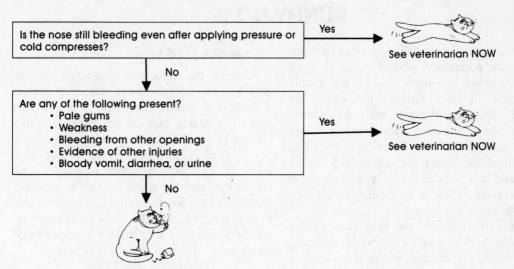

Is the nose still bleeding even after applying pressure or cold compresses?

Yes → See veterinarian NOW

No ↓

Are any of the following present?
- Pale gums
- Weakness
- Bleeding from other openings
- Evidence of other injuries
- Bloody vomit, diarrhea, or urine

Yes → See veterinarian NOW

No ↓

Follow home treatment

RUNNY NOSE

The nose is responsible, in large part, for your cat's perception of the world. A cat's sense of smell is remarkable. All the smells of the world filter through it—but so do viruses, bacteria, pollens, and, sometimes, thorns. These "invaders" can cause a runny nose. Nasal secretions contain antibodies and tissue fluid that fight these unwanted particles and flush them outside the body. The sneeze is a remarkable reflex in your cat's body to attempt to expel the irritant.

If your cat's nose and eyes have a thick yellowish discharge and your pet is lethargic, breathes heavily, coughs, and/or has a fever, a serious respiratory infection, such as rhinotracheitis, may be present.

A discharge from one nostril may be due to a thorn or other object that has lodged in the nose as your cat inspected its environment. Older cats can have sinus infections or tumors involving one side of the nose. An uncommon cause of runny noses in cats is allergies.

Cats with a clear, watery nasal discharge and sneezing will often have other signs simultaneously, such as paw licking, face rubbing, watery eyes, and scratching. This problem lasts longer than a viral infection (often for weeks or months) and occurs most often seasonally, when pollen particles or other allergies are in the air. House dusts and molds may aggravate the allergic runny nose.

Whether your pet's nose is cool and moist or warm and dry is not a good indication of its health or body temperature.

Home Treatment

Since the cat's nasal passages are so complex, any infection there is difficult to treat without your veterinarian's help. If you suspect that the problem may be an allergy, see that section (page 178) for more information.

You will need to contact your veterinarian to treat respiratory infections properly. Increase the humidity in the air with a vaporizer, especially in a small room, such as the bathroom, to help liquefy the nasal discharge. Humidifiers also help stop irritation when heated air dries out the respiratory passages.

What to Expect at the Veterinarian's Office

Your doctor will make a thorough examination of your cat's nose, mouth, and throat. If a respiratory infection is suspected, antibiotics may be dispensed. Steroids and/or antihistamines will help if the runny nose is an allergic sign. A foreign body in the nose must be removed, with or without anesthesia.

Severe respiratory infections, trauma, or poisoning may demand more intensive treatment, laboratory tests, and radiographs (X-rays).

Cats with recurrent respiratory infections should be tested for feline leukemia, the FTLV (AIDS-like) virus, and yeast infection (cryptococcosis).

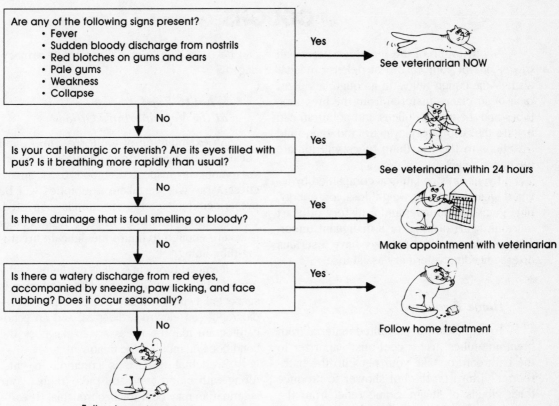

Are any of the following signs present?
- Fever
- Sudden bloody discharge from nostrils
- Red blotches on gums and ears
- Pale gums
- Weakness
- Collapse

Yes → See veterinarian NOW

No ↓

Is your cat lethargic or feverish? Are its eyes filled with pus? Is it breathing more rapidly than usual?

Yes → See veterinarian within 24 hours

No ↓

Is there drainage that is foul smelling or bloody?

Yes → Make appointment with veterinarian

No ↓

Is there a watery discharge from red eyes, accompanied by sneezing, paw licking, and face rubbing? Does it occur seasonally?

Yes → Follow home treatment

No ↓

Follow home treatment

COUGHS

Any irritation of the breathing tubes will trigger one of your cat's best defense mechanisms—the cough reflex. In a cough, a violent rush of air cleans material from the breathing tubes and the lungs. Pollens and pollution can irritate the respiratory system, and even mild irritations to the breathing tubes will initiate the cough reflex.

If your cat's cough is accompanied by fever, difficult breathing, weight loss, low energy, blue gums and tongue, and a history of heart murmur, heart disease, or a malignant tumor, see your doctor. Your pet may have a serious disease needing veterinary assistance.

Home Treatment

To help clear the unwanted material from breathing tubes, use a cool-mist vaporizer in the bathroom or take your pet into the bathroom and turn on the hot shower to produce thick clouds of steam. Some relief from the congestion should be seen in fifteen minutes. If there is no improvement, see your doctor. If your pet becomes more distressed in the "steam room" or when using the cool-mist vaporizer, stop the treatment and see your doctor. Cough syrup containing just guaifenesin can be used. See Your Cat's Home Pharmacy, page 85.

What to Expect at the Veterinarian's Office

An examination of the throat, neck, and chest will be made. If pneumonia or lung involvement is suspected, blood tests and a chest X-ray will be taken. Antibiotics will be prescribed if a bacterial infection is suspected. Cough depressants may be given if the cough is severe enough to injure the delicate breathing-tube lining.

If a heart problem such as cardiomyopathy or metastasis (spread) of a malignant tumor is suspected, heartworm blood tests, urinalysis, radiographs, an electrocardiogram, and an echocardiogram may be necessary to diagnose the condition and monitor the treatment.

Bronchial disease is common in cats. Along with blood tests and radiographs, your veterinarian may do a tracheobronchial (breathing-tube) wash and endoscopy to evaluate your cat's condition. Your doctor will prescribe antibiotics, bronchodilators (breathing-tube openers), and/or steroids. Feline bronchitis is easier to manage than to cure. A consultation with a veterinary respiratory specialist may be advised.

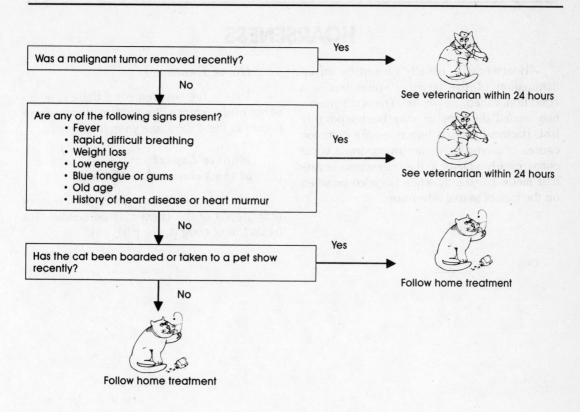

Was a malignant tumor removed recently?

Yes → See veterinarian within 24 hours

No

Are any of the following signs present?
- Fever
- Rapid, difficult breathing
- Weight loss
- Low energy
- Blue tongue or gums
- Old age
- History of heart disease or heart murmur

Yes → See veterinarian within 24 hours

No

Has the cat been boarded or taken to a pet show recently?

Yes → Follow home treatment

No

Follow home treatment

HOARSENESS

Hoarseness is usually caused by an inflammation of the larynx ("voice box"), a condition called *laryngitis*. The cat's meow may sound different or may be temporarily lost. Bacterial or viral infections are common causes of laryngitis, as are overworked vocal cords, clearly a factor in the hoarseness of cats that meow constantly when boarded or when on the trail of sexual adventure.

Home Treatment

Time is the best remedy if there is no fever or other signs of illness. If no improvement occurs in three days, see your veterinarian.

What to Expect at the Veterinarian's Office

If an infection is suspected, blood tests or radiographs of the chest may be needed. For treatment of coughs, see page 208.

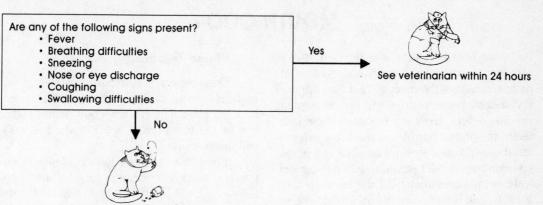

Are any of the following signs present?
- Fever
- Breathing difficulties
- Sneezing
- Nose or eye discharge
- Coughing
- Swallowing difficulties

Yes → See veterinarian within 24 hours

No ↓ Follow home treatment

MOUTH ODOR

Bad breath in cats is commonly due to problems involving the teeth and gums. Cats develop *plaque* (the mucous film that appears if you don't brush your teeth), just as humans do. Since very few owners brush their pets' teeth, the plaque hardens into a brownish material called *tartar* or *calculus.* The tartar that you *don't* see (under the gum) loosens the delicate membranes that hold the teeth in their sockets, and infections develop around the receding gums and teeth. This is called *periodontal disease,* and it is not easily missed by the owner: the odor is quite powerful, the tartar is prominent on the canine teeth and molars, and the gums are red and swollen. In addition, your cat may drool or have trouble chewing.

Tumors and overgrowth of gum tissue will also cause a foul mouth odor. The cat needs veterinary care. A very sweet mouth odor combined with lethargy and increased water intake, urination, and appetite may indicate diabetes. See your doctor and take a urine sample to be checked for sugar. Kidney disease may also produce bad breath.

Cats rarely need to have a cavity filled, because they don't get cavities very often.

Cats with chronic mouth infections and gum inflammation should be tested for the leukemia and FTLV (AIDS-like) viruses.

Home Treatment

Don't worry if your kitten is only a few months old and has "garlic breath"; this is normal. It is caused by certain "good" bacteria that live in the mouth. In a few months this odor will disappear.

Prevention of periodontal disease is important, since chronic mouth infections constantly spread bacteria and toxins to the kidneys and other organs. In time, this takes its toll on your pet. If the tartar is just forming, scrape it off with your fingernail, but keep in mind that the culprit is the tartar that you *don't see,* under the gum.

What to Expect at the Veterinarian's Office

If the mouth odor is caused by dental tartar and gum inflammation, a teeth cleaning (and possibly an extraction) is necessary. Very few cats will tolerate their teeth being scraped by the special instrument called a tartar scraper—and *no* cats will tolerate the ultrasonic teeth cleaners while they are awake, so sedatives or anesthesia are necessary. If your cat is middle-aged or older, your doctor may perform a blood test to check the health of the kidneys before using a sedative or anesthesia.

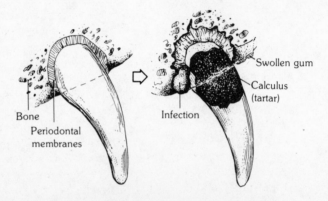

Bone
Periodontal membranes

Swollen gum
Calculus (tartar)
Infection

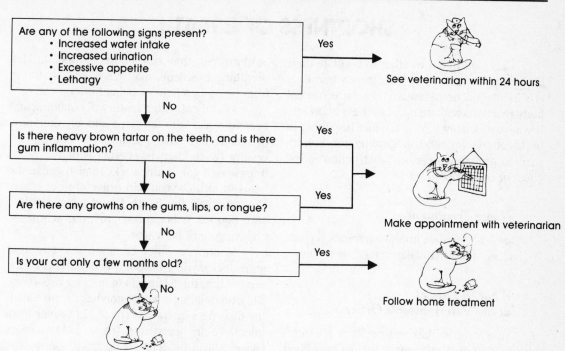

Are any of the following signs present?
- Increased water intake
- Increased urination
- Excessive appetite
- Lethargy

Yes → See veterinarian within 24 hours

No ↓

Is there heavy brown tartar on the teeth, and is there gum inflammation?

Yes → Make appointment with veterinarian

No ↓

Are there any growths on the gums, lips, or tongue?

Yes → Make appointment with veterinarian

No ↓

Is your cat only a few months old?

Yes → Follow home treatment

No ↓

Follow home treatment

The heart will be monitored before, during, and after the teeth cleaning.

If teeth need to be extracted or if the teeth and gums are very unhealthy, your doctor will prescribe antibiotics. Since the bacteria can spread through the bloodstream, antibiotics will prevent an infection from developing in the mouth or in some distant organ (the liver or kidneys, for instance). They may be started a few days before the teeth cleaning.

Prevention

The time to prevent future dental problems is before tartar forms, or after your doctor cleans the teeth. Cleaning your cat's teeth at least twice weekly with a children's toothbrush or a gauze pad is the ideal way of increasing the interval between professional teeth cleanings. Most cats don't like the foaming and fizz-

ing of human toothpastes, so use a salt-water or bicarbonate of soda solution to clean the outer surface of the gums and teeth. The inner surface collects tartar much more slowly, and since most pets resist having this area cleaned, don't bother trying. It is best to start this routine when your pet is a kitten. Handle your cat firmly but gently. You can clean the outside of the teeth rapidly, in about thirty seconds.

Set up a regular teeth-cleaning schedule with your veterinarian and have him or her send you a reminder card. Some cats need a teeth cleaning every six months; others can go a year or two between cleanings.

I'm not a big believer in hard bones, hard rubber toys, dry food, or hard biscuits that purport to clean teeth. If these *were* helpful, I'm sure your dentist would suggest that you chew on a soup bone while you're watching television.

SHORTNESS OF BREATH

Cats pant in hot weather to regulate their body temperature. They also pant when they are frightened or nervous. These are normal body reactions and are *not* shortness of breath. If your cat is truly having trouble breathing in or breathing out and is gasping for breath, there is probably a serious obstruction in the chest or breathing tubes.

Home Treatment

EMERGENCY   Give artificial respiration (page 98) and see your veterinarian immediately.

What to Expect at the Veterinarian's Office

Your veterinarian will perform a careful examination of all systems. Your pet may need oxygen at this time. If there has been evidence of trauma (such as an auto accident), X-rays will be taken when your cat is stabilized. An outdoor pet that has no fever and sudden breathing problems may have a chest injury from being in a fight or being hit by a car.

An old cat with a history of coughing and heart disease who develops sudden shortness of breath may have a failing heart. Cardiomyopathy (a sudden degeneration of the heart muscle of a cat at any age) can also cause the heart to fail. Oxygen and drugs are necessary to strengthen the heart. Blood tests, electrocardiograms, echocardiograms, thoracentesis, and X-rays are indicated.

There are other common diseases that your doctor will consider if your cat has shortness of breath: eclampsia in nursing cats (page 246), anemia, internal hemorrhage from bleeding disorders or trauma (page 124), fever from infection or heatstroke (page 134), tumors (page 196), or feline infectious peritonitis (page 149). Hospitalization is almost always necessary for a pet that has shortness of breath.

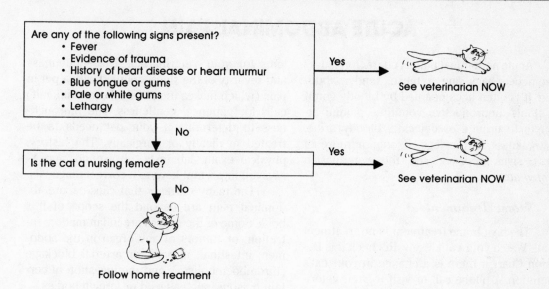

Are any of the following signs present?
 • Fever
 • Evidence of trauma
 • History of heart disease or heart murmur
 • Blue tongue or gums
 • Pale or white gums
 • Lethargy

Yes → See veterinarian NOW

No

Is the cat a nursing female?

Yes → See veterinarian NOW

No

Follow home treatment

ACUTE ABDOMINAL PAIN

Acute abdominal pain is characterized by a hunched back and a tense, tender abdomen. It is often accompanied by bloody vomit or stools, unproductive vomiting, painful attempts to urinate or defecate, bloody urine, or weakness in the legs. If one or more of these signs appears, see the veterinarian *immediately*.

Home Treatment

The best home treatment is no treatment at all. Watch your cat closely. Recheck this Decision Chart if there is a change in your cat's condition. A phone call or visit to your veterinarian may be necessary.

What to Expect
at the Veterinarian's Office

Acute abdominal pain is one of the most challenging diagnostic and procedural problems for your veterinarian. The suddenness and severity of the signs, coupled with a pet in pain (which makes the physical exam difficult) calls for patience, gentleness, and thoroughness to determine if your pet needs to be treated medically or surgically. The history, physical exam, lab tests, ultrasound, and X-rays are important keys to a correct diagnosis.

The many diseases that cause acute abdominal pain are beyond the scope of this book. Some of the causes are inflammation, infection, or tumors of any organ in the abdomen; intestinal, urinary, or arterial blockage (thromboembolism); and the ingestion of certain poisons, such as lead or foreign bodies.

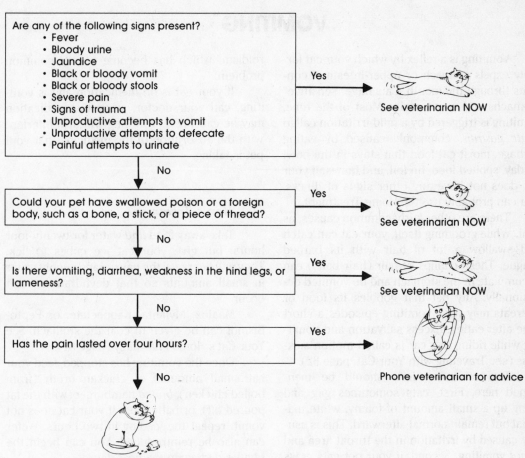

Are any of the following signs present?
 • Fever
 • Bloody urine
 • Jaundice
 • Black or bloody vomit
 • Black or bloody stools
 • Severe pain
 • Signs of trauma
 • Unproductive attempts to vomit
 • Unproductive attempts to defecate
 • Painful attempts to urinate

Yes → See veterinarian NOW

No ↓

Could your pet have swallowed poison or a foreign body, such as a bone, a stick, or a piece of thread?

Yes → See veterinarian NOW

No ↓

Is there vomiting, diarrhea, weakness in the hind legs, or lameness?

Yes → See veterinarian NOW

No ↓

Has the pain lasted over four hours?

Yes → Phone veterinarian for advice

No ↓

Follow home treatment

VOMITING

Vomiting is a reflex by which your cat forcibly expels stomach or upper-intestinal contents through the mouth. Cats have "sensitive" stomachs and vomit easily. Most of the time, vomiting is triggered by a mild irritation called *acute gastritis,* commonly caused by eating garbage, moist cat food that stays in the bowl all day, spoiled food, tin foil, and bones. If your pet does not have any other signs of illness, you can probably use the Home Treatment.

There are other fairly common causes, as well. While grooming itself, your cat can catch and swallow a lot of hair with its barbed tongue. These clumps of hair (hair balls) can accumulate in the stomach and be vomited occasionally. Any pet that gobbles its food or overeats may have vomiting episodes a short time after eating. Excess salivation and vomiting while riding in a car is called motion sickness (see Traveling with Your Cat, page 62).

Two misconceptions should be mentioned here. First, cats sometimes gag and bring up a small amount of foamy, white material but remain normal afterward. This is usually caused by irritation in the throat area and is *not* vomiting. Second, if your pet eats grass and does not vomit, it usually means only that your pet likes grass, not that there is something wrong.

See your veterinarian if the Decision Chart advises a visit. Vomiting can indicate inflammation of the pancreas, the presence of foreign bodies, intestinal obstructions, liver disease, kidney failure, or infections such as panleukopenia. Any vomiting cat over seven years of age should be checked for hyperthyroidism, which has become a very common problem.

If your cat is on medication and is vomiting, call your doctor, since the medication may be causing it. Vomiting will also interfere with the absorption of the medicine that your pet is taking.

Home Treatment

Take away food *and* water for twenty-four hours, but give your cat ice cubes to lick. They will decrease the nausea and supply water in small amounts so that deyhdration won't occur.

Maalox, Mylanta, Kaopectate, or Pepto-Bismol can be given to coat the stomach. See Your Cat's Home Pharmacy (page 81).

Once the vomiting has stopped, feed your cat small amounts of chicken broth (from boiled chicken), *boiled* hamburger (with the fat poured off), or baby food. If your cat does not vomit, repeat the feeding in two hours. Water can also be reintroduced. You can begin the regular diet again the next day.

If the cat occasionally vomits hair balls and shows no other signs of illness, more regular combing and brushing will remove the loose hairs and decrease the formation of hair balls. Smear one-half teaspoon of white petroleum jelly per ten pounds of body weight on the cat's nose or paw. The cat will lick it off, and the jelly will coat the hair ball. Also, commercial medications are available from your pet store or your veterinarian.

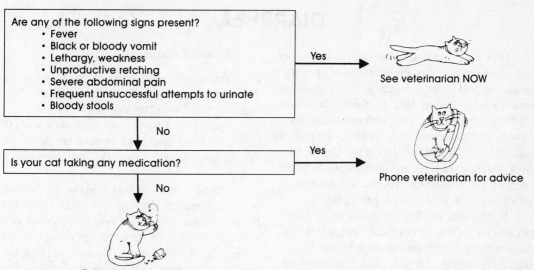

Are any of the following signs present?
- Fever
- Black or bloody vomit
- Lethargy, weakness
- Unproductive retching
- Severe abdominal pain
- Frequent unsuccessful attempts to urinate
- Bloody stools

Yes → See veterinarian NOW

No

Is your cat taking any medication?

Yes → Phone veterinarian for advice

No

Follow home treatment

What to Expect at the Veterinarian's Office

The doctor will conduct a complete history and physical exam. If your cat is dehydrated, fluids will be given subcutaneously or intravenously. Blood tests, a urinalysis, a stool sample, X-rays, ultrasound, and endoscopy may be necessary to determine the cause of the vomiting.

DIARRHEA

One of the most common problems in cats is diarrhea, the elimination of watery, runny, or soft stools. Usually, the condition lasts for only twenty-four to thirty-six hours and home treatment is fine, unless the diarrhea persists and your pet gets severely listless. If your cat has bright-red blood in the stools; black, tarry stools; severe abdominal pain; or fever; or if it persistently vomits or attempts to vomit, see your veterinarian promptly.

Sometimes medication such as antibiotics can change the number and kind of bacteria that normally live in your pet's intestines. This can cause diarrhea. If your cat is on medication, call your veterinarian.

Many cats do not have enough of an enzyme called *lactase,* which breaks up a large sugar molecule in milk called *lactose.* Consequently, the lactose "pulls" water into the intestinal tract to soften the stools.

Very often diarrhea is caused by diet—that is, by eating "exotic" things, such as garbage, tin foil, candy, the family's table food (especially spicy foods), and bones. Excess fat in the diet, or sudden pet-food changes, can sometimes cause diarrhea as well.

Worms and other intestinal parasites can irritate the intestine and cause diarrhea that is sometimes bloody.

Kittens with diarrhea may quickly develop a severe fluid loss. Be sure to maintain adequate fluid intake. Assessing dehydration is discussed on page 31.

If you suspect a chemical or plant to be the cause, see Swallowed Poisons (page 136). However, neither is a common cause of diarrhea. Any cat over seven years of age with diarrhea should be checked for hyperthyroidism.

Home Treatment

You can manage diarrhea by changing the diet and giving Kaopectate to coat the intestinal tract and firm the stools.

Except for kittens, who have only a small caloric reserve, no food should be given for twenty-four hours. *Note:* Do *not* take away water.

After the one-day fast, you can give small, frequent feedings (four to five small meals) of *boiled* hamburger or chicken with boiled rice for four or five days. Cooked eggs and cottage cheese can then be added. Be sure to bring the food to room temperature before feeding, because food that is too hot or too cold can cause diarrhea. The small, frequent feedings give the intestine enough time to digest the food. Over the next few days, mix this diet with an increasing amount of your cat's regular food.

If the diarrhea persists beyond forty-eight hours, contact your veterinarian.

What to Expect at the Veterinarian's Office

The doctor will conduct a complete physical exam, paying particular attention to the abdomen. Blood tests, a fecal exam, and a urinalysis may be needed if an infectious (panleukopenia) or systemic (kidney disease, thyroid disease, diabetes, pancreatitis) disease is suspected. An X-ray, barium series, ultrasound, or endoscopy may be necessary to define the area of inflammation or the intestinal obstruction (such as string or a rubber ball). Sometimes, *intussusception* (telescoping of a loop of the bowel into the adjacent loop of bowel) is obstructing the digestive tract. Intestinal obstruc-

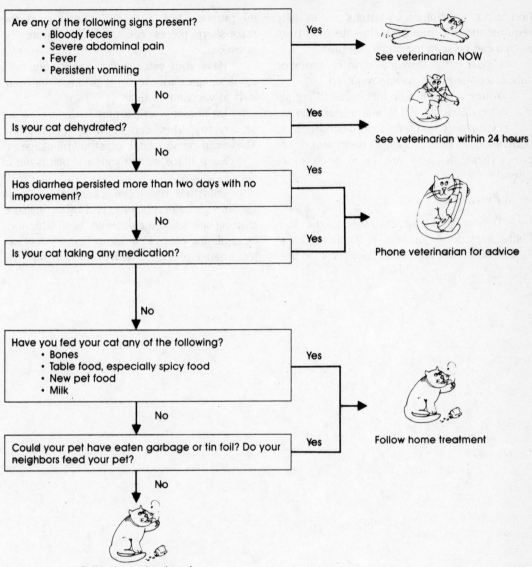

Are any of the following signs present?
- Bloody feces
- Severe abdominal pain
- Fever
- Persistent vomiting

Yes → See veterinarian NOW

No ↓

Is your cat dehydrated?

Yes → See veterinarian within 24 hours

No ↓

Has diarrhea persisted more than two days with no improvement?

Yes →

No ↓

Is your cat taking any medication?

Yes → Phone veterinarian for advice

No ↓

Have you fed your cat any of the following?
- Bones
- Table food, especially spicy food
- New pet food
- Milk

Yes →

No ↓

Could your pet have eaten garbage or tin foil? Do your neighbors feed your pet?

Yes → Follow home treatment

No ↓

Follow home treatment

tion is not uncommon in kittens and usually requires surgery. Tumors of the intestinal tract in cats can be seen in lymphosarcoma.

If your cat is dehydrated, intravenous or subcutaneous fluids may be required.

Your cat should also be checked for giardia, campylobacter, FTLV, feline leukemia virus, cryptosporidium, and toxoplasmosis if its diarrhea does not respond to treatment or recurs. These diseases are being seen more often.

Prevention

Do *not* give your cat table food (especially spicy food) or milk if it causes loose stools. Do *not* feed it bones. They serve no useful purpose but they *do* splinter, and the razor-sharp pieces can cut or perforate the intestines.

Have your veterinarian check your cat's stool samples for worm eggs often—particularly at vaccination time.

Do *not* let your cat play with yarn, string or any toys they can chew up or swallow. These can cause a fatal intestinal blockage.

Keep all toxic chemicals and plants out of your cat's way.

Cats that run loose, unsupervised, can get into garbage, poisons, and other disease-causing snacks. You can avoid these situations by confining your pet indoors. House cats have less chance of finding dangerous things to eat.

CONSTIPATION

Constipation is characterized by straining to move the bowels or by having infrequent bowel movements. If your cat is not straining, is alert and active, and is eating well but has not defecated in two or three days, don't panic. Not even Amtrak is always on time, so why should your cat's bowel movements be on such a strict schedule?

Ingesting bones, wood, or other indigestibles is the leading cause of constipation. Less common causes are the ingestion of hair balls from cats cleaning themselves and the slower intestinal movements of older animals.

A cat that has impacted feces (hard feces in the colon) makes frequent, straining attempts to defecate. The animal may be listless or *anorectic* (without appetite) and may vomit or pass small amounts of blood-streaked, foul-smelling feces. Some long-haired cats get feces stuck and matted over their anus. Consequently, they cannot defecate. This is called *pseudocoprostasis.*

Note: Male cats strain with a urinary blockage that many owners confuse with constipation. If your male cat squats with no elimination, see Painful, Frequent, or Bloody Urination, (page 230).

Home Treatment

Take your cat's temperature (page 31). It may be normal or slightly elevated. You can try to relieve mild constipation by adding over-the-counter laxatives such as Metamucil or Mucilose to the food. Adding water to a dry-food diet may also be helpful. Also try adding mineral oil, which lubricates and softens the stools, to the food. Add one teaspoon per ten pounds of body weight, but don't give mineral oil for more than three days—prolonged use decreases the absorption of vitamins. *Note:* Do *not* administer it directly into the mouth, as it is very bland and may pass into the respiratory system before your cat can cough. Mineral oil in the lungs will cause a pneumonia.

If your cat is straining to pass small amounts of blood-streaked, foul-smelling feces, you can try a pediatric Fleet mineral oil enema if your veterinarian recommends it. Follow the directions on the package and stay in touch with the veterinarian.

Pseudocoprostasis is cured very simply by trimming the hair and matted feces from the anus using scissors. Bathe the area and apply a soothing cream if it is irritated.

What to Expect at the Veterinarian's Office

If your cat has impacted feces trapped in the colon, your doctor will perform a complete physical. He or she will palpate the impacted feces in the colon and do a rectal exam. In addition, your doctor may suggest a radiograph, ultrasound, or endoscopy to study the extent and cause of the impaction. Sometimes a piece of bone is found lodged in the rectum.

Repeated warm-water enemas will probably be necessary to relieve the blockage.

Keep your cat's water bowl filled. Dehydrated pets can have hard, dry feces.

When cats groom themselves, their barbed tongues can capture large clumps of hair, which are then swallowed. These hair balls can contribute to constipation. An oil-based gel such as Laxatone, Kat-a-lax, or white petroleum jelly can prevent problems (see Your Cat's Home Pharmacy, page 81).

As your cat ages, so does the muscle in the intestine. It becomes lazy and moves the feces through the intestines much more slowly. The longer the feces stay in the intestine, the more water is removed from them, making the stool much drier. Give an oil-based gel and mix stewed or raw fruits and vegetables in the food—prunes live up to their reputation! Be sure that an old cat's water bowl remains filled, because adequate fluid intake is very important.

To help prevent pseudocoprostasis, keep the anal area of your long-haired cat clipped of excess hair.

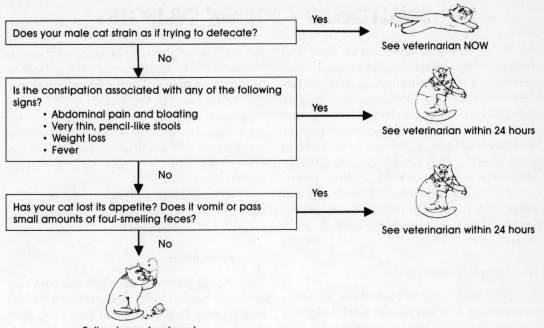

Does your male cat strain as if trying to defecate?

Yes → See veterinarian NOW

No ↓

Is the constipation associated with any of the following signs?
- Abdominal pain and bloating
- Very thin, pencil-like stools
- Weight loss
- Fever

Yes → See veterinarian within 24 hours

No ↓

Has your cat lost its appetite? Does it vomit or pass small amounts of foul-smelling feces?

Yes → See veterinarian within 24 hours

No ↓

Follow home treatment

SWALLOWED FOREIGN OBJECTS

Cats (especially kittens) can chew and swallow enough paraphernalia to stock a moderate-sized department store. If your cat has swallowed a foreign object and is vomiting or attempting to vomit, coughing, bleeding from body openings, or having abdominal pain or breathing problems, a blockage or perforation of the digestive tract (esophagus, stomach, or intestine) may have occurred. See your veterinarian *immediately*. If your cat has swallowed a known chemical or medicine or a suspected poisonous plant, see the appropriate Decision Charts.

Home Treatment

EMERGENCY   You will usually need veterinary assistance. If you cannot reach a doctor, feed your cat a large meal of cat food and bread or cotton balls soaked in milk or broth to coat the object and cushion its passage through the digestive tract, so that it passes out in a bowel movement without causing injury. This is especially important if you suspect that a pin or piece of glass has been swallowed. Check with your doctor as soon as possible and check the feces daily for the object.

What to Expect at the Veterinarian's Office

Your doctor may take plain X-rays, do a barium series, or do ultrasound to determine the position of the foreign object. Surgery is necessary if the foreign object is too large or too sharp to pass out in the feces. Sometimes the doctor can remove foreign bodies in the esophagus or stomach without surgery, by using scopes. However, these are very expensive instruments and are usually available only at university veterinary medical centers or some central hospitals.

Some doctors will expect the object to pass with no problem and will discharge your cat with instructions to check the feces daily.

Prevention

Do not give your cat chewable toys that are small enough to be swallowed or toys that may splinter. Keep string and yarn away from kittens (a string obstruction of the intestine is a *very* serious surgical emergency). Do not give your pet bones to chew, because they are also a frequent cause of digestive inflammation and obstruction. Watch your kittens carefully during the teething stage, because anything is "fair game" for swallowing. If you have a young child *and* a kitten in the house, you have double trouble—you need four eyes. After a play period, be sure that all your child's playthings are accounted for and have not been chewed by your pet. After sewing, account for all thread and needles.

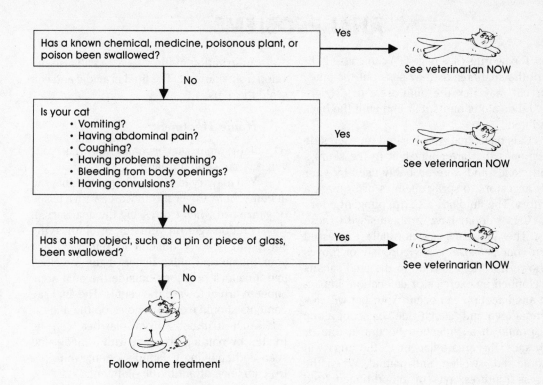

Has a known chemical, medicine, poisonous plant, or poison been swallowed?

Yes → See veterinarian NOW

No

Is your cat
- Vomiting?
- Having abdominal pain?
- Coughing?
- Having problems breathing?
- Bleeding from body openings?
- Having convulsions?

Yes → See veterinarian NOW

No

Has a sharp object, such as a pin or piece of glass, been swallowed?

Yes → See veterinarian NOW

No

Follow home treatment

ANAL PROBLEMS

Tapeworms (see page 55) can cause itching of the anal area as they pass out the anus. Your cat may lick the anal area, or "sleigh-ride": slide along on its rear end with the back legs lifted.

Cats have anal sacs located on each side of the anus that are equivalent to the skunk's scent glands and were probably used by your pet's ancestors to spray enemies or to mark a territory. The fluid has a sharp, pungent odor.

Cats seldom have problems with these sacs. The anal sacs are normally expressed when your pet exercises vigorously or moves its bowels. If the secretion in the anal sacs is not emptied by exercise or defecation, impaction and infection can occur. Your pet will lick the anal area and "sleigh-ride" or scoot along the ground. If an infection occurs in one or both sacs, the area adjacent to the anus will become red, swollen, and painful. When the abscess ruptures, pus or blood-tinged fluid may drain from it.

An irritation of the anal area can also develop from diarrhea. The fluid is acidic and can scald the anus.

Home Treatment

If the anal sac becomes infected, your veterinarian should treat it.

You may try to treat an impacted anal sac at home. *Note:* Cover the anal area with a tissue or gauze pad when expressing the anal sacs. If the secretions get on your rug or clothes, the smell can be very difficult to remove. Place your thumb and index finger at the 3 o'clock and 9 o'clock positions outside the anal area. Squeeze firmly toward the center. The anal sac contents should exit from holes on the anus.

Anal irritations from diarrhea can be treated by bathing your cat with a medicated soap and applying calamine lotion, white petroleum jelly, or antibiotic ointment.

What to Expect at the Veterinarian's Office

Anal-sac infections can be treated by flushing the sac with sterile water and antibiotics. Your doctor may hospitalize your pet for a few days or may treat the animal on an outpatient basis. Anal abscesses need more vigorous therapy.

Chronic anal-sac infections are best treated by removing the sacs surgically.

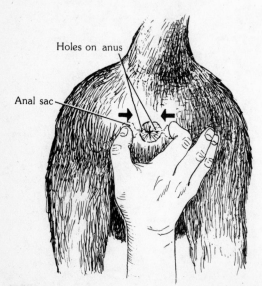

Holes on anus

Anal sac

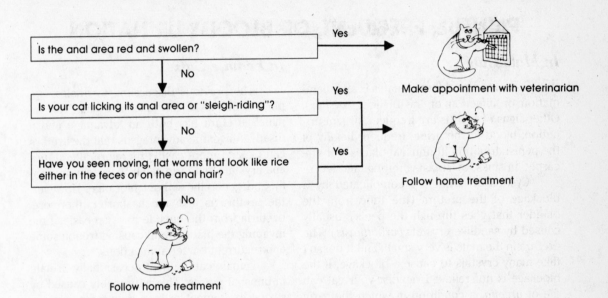

Is the anal area red and swollen? — Yes → Make appointment with veterinarian

No

Is your cat licking its anal area or "sleigh-riding"? — Yes

No

Have you seen moving, flat worms that look like rice either in the feces or on the anal hair? — Yes → Follow home treatment

No

Follow home treatment

Prevention

Since cats express the anal sac while running, regular exercise is very important.

If your pet is prone to impactions, frequent expressing of the sacs by you or your doctor will lessen the chances of anal infections or abscesses.

Controlling fleas and keeping your cat indoors will prevent tapeworms.

PAINFUL, FREQUENT, OR BLOODY URINATION

In Male Cats

A common problem in males is an inflammation or infection of the bladder (*cystitis*). Other signs of cystitis are frequent, urgent urination; blood in the urine; frequent licking of the penis; urination in unusual places—on the carpet, in sinks, on sofas; vomiting; and fever.

Cystitis is frequently complicated by a blockage of the urethra (the tube from the bladder that goes through the penis), usually caused by sandlike crystals (*urolithiasis*). The urethra in the male is very small, and it doesn't take many crystals to cause a blockage. If the blockage is not relieved rapidly, your cat can die of *uremia,* a condition in which the toxic products that are normally eliminated in the urine build up in the blood. Loss of appetite, vomiting, weakness, and dehydration are ominous signs of a very serious situation, such as impending kidney failure or death.

Trauma such as being hit by a car or being kicked can injure or rupture the bladder. You may see blood in the urine, or perhaps the evidence can be checked only microscopically, by your doctor.

If your pet is urinating more than usual and is drinking excessive amounts of water, diabetes, thyroid disease, or kidney disease may be the cause.

In Female Cats

The previous discussion, for males, applies with just a few qualifications. The female's urethra has both an advantage and a disadvantage: the advantage is that the urethra can expand more easily; therefore, the stones and crystals that form can be passed more easily and generally without blockage. However, the urethra is also much shorter; therefore, bacteria from the outside have an easier time invading the bladder and causing troublesome and recurrent bacterial infections.

Female cats in heat occasionally urinate in unusual places. This is probably caused by sexual excitement or by a mild temporary inflammation of the urinary opening. If your pet seems to be healthy and happy but the strange urination doesn't stop in a few days, see your veterinarian.

Home Treatment

EMERGENCY If your cat is straining to urinate, seek veterinary aid *immediately.* A cat that hasn't been able to urinate for twenty-four hours may die. If your male cat is urinating a good stream, but there is blood in the urine, you should see your veterinarian. It may be only an inflammation or infection of the lower urogenital tract (bladder, prostate, or urethra), but it could lead to a blockage. Give your pet vitamin C or cranberry or tomato juice to acidify the urine (see Your Cat's Home Pharmacy, page 81). Either will act as a natural antibiotic if bacteria are present. Most cats like tomato juice better than sweet cranberry juice.

What to Expect at the Veterinarian's Office

Try to collect a urine sample: place only a few granules of kitty litter in a clean, dry litter box. Transfer the urine collected there to a clean, dry container. Refrigerate the sample if your appointment is an hour or more away from collection time.

Your veterinarian will perform a complete physical examination. If there is a partial or complete obstruction of the urethra, the bladder may be as large as an orange and painful to the touch. In this case, your cat will have to be *catheterized* (i.e., a tube will be placed into the urethra), and the blockage of crystals will be dispersed by flushings with sterile water. This procedure is usually done under general anesthesia. The health of the kidneys may be determined by blood tests before the anesthesia is given. At the time of catheterization, a sterile urine sample may be collected to determine if bacteria are causing or complicating the cystitis and, if so, what antibiotic will

be effective. X-rays or ultrasound may be taken of the bladder to rule out bladder stones or tumors. Fluids are usually given intravenously or subcutaneously to increase urine flow and to remove the toxic products that were retained during the obstruction. Antibiotics, *antispasmodics* (to relax the muscles of the bladder and relieve pain), and *urinary acidifiers* (if the crystals are found only in neutral or alkaline urine and the kidney tests are normal) will be used. It is necessary to hospitalize and carefully monitor your pet's kidney function and urination.

Urolithiasis is one of the most frustrating conditions that your veterinarian has to treat, and the blockage can recur very easily. Recurrent blockages are best treated with a surgical procedure called a *urethrostomy,* in which a larger opening is made in the urethra. This does not cure the disease, but it provides a larger hole for the passage of the crystals and decreases the chance of another blockage. If there are stones in the bladder, they can be removed by *cystotomy* (bladder surgery).

If a bacterial infection is present (this is uncommon), an antibiotic should be prescribed. Months of treatment may be necessary to clear up the infection. Bacteria can move up into the kidney or *seed* (multiply) in the bladder wall and can be difficult to eradicate. Culture, sensitivity, and urine tests—not just the outward appearance of a cure—are important follow-ups. Many times, infections can move up the urinary tract and remain "silent," while slowly deteriorating your cat's kidneys.

If your cat has been injured and there is visible or microscopic blood in the urine, your doctor will want to monitor the damage and repair to the urinary system with blood tests and urinalyses.

Prevention

Since the cause of the male cat's urinary problem is not known, methods for preventing a recurrence are controversial. A few suggestions that seem to help are adding just a pinch of salt to the food to increase water intake and thus increase urination, thereby flushing out the bladder and decreasing crystal formation. Feeding cat foods low in ash (magnesium and other minerals) may help. Both dry and moist cat foods that contain more than 3.5 percent ash (wet weight) and high magnesium levels should be avoided. Long-term urinary acidifiers may be recommended. Two acidifiers that can be purchased in drugstores or your pet store are DL-Methionine (250 milligrams three times daily) or ascorbic acid (vitamin C) tablets. One vitamin C tablet (100 milligrams) three times daily should acidify the urine. Any long-term medicine should only be given with your doctor's consultation. Litmus paper can be used to check the effectiveness of the acidifiers.

Recurrence of bacterial infections and/or bladder stones may be prevented by antibiotics, acidifiers, or alkalinizers, depending on the type of bacteria isolated and the type of stone formed. Unfortunately, these problems often recur.

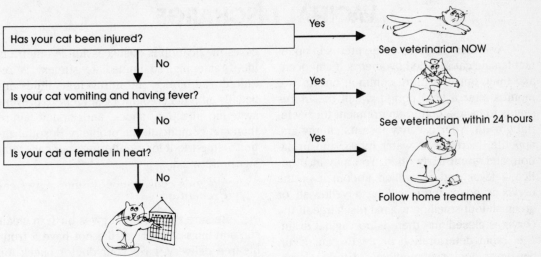

Has your cat been injured? — **Yes** → See veterinarian NOW

No

Is your cat vomiting and having fever? — **Yes** → See veterinarian within 24 hours

No

Is your cat a female in heat? — **Yes** → Follow home treatment

No

Make appointment with veterinarian

VAGINAL DISCHARGE

A serious infection of the uterus in an intact female cat is called *pyometra.* It can occur any time, but it is more common one to two months after a heat period, when the uterus seems to have a better environment for bacterial growth. Your cat may lose its energy and appetite, increase its water intake and urination, and vomit fairly often. You may also notice a fever and a swollen abdomen. If the cervix is open, there will be a yellowish or greenish foul-smelling vaginal discharge. If the cervix is closed and there is no vaginal drainage, rapid deterioration or death can occur. See your doctor *immediately.* Uterine infections can also be seen a few weeks after the birth of kittens. A red or brownish discharge is present, along with some of the signs seen in pyometra. Again, see your doctor as soon as you can.

An infection of the vagina is not very common in cats.

Home Treatment

No treatment is necessary for the slight mucous discharge of the female just entering or in heat. For other discharges, professional care is necessary.

What to Expect
at the Veterinarian's Office

An ovariohysterectomy is the treatment of choice for uterine infections, since in most cases medication is unsuccessful. Pyometra is life-threatening, so immediate surgery is required. Antibiotics and intravenous fluids are usually administered during surgery to prevent systemic infection, shock, and kidney failure than can complicate the problem. Hospitalization is important for monitoring your cat's vital signs afterward.

Prevention

Be sure that your cat gives birth in clean surroundings. If your cat did not have a trouble-free delivery, have your doctor check for retained fetuses or placenta within twenty-four hours, and ask him or her to give an injection of hormones to involute the uterus.

Watch your cat carefully for one to two months after a heat period. If any signs of pyometra are present, see your doctor immediately.

If you do not intend to breed your cat, schedule an ovariohysterectomy *before* the first heat. Besides eliminating the chance of your cat contracting pyometra, having the procedure done this early may prevent breast cancer (see Lumps and Swellings in the Breast, page 194).

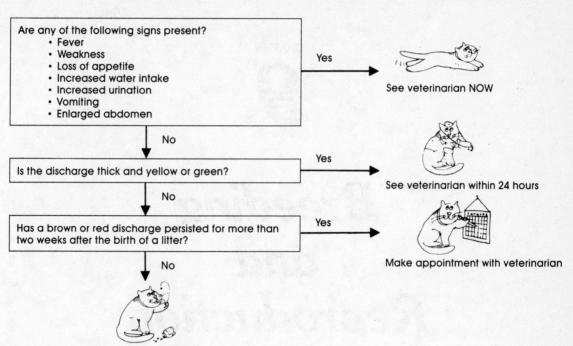

Are any of the following signs present?
- Fever
- Weakness
- Loss of appetite
- Increased water intake
- Increased urination
- Vomiting
- Enlarged abdomen

Yes → See veterinarian NOW

No

Is the discharge thick and yellow or green?

Yes → See veterinarian within 24 hours

No

Has a brown or red discharge persisted for more than two weeks after the birth of a litter?

Yes → Make appointment with veterinarian

No

Follow home treatment

Breeding and Reproduction

Breeding, pregnancy, delivery, and nursing require a healthy mother cat. This section is provided to make your care easier and more organized before and during breeding and when your cat is pregnant. If all the steps are followed, delivery should be very easy. Most cats have no problems during delivery and nursing, but just in case, a delivery chart is provided to inform you of the general process and to let you know situations when your veterinarian's help might be needed.

BREEDING AND MATING

Once you have decided to breed your cat, the first step is to have it examined by the veterinarian. Besides updating vaccinations (see page 41) and checking for internal parasites (see page 48), your doctor will also be on the lookout for any genetic traits or diseases that might be a problem in the kittens. Your veterinarian might suggest that both cats be tested for feline leukemia, FTLV (AIDS-like virus), and feline infectious peritonitis. If you have picked your cat's mate, it's wise to collaborate with the other owner so that all pertinent information is available for the physical examination. If the mate hasn't been chosen, ask your veterinarian to recommend a good breeder.

Ideally, the two cats should meet at least once before they mate, preferably at the breeding site. Since male cats can be finicky about breeding away from familiar surroundings, I recommend breeding at the tom's home.

The cat has to be the most passionate creature alive—next to its "friend," the flea, that is. The flea is the champ for longest lovemaking (up to nine hours), but the cat gets the award for most vocal!

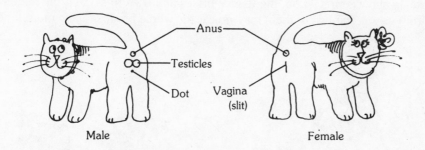

Cats have no problem finding a member of the appropriate sex for mating, but many cat owners "can't tell the players without a scorecard." To tell the sex of your pet, first lift up the tail. Below the anus is either a dot (●) or a slit (|). The dot indicates a male cat, the slit a female. Male cats reach sexual maturity in eight months to one year; females, from the age of five months to eight months. A mature male (tom) will establish its "territory"—even on another cat's "territory"—by spraying: that is, backing up to a vertical object, lifting its tail, and squirting urine against it. It could be a neighbor's bush or your antique grandfather clock; the cat isn't particular. Howling, crying, and pacing for a "sweetheart" are also part of a male's repertoire.

For females (queens), the signs of maturity are a little more dramatic, as this scenario indicates:

> *"Doctor, my cat's dying! I think she was poisoned!"*
> *"What's the matter?"*
> *"She's screaming and rolling on the floor in pain. Now she's crouching, with her tail in the air, still screaming and treading her back feet!"*
> *"How old is she?"*
> *"Six months. I'm afraid she's going to die. . . ."*
> *"She's going to die of a broken heart if she can't mate. Your cat is in heat!"*

If the female is not bred, it will be in heat every two or three weeks. Queens are different from other female animals in that their eggs will not be released from the ovary (*ovulation*) until *after* intercourse.

The female selects a mate with a majestic display of vocalizing, rolling, foot treading, and crouching. (Fights may break out if more than one tom wants to mate with a single queen in heat.) The chosen partner grabs the queen by the back of the neck with its teeth. The female crouches and raises its rear end, the tail to one side. The tom thrusts its penis into the queen's vagina, ejaculates, and quickly dismounts, while the female lets out a shrill cry. The tom dismounts quickly, because, to show appreciation, the female hisses and tries to scratch the mate with its front claws. The two of them may repeat the whole process a few more times.

"The dating game"

Breeding Checklist

☐ Schedule a veterinary exam for
    ☐ Intestinal parasites
    ☐ Vaccinations
    ☐ FLV, FTLV, and FIP
    ☐ Genetic diseases
☐ Choose a responsible breeder
☐ Introduce the cats before they mate, if possible
☐ Let them breed in the male's home, if possible

PREGNANCY

Your female is now probably pregnant, but you should look for certain telltale signs to be sure. First, your cat's appetite and body weight will increase. After thirty-five days, the belly and breasts will start to enlarge. A physical exam at this time will be done to confirm pregnancy and monitor the health and nutritional status of the cat.

Your doctor should also tell you when to expect the kittens, and he or she should help you formulate an emergency plan, in case problems arise during delivery.

The phase of pregnancy in which the uterus prepares for the development of the fetuses is called *metestrus*. The egg is released, gets fertilized, and attaches to the wall of the uterus (*implantation*) to grow. Pregnancy lasts an average of sixty-three days after conception. After fifty days milk production will begin, and a few days before your cat gives birth, the breasts may secrete a milklike substance.

239

If the pregnant queen does not seem to be in good condition, your doctor may perform a few blood tests, such as hemoglobin and serum protein, and suggest supplementing the daily balanced diet. Undernutrition is a major factor in the birth of kittens that are too small to survive the postnatal period. Also, an undernourished cat may not care for the kittens properly, and the milk production may be inadequate.

For healthy cats, a normal commercial cat-food diet should provide adequate nutrients, although supplements of high-quality proteins, such as milk products and cooked eggs, certainly won't hurt. Vitamin and mineral supplements are a rather controversial topic; I suggest you discuss this with your veterinarian.

The primary difference in the pregnant cat's diet is that the queen needs more food, more calories, and more protein during the second month of pregnancy. Divide the total daily ration into three or four smaller meals to aid digestion (see Nutrition, page 34).

Exercise is beneficial—it will keep your cat from getting too heavy and having a difficult delivery. Therefore, do not at first restrict exercise, but don't let the cat roam far without supervision. Most queens will themselves limit their exercise as the pregnancy progresses, but you should restrict all strenuous exercise three days before the due date.

Drugs taken during pregnancy are potentially dangerous to the fetuses. Consult your veterinarian before giving your pregnant cat any medication. Some medications to avoid are aspirin, acetaminophen (Tylenol), antihistamines, antibiotics (especially tetracycline, kanamycin, streptomycin, and sulfa drugs), hormones, tranquilizers, and most worming medications.

Pregnancy Checklist

- [ ] Feed high-quality food:
  - [ ] Well-balanced commercial food
  - [ ] High-protein supplements (milk products, cooked eggs)
- [ ] Divide the daily ration into 3 or 4 smaller portions
- [ ] Discuss vitamin supplements with your veterinarian
- [ ] Schedule a midgestation veterinary exam for
  - [ ] Confirmation of pregnancy
  - [ ] Health check
  - [ ] Ultrasound
- [ ] Let exercise continue, but not unsupervised
- [ ] Avoid giving your cat drugs
- [ ] Arrange the nursing box
- [ ] Have this book handy, open to the Delivering the Kittens chart (page 243)
- [ ] Have all utensils handy
- [ ] Have your emergency plan ready
- [ ] Stop strenuous exercise 3 days before the due date

False Pregnancy

Although it is rare, some females may experience a false pregnancy: they have all the signs of the "real thing"—even labor pains—but no kittens are born. In their place, the "mother" will drag slippers, socks, or other soft objects into the "nest," wherever it is. In fact, the "babies" may even be shredded clothing or newspapers.

To check the reality of your queen's signs, palpate the abdomen very gently after thirty-five days have elapsed. If you can't feel anything, or if your cat is especially large or fat, your veterinarian can help you tell for sure. An X-ray may be necessary to determine the existence of kittens.

If the pregnancy is false, hormone injections can be given to lessen or alleviate the signs, but I suggest that you just wait it out and let your cat "nurse" your slippers. The less hormone therapy, the better, because hormones can affect so many different body processes. However, I recommend spaying to prevent the almost certain recurrence of false pregnancy—probably after the very next heat.

PREPARING FOR DELIVERY

Introduce your queen to the maternity box two weeks before delivery. It should be large enough for the cat to stretch out and nurse the kittens comfortably. The sides should be high enough to keep the kittens inside, but low enough for the mother to get in and out. Line the bottom with several layers of newspaper, towels, or sheets, but whatever is used, clean the box regularly. Be sure that any material that lines the bottom goes to the edge of the box so that the newborn kittens will not get caught underneath and smother.

The temperature in the maternity box should be about 80°F, because chilling is a frequent cause of kitten mortality. Since newborn kittens have a difficult time regulating their own temperature, a 250-watt infrared (heat) bulb can be placed above the box, so that half of the box is heated. (Otherwise, a nearby radiator or electric heater may be adequate.) Attach a thermometer to the box to monitor the temperature. The "delivery room" should be a familiar area—perhaps the cat's regular sleeping area—as long as it's warm and draft-free. Place the maternity box there.

After all your preparations, the mother cat may just decide that your own bed or closet is the best choice! If this happens, gently place it back in the maternity box. If the cat still insists on delivering elsewhere, let it. You can move mother and kittens back to the box later.

The "delivery room" should also be supplied with

- This book, open to the delivery section
- Thread dipped in alcohol
- Scissors dipped in alcohol
- Warm, rough towels
- A bowl of water for the mother
- Your veterinarian's phone number

After delivery, do not disturb the maternity box, especially if it's the cat's first pregnancy. Some mother cats, if they are disturbed, will attack those in the room or even eat their own young during the first few days after birth. Of course, each cat is an individual and many will be happy to have you around as long as you are quiet and gentle, so play it by ear. Clean the box after the third day.

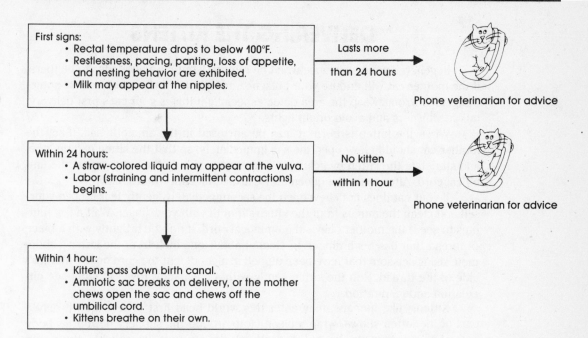

First signs:
- Rectal temperature drops to below 100°F.
- Restlessness, pacing, panting, loss of appetite, and nesting behavior are exhibited.
- Milk may appear at the nipples.

Lasts more than 24 hours → Phone veterinarian for advice

Within 24 hours:
- A straw-colored liquid may appear at the vulva.
- Labor (straining and intermittent contractions) begins.

No kitten within 1 hour → Phone veterinarian for advice

Within 1 hour:
- Kittens pass down birth canal.
- Amniotic sac breaks on delivery, or the mother chews open the sac and chews off the umbilical cord.
- Kittens breathe on their own.

DELIVERING THE KITTENS

In general, your assistance won't be required, but it's a good idea to be there, if the mother cat will endure your presence, to monitor the process in case something goes wrong. Keep the area quiet, especially if this is your cat's first delivery; talk in whispers and avoid bright lights.

When the kitten is born, it may be enclosed in the amniotic sac. If so, the mother cat should chew open the sac immediately, so that the kitten can breathe, and stimulate the kitten by licking it. The mother should then chew apart the umbilical cord. After birth, the queen may eat the placenta—that's okay.

If your cat does not chew open the sac immediately, gently tear it open yourself and clean the mucus from the kitten's mouth with your finger. Wait a few minutes to see if the mother chews the umbilical cord. If not, tie it tightly with a piece of thread that has been dipped in alcohol about one inch from the kitten's abdomen. Using scissors that have been dipped in alcohol, cut the cord on the mother's side of the thread. Rub the kitten gently with a clean, soft towel to stimulate circulation and respiration.

Kittens, like humans, may enter this world head first or feet first. If only a part of the kitten shows, wrap a clean cloth around the slippery newborn's body and, as the mother strains, pull it gently all the way out. Pause when the queen relaxes. Call your doctor if you are not able to deliver the kitten.

If a kitten is not breathing, wrap it in a warm towel with its head down (but support the head so it doesn't wobble) and shake it downward. This should stimulate respiration and remove fluid from its breathing tubes. If a breath *still* is not taken, gently blow into the kitten's nose until its chest expands, and try rubbing it in a warm, rough towel to stimulate respiration.

The mother cat may rest anywhere from fifteen minutes to two hours between deliveries. After all the kittens are born, the mother will stop straining. Instead, your cat will comfortably lick and clean the new kittens.

Within twenty-four hours after the delivery, which in most cases occurs with no problems, the mother and kittens may be examined by your doctor. In general, however, most veterinarians don't feel that cats need to be checked or given a hormone injection after a trouble-free delivery. Be sure to keep the kittens warm if a trip to the office is necessary. A snug blanket placed in a box is perfect.

The doctor will palpate the queen's abdomen to make certain all the kittens were delivered. The mother will be given an injection of a hormone (*oxytocin*) to *involute* (shrink) the uterus and to stimulate milk flow from the breasts. Your veterinarian will determine the little ones' sexes, weigh them, and check for birth defects, such as cleft palates, harelips, heart problems, and umbilical hernias.

If there are any problems at all during delivery, *telephone your doctor.* If a kitten is stuck in the birth canal and you have tried gentle help, professional manipulation may solve the problem. Sometimes an *episiotomy* (an incision between the upper end of the vagina and the anus that enlarges the vaginal opening and eases the birth of the kitten) is necessary.

Occasionally, *uterine inertia* (weak contractions of the uterus) will occur during delivery. If the mother is obese, old, or upset by many people in the room, or has been straining for a long time, the uterus may become tired and stop squeezing the kittens out efficiently. Injections of oxytocin may help.

In some instances, a *caesarean birth* (surgical removal of the kittens through the abdominal wall) is necessary. Timing is very important, but the surgery is generally fast and safe. After recovery from the anesthesia, the mother can nurse the kittens and go home. The sutures are removed in ten days.

THE NURSING PERIOD

Usually, this is pleasant for all concerned—mother, kittens, and you. Remember not to disturb your new cat family any more than necessary for about three days. But you *do* have a few important jobs during this time: cleaning the maternity box and the mother's breasts, watching for signs of illness or malnutrition, and initiating solid foods (*weaning*).

The kittens will soil the maternity box, so on the third day, when the mother goes to relieve itself, change the newspapers or towels. Wash the queen's breasts once daily with warm water and a clean washcloth, but do *not* use soap.

The milk produced during the first twenty-four hours is called *colostrum* and is rich in antibodies that protect the kittens from such diseases as panleukopenia for a few weeks. But if you see any signs of illness, see your veterinarian *immediately*. Most kitten illnesses need professional attention.

Appearance and milk production are the best indication of the mother's nutritional status. A well-balanced, commercial cat food is adequate for lactating queens. If necessary, supplement this with high-protein foods, such as milk products and cooked eggs. A general rule is to feed an additional 100 calories per pound of kitten. By the end of the lactation period, your cat may be eating three times the prebreeding level. Vitamin and mineral and extra calcium supplements should be fed to heavy lactaters with large litters.

Using an ounce or gram scale, weigh the kittens about two weeks after birth. At that time they should be double their birth weight. Their eyes will open about ten days following birth.

Later in nursing, the kittens' teeth and nails may irritate the breasts, and the mother will lose patience and leave the kittens for longer periods of time. Although you can help by trimming the kittens' nails, this is actually nature's way of telling the kittens to try some solid food. Now is the time to try weaning.

Hand Feeding

Hand feeding the kittens may be necessary if the mother becomes ill or dies, if a kitten is too weak to nurse, or if the litter is unusually large. Borden's KMR is a very good commercial milk substitute. Cow's milk does not contain the level of protein, calcium, phosphorus, or calories kittens need, but in an emergency, you can use one cup of homogenized milk mixed with two egg yolks, one-half teaspoon corn syrup, and a pinch of salt. The kittens should be fed six times a day at four-hour intervals. One teaspoon per day for each ounce of body weight is each kitten's daily ration. Divide this into six equal feedings.

First, warm the formula to body temperature (100°F). Feed the kittens using a doll-sized baby bottle with a nipple or a Pet-Nip, which is sold in pet stores or by your doctor. *Note: Never* use an eye dropper for feeding. The kitten may aspirate the milk into the lungs and get pneumonia. The formula should drip out slowly when the bottle is inverted; a heated needle can enlarge the hole in the nipple, if necessary. Place the kitten on its stomach, open its mouth with your finger, and position the nipple on top of the tongue. As an extra treat, place a towel within reach so the kitten can knead. The kitten will suck vigorously and be very happy. At the end of a feeding, its abdomen should be enlarged, not bloated.

The kitten should be burped and stimulated to urinate and defecate after each feeding. Burp the kitten as you would a human baby. Hold it against your shoulder and gently pat its back. A warm, moist cotton ball washed against the anal, genital, and abdominal areas will simulate the mother's tongue (which normally would do this) to initiate urination and defecation. The bowel movements should be yellow and formed.

If the kittens are orphaned, the environmental temperature must compensate for the mother's absence. The kitten box should be kept at 85°F to 90°F for the first week, 80°F for the second week, 75°F for the third and fourth weeks, and 70°F thereafter. A heating pad on "low" draped over one side of the box and covering a few inches of the bottom will suffice. This way the kitten can choose to be near the heat source, or if too warm, it can crawl away to the cooler side. The heating pad should be covered with a sheet or towel to avoid burns. Whatever external heat source is used, be sure it doesn't burn or overheat the kittens.

If you find that the kittens' skin is getting irritated from sucking on each other, separate them for a week.

Nursing Problems

There are some serious problems during nursing that require immediate co-operation between you and your doctor. Since pregnancy and milk production may demand more calcium than the mother can spare, *eclampsia* (low blood calcium) may be seen during nursing. The signs are nervousness, crying, stiffness, staggering, fever (as high as 107°F), muscle spasms, and convulsions. Eclampsia usually

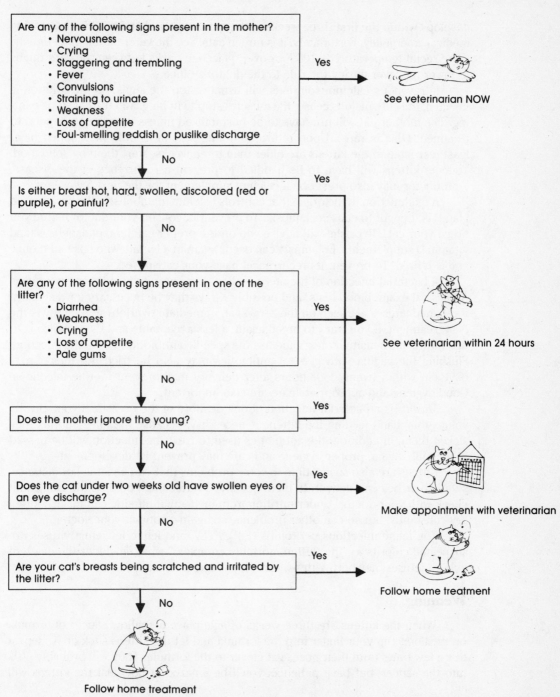

Are any of the following signs present in the mother?
- Nervousness
- Crying
- Staggering and trembling
- Fever
- Convulsions
- Straining to urinate
- Weakness
- Loss of appetite
- Foul-smelling reddish or puslike discharge

Yes → See veterinarian NOW

No ↓

Is either breast hot, hard, swollen, discolored (red or purple), or painful?

Yes →

No ↓

Are any of the following signs present in one of the litter?
- Diarrhea
- Weakness
- Crying
- Loss of appetite
- Pale gums

Yes → See veterinarian within 24 hours

No ↓

Does the mother ignore the young?

Yes →

No ↓

Does the cat under two weeks old have swollen eyes or an eye discharge?

Yes → Make appointment with veterinarian

No ↓

Are your cat's breasts being scratched and irritated by the litter?

Yes → Follow home treatment

No ↓

Follow home treatment

develops within the first three weeks of the nursing period and is a life-threatening medical emergency. Fortunately, it is rare in cats. See the veterinarian *immediately.* If the rectal temperature is 106°F or over, place ice packs between the cat's thighs to lower the fever during the ride to the doctor's office.

Intravenous calcium solutions will usually stop the signs. As the solution is injected, the convulsions cease, the muscles stop twitching, and the cat stops panting. The mother cat will not have to be hospitalized unless it does not respond to treatment (this is rare). Upon returning home, nursing should be stopped or at least restricted. If the kittens are older than three weeks, start them on solid food. Younger kittens will have to be handfed to prevent a recurrence of the disease. Your doctor may also prescribe a calcium supplement for the next few weeks.

A malfunction in the organ that controls calcium metabolism (the parathyroid gland) is thought to cause eclampsia. To prevent it, consult your doctor before you breed your cat. He or she will advise you on the proper calcium, phosphorus, and vitamin D supplements. Eclampsia can occur again in a female who has had it once and is rebred. To prevent its recurrence, have your cat spayed.

A bacterial infection of the uterus called *acute metritis* is another emergency. A physical exam, blood tests, and possibly X-rays may be necessary for diagnosis. If retained fetuses are seen on the X-rays, an immediate ovariohysterectomy is the best treatment. If you want to breed again, a less acceptable and risky choice is to do culture and sensitivity tests and use the specific antibiotic to treat the infection. Flushing the vagina with general antibiotics may also be tried. An injection of oxytocin within twenty-four hours after delivery may prevent uterine infections. Good hygiene and appropriate care are also important.

Mastitis is a bacterial infection of one or more of the breasts. If your cat develops this, hand feeding the kittens is necessary, because the infected milk may sicken them. In addition, the antibiotics used to treat the infection will be passed in the milk. Again, proper hygiene and care may prevent its development.

Kittens are also susceptible to some problems that can be fatal. For instance, simple diarrhea can dehydrate them quickly. Overfeeding could be the cause, but check with your doctor. Undernutrition from ineffectual nursing can make a kitten cry constantly, but so can other problems, so again—contact your doctor.

The feline infectious peritonitis (FIP), FTLV, and feline leukemia viruses are suspected culprits for the "kitten mortality complex," which includes the death of unborn fetuses, newborn kittens, and very young kittens.

Weaning

When the kittens are three weeks of age, place a shallow saucer of formula on the floor. Dip your finger into the formula and let the kittens suck on it. Repeat this a few times until their noses get closer to the formula. They will probably walk into the saucer, but have patience; you'll be amazed at how fast the kittens will pick up your message. Moistened commercial kitten food or high-protein pablum can be added to the formula to make a thin gruel. The mother cat will still let the kittens have a free lunch until they have all their baby teeth (about five weeks of age), but then their teeth will start to irritate the breasts.

The mother will be happy to cooperate with your weaning program. Keep the cat away from the kittens for a few hours during the day. After a week, let them be together just at night. At the same time, decrease the mother's food intake accordingly, to decrease milk production. If the breasts become engorged, which does occasionally happen, compresses may help. Contact your doctor if things don't improve in two or three days.

PREVENTING PREGNANCY

If you do not want to breed your cat, *please* have it neutered, for its own health and as a contribution to reducing the pet population. It is *not* true that neutering causes obesity and laziness; overeating and getting too little exercise are to blame.

The best time for the female's ovariohysterectomy is *before* the first heat (but not before five or six months of age). The estrogens secreted during the heat period may prime the breast tissue for later tumor development, and approximately 90 percent of them are malignant. Spaying early may help prevent tumors from developing.

The ovariohysterectomy is the surgical removal (*"ectomy"*) of ovaries (*"ovario"*) and the uterus (*"hyster"*) through an abdominal incision. The size of the incision does *not* indicate your doctor's surgical skill. Some doctors make small incisions, and others like to have good exposure of the surgical area. The size of the organs to be removed will vary among animals as well.

Spaying is common surgery, but every pet is unique, and special care will be taken. A careful and thorough preoperative exam will determine your cat's ability to undergo surgery. Modern anesthesia (gas or inhalants) is very safe: an anesthetic-caused death is extremely rare in a healthy pet. Your doctor will instruct you not to feed your cat for twelve hours before surgery, which will allow the stomach to empty. If there is food in the stomach during surgery, it may be vomited and pass into the breathing tubes and lungs, and an aspiration pneumonia could occur. If the monitoring equipment (which keeps track of breathing and heart functions during surgery) indicates a potential problem, your cat can be brought out of the anesthesia in a few minutes. Many veterinary hospitals have the same heart monitors used for humans in hospital intensive care units. Emergency fluids and drugs, which are rarely needed, are readily available.

Postoperative complications (such as infection) are also very rare because of aseptic surgical techniques: the operating room is well sterilized, as are the instruments, drapes, caps, masks, and gowns. Modern anesthetics allow most cats to be on their feet minutes after surgery, which also probably lessens the postoperative discomfort. Your cat may be home the same day or the next day, depending on the veterinary hospital procedure.

Home care after surgery consists of keeping the incision clean (don't allow your pet to lie on dirt), restricting your cat's exercise (cats will normally restrict their own activity), and checking the incision for swelling, redness, or discharge. If any infection develops, call your doctor. The sutures can be removed in a week.

Castration (surgical removal of the testes) is recommended to prevent or eliminate roaming, spraying, fighting, and breeding in male cats. The testicles are removed through a very small incision in each scrotal sac after the cat has been anesthetized. Most cats are sent home the same day, and surgical recovery is uneventful. In fact, when our male cat Pu was castrated, he was out of the anesthesia in five minutes. I drove him home shortly afterward, and no sooner had we arrived home than he gobbled down some cat food and briskly mounted Mitzi, our tolerant female Siamese! Now that's what I call a recovery!

It may take up to a month for the roaming, spraying, fighting, and mounting behavior to stop, because it will take a few weeks for the male hormones still circulating in the body to be used up. A very small percentage of cats may still have some residual objectionable behavior. The best time for the surgery is before the behavior patterns develop—about six months of age.

Rarely, a male cat will have only one testicle (*monorchid*) or none at all (*cryptorchid*) in the sacs (*scrotum*). Although sperm will not be produced in the undescended testicle, male hormones will still be manufactured: your cat will continue to strut around like the neighborhood lover. One problem with undescended testicles is that they frequently form a large sertoli cell tumor after seven years of age. Again, this is extremely rare in cats.

If your female cat has been *mismated* (accidentally bred), an estrogen injection, followed by estrogen tablets given at home, is usually successful at preventing pregnancy if given within twenty-four hours of the breeding. The injection makes the uterine environment hostile to the sperm and egg; therefore, implantation won't occur. Estrogen can have toxic side effects, however, so this treatment is discouraged. Unless you really want to breed your cat, I recommend an ovariohysterectomy.

Genetics and
Hereditary
Diseases

The Austrian empire in the mid-1800s was *the* important center of the arts, litera-ture, and music. At the same time that Brahms produced his brilliant *Variations on a Theme by Handel* (1861), another genius, an Austrian monk named Gregor Men-del, was making one of the most important biological discoveries ever made: an organism's traits, such as height, are regulated by two particles we now know as *genes* (Greek for "to give birth to"), one particle contributed by the female and the other by the male. Mendel performed his experiments on garden pea plants. He noticed that when he bred tall pea plants to short pea plants, all the offspring were tall. Mendel called this characteristic the *dominant* trait, and the characteristic that "seemed to disappear," he termed *recessive.*

When Mendel bred the offspring to each other, the result was three tall pea plants for every short pea plant—a ratio of three to one. Mendel surmised that each offspring of the first breeding carried one dominant and one recessive particle and that in the breeding of the offspring, one short pea should be produced for every three tall pea plants.

Unfortunately, Vienna and the rest of the world neither understood nor cared about the biological sciences, which were considered antireligious. Gregor Men-del's papers were burned after his death in 1884, and his great findings were not "rediscovered" until the beginning of the twentieth century.

What is this genetic material, which determines that like shall beget like? Genes are composed of *deoxyribonucleic acid* (DNA). This DNA is found in long strands called *chromosomes* in the nucleus of the billions of cells in your pet's body. Every cell of your cat contains nineteen pairs of chromosomes.

Each gene controls the synthesis of one protein. Protein makes up about three-fourths of the body solids and is the building block of life. The majority of proteins are enzymes that regulate the chemical reactions in the cells. Blood, bone, hair, and muscle are primarily protein. Hormones such as insulin are also proteins. Structural protein called *connective tissue* gives the skin its elasticity and the hair its form.

Throughout a lifetime there is a constant turnover of cells—daily wear and tear destroy skin, hair, and blood cells, but they are constantly being replaced, thanks to the cells' ability to duplicate themselves. Before the cell divides, the chromosome forms a replica of itself (a process called *replication*). Each new cell has the exact number and order of genes as the original cell. Thousands upon thousands of activities occur and renew themselves daily in your pet's body, thanks to a biological "blueprint," called the *genetic code,* in the chromosomes.

Every part of your pet's body (and even its temperament, to a large extent) is dependent on the chromosomes that were combined when its parents mated. The fertilized egg is a complete cell containing all the information that determines hereditary makeup. That cell divides in the mother cat's uterus, and the developing embryo contains the identical genetic makeup.

Let's suppose you bred your pure tabby to a pure black cat. What color would you expect in the kittens? Tabby is dominant, and black is recessive. If a creature has two dominant genes for a trait, such as tabby, it is called *homozygote*. Let's use the letters TT for our homozygote female's genes, and tt for the male's recessive black-coat genes. The kittens will all have one gene from each parent (Tt); this pairing of dominant and recessive genes is called *heterozygote*. Because tabby genes are dominant, all the kittens will be tabby. What if you bred one of these kittens to another heterozygote just like it? Using a chart called Mendel's Checkerboard, we can predict the probability of genetic traits in cats, pea plants, or any other living thing.

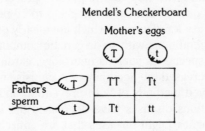

Mendel's Checkerboard

In the next generation, one of four kittens will have dominant tabby genes, two will be tabby heterozygotes like their parents, and one will have a pair of the parents' recessive black-coat genes. In other words, two tabby parents can produce a black cat!

By now, you're probably wondering what all this has to do with your cat's health. It has a *lot* to do with it! As you already know, one gene carries the message for the production of one protein. But if the DNA gets mixed up, the gene carries an abnormality known as a *mutation,* a change from the normal pattern of inheritance that appears as a new or altered characteristic.

Inbreeding (mating closely related individuals, such as mother to son, father to daughter, or brother to sister) or *linebreeding* (mating more-distant relatives such as cousins) increases the chance of defects that require two recessive genes to come together or defects that require a polygenic union. Before breeding, the male and female should be checked by a veterinarian for defects or diseases that have a hereditary basis.

A disease called *globoid cell leukodystrophy* has been seen in a few kittens in which a genetic enzyme deficiency causes progressive degeneration of the nervous system and death in kittens between two and six months of age. It has a *recessive pattern of inheritance:* i.e., a kitten must receive two abnormal genes to produce the disease. A cat that has one normal gene and one abnormal gene is called a *heterozygote carrier* and will appear normal but can pass the abnormal gene to its offspring.

At the University of Pennsylvania Veterinary School, Doctors Donald Patterson and Peter Jezyk and their co-workers are studying the "fading puppy syndrome." In human neonates and infants, genetic enzyme defects such as *phenylketonuria* (PKU) have been identified. Newborn infants can be screened for these hereditary metabolic defects and treated before mental retardation, liver or kidney dysfunction, or death occurs. Neonatal kittens that fail to thrive (they lose weight, have problems moving, and can't maintain body temperature) may have similar disorders.

Metabolic screening is a new and important procedure in veterinary medicine. Dr. Jezyk points out, "In human medicine, 5 to 10 percent of all admissions to pediatric hospitals are for disorders which are clearly genetic, while another 10 to 15 percent are for conditions with some genetic component." The development of veterinary clinical specialties such as neurology, cardiology, dermatology, and ophthalmology has increased the accuracy of diagnosis and the recognition of genetic diseases. Improved methods of both prevention and treatment of parasitic, nutritional, and infectious diseases have decreased the importance of these illnesses and have brought to light diseases that are entirely or partially genetic in origin.

11

Cancer—
A Chronic
Disease

The improvements in the prevention and treatment of infections, parasites, and nutritional diseases have lengthened the life span of our pets. Consequently, a cat living into its middle and later years will develop other health problems. Probably the most dreaded disease of mid- and later life is cancer (although there are some cancers, such as lymphosarcoma [leukemia] that affect primarily younger cats). Yearly, there are almost 160 new cases of cancer per 100,000 cats.

Cancer begins as a biologically abnormal change in a single cell in one of your pet's organs. This cell divides repeatedly, producing more abnormal cells. These new cells also divide at an extremely rapid rate and cannot be stopped by your cat's normal internal monitoring system, which makes normal cells behave. These abnormal cells are biologically destructive: they form solid tumors and invade and destroy surrounding tissue. Malignant tumors produce chemical substances that aid the cellular destruction and help stimulate a blood supply (to obtain oxygen and nutrition) for the tumors. Malignant cells frequently spread throughout the body by way of veins or lymph vessels and thus bring their destructive ways to other organs in your cat's body. This process is called *metastasis*.

WHAT IS CANCER?

Why should normal cells in your cat's body suddenly transform into malignant cells? Researchers feel that cancer is caused by one or more of the following factors: contact with harmful environmental agents, heredity, viruses, immunologic factors, or body hormones.

Harmful Environmental Agents

Chemical *carcinogens* (agents that produce cancer) are being identified in our air, water, and food. Our pets share this unhealthy environment and share the carcinogens, most of which alter cellular genetic material. Asbestos workers and cigarette smokers have a high incidence of lung cancer. Since cats don't smoke and don't work—especially around asbestos—they have a very low incidence of lung cancer. However, white cats that are excessively exposed to sunshine have a high incidence of skin cancer, just as do fair-skinned humans.

Heredity

Certain breeds seem to have a predisposition for and a high incidence of specific cancers.

Viruses

Tumor-causing viruses are being identified. These viruses change the genetic code in cells, transforming them into malignant cells. The most publicized cancer-inducing virus is the feline leukemia virus (see page 47).

Immunologic Factors

Tumor cells have antigens (see page 41) on their surfaces. Your cat's immune system (antibodies, lymphocytes, and *macrophages*) recognizes these "foreign" cells and attempts to destroy them. It has been speculated that our pets (and our bodies) produce cancer cells quite often but the immunologic defenses in healthy humans and cats destroy these cells before they can get established. This is called *immunologic surveillance.* If the immune system fails for any reason, the cancer cells can start their destruction.

Body Hormones

Although it has not been established empirically, having an ovariohysterectomy for your cat *before* her first heat may help avert breast cancer in later years.

Cancer will be prevented only when we understand how and why these factors cause normal cells to transform into cancer cells. For example, if air pollution and smoking induce lung cancer in humans, why don't *all* exposed humans develop cancer?

If your pet develops cancer, don't feel that all is hopeless. In many cases, modern veterinary medicine, just like human medicine, has therapy available to help your pet. The chance for a cure or *remission* will depend on the type of tumor, its location(s), the type of therapy used, and your cat's general health (for example, whether general anesthesia or chemotherapy can be tolerated).

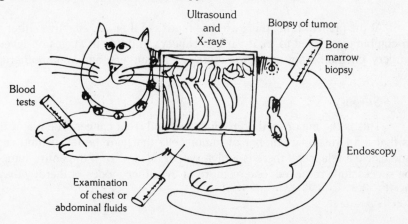

Ultrasound and X-rays

Biopsy of tumor

Bone marrow biopsy

Blood tests

Examination of chest or abdominal fluids

Endoscopy

First, you and your doctor must be *sure* that your cat has cancer. Most types of cancer cannot be diagnosed by looking at your pet. Some of the signs, such as loss of appetite, gradual weight loss, weakness, lumps in the abdomen, and even ugly skin growths, could indicate a simpler problem. Your doctor must perform certain tests and take radiographs to verify that cancer is present, to determine the type and extent of the cancer, and to decide on the best type of treatment, if any, for the malignancy (see Laboratory Tests, page 72, and Noninvasive Diagnostic Techniques, page 77). Your veterinarian may select some or all of these diagnostic tools to give you clear assessment of your cat's situation.

Once the lab tests and X-rays have been studied, the doctor can determine the next step. If there is cancer and it is treatable, you should receive the following information so that you and your doctor can reach a common understanding and decision in your cat's best interest.

- What are the chances for a cure or remission?
- If we can expect a remission, how much time does this give my cat to live free of pain and discomfort?
- What type of therapy will be used?
- What are the side effects of the therapy?
- What is the cost of the therapy?
- How much of my time will be taken up by visits to the veterinary hospital for therapy and follow-up exams?
- Is there any new cancer therapy that will not cause my cat discomfort and that may benefit it and contribute to current human cancer studies?

THERAPY

At the present time, there are five modes of therapy, effective either singly or in combination, used to treat various cancers in different stages of development: surgery, chemotherapy, radiation therapy, cryosurgery, and immunotherapy.

Surgery

This is the major method to diagnose and treat cancer. The major drawback is that a microscopic number of tumor cells that may be left behind can spread and cause a relapse. If there is a high risk of relapse, or if the entire tumor cannot be successfully removed, one or more of the other modes of therapy may also be used.

Chemotherapy

The hope of chemotherapy is in using a drug or chemical agent that will kill tumor cells while doing as little damage as possible to your cat's healthy cells. The drawbacks of chemotherapy are its expense (unless the therapy is supported by governmental grants to a university or private veterinary medical center) and the potential toxic effects on healthy tissue.

Radiation Therapy

Radiation therapy is an important and effective mode of cancer treatment in human medicine. It is now being recognized as an important form of general cancer therapy. Unfortunately, the cost of the equipment and facilities has limited its use to university and private veterinary medical centers.

The cells of certain tumors seem to be more susceptible to therapeutic doses of *ionizing radiation*. These *ions* seem to kill tumor cells by disrupting their "code of life"—the DNA and chromosomes. The cells die when their attempt at division is ineffective. Susceptible tumors are termed *radiosensitive*.

Cryosurgery

Certain tumors—especially some skin and mouth tumors—have been successfully treated with cryosurgery. This is a technique using liquid nitrogen or a compressed gas such as nitrous oxide to kill tumor cells by alternately freezing and thawing the tissue. A temporary but odorous and oozing wound is the main disadvantage until healing occurs.

Immunotherapy

A new form of therapy that seems to hold some promise, especially when combined with surgical treatment, is immunotherapy. Your own and your pet's immune system protects the body against "foreign" cells such as bacteria, viruses, and tumor cells. In cancer, the immune system is suppressed or blocked from destroying the tumor cells. Certain biological and chemical substances called *immune adjuvants* are being used to stimulate the immune system in hopes of getting remissions in breast cancer.

Early diagnosis and treatment are most important if therapy is to be successful. If your cat is over five years old and you suspect the presence of cancer, see your veterinarian.

Most cat owners are willing to prolong their pet's life if it will be free of pain and suffering. If you and your veterinarian reach an understanding that this is not possible, it is in your pet's best interest to administer euthanasia (page 265). In this way, pets do not have to suffer through the pain and misery of cancer that has spread throughout the body. But please consider euthanasia only as one option. Just like heart disease, cancer can be considered a chronic illness that can, in many cases, be controlled—that is, your cat can live free of pain and discomfort. Euthanasia should be used only if treatment has failed or if your cat has a form of cancer that is completely hopeless.

Skin cancer, lymphosarcoma, and breast cancer are three forms of cancer commonly seen in cats.

SKIN TUMORS

Any growth in or on your cat's skin should be examined by your veterinarian. Most skin tumors, such as the three shown, are benign, but any growth that increases in size rapidly and infiltrates the surrounding tissue may indicate malignancy. Early surgical removal is curative for the majority of skin tumors.

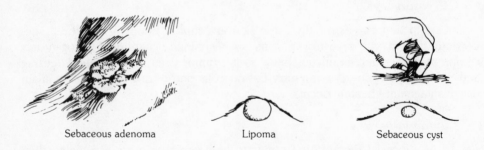

Sebaceous adenoma   Lipoma   Sebaceous cyst

Sebaceous Adenoma

This skin growth looks very much like a cauliflower: there are several small clumps of greyish matter growing from a common base. If the adenoma gets irritated, it may become red and ulcerated. You should be able to get your fingers around the growth, because it does not infiltrate adjacent tissue.

Lipoma

The more common term for this growth is "fatty tumor." It grows under the skin, but you can feel it. A lipoma can get very large, although it grows slowly. Again, it should move freely because it does not spread to surrounding cells.

Sebaceous Cyst

This is similar to a lipoma in that it is a freely moving growth under the skin. However, this cyst is composed of cheeselike matter and remains fairly small, about the size of a marble. This, too, does not harm adjacent tissue.

LYMPHOSARCOMA (LEUKEMIA)

Since the early 1900s, viruses have been known to cause cancer in animals. In 1964, a virus called the feline leukemia virus (FLV) was found in a household of cats with a high percentage of leukemia cases. Since 1964, major developments have been made in understanding the nature and transmission of this virus, detecting it in the cat population, and studying leukemia and other disease states attributed to the virus. At this writing, there is no evidence that the feline leukemia virus can infect humans or other animals. A vaccine that protects cats against the virus is available.

Lymphosarcoma is a cancer of the blood-forming cells—more specifically, the lymphoid tissue (such as the lymph nodes). The virus FLV is spread by the saliva and urine of infected cats, and it can also be transmitted in the uterus to unborn kittens and in the milk to nursing kittens. Since it is found in the blood, such blood-sucking insects as cat fleas and mosquitoes probably transmit the FLV to other cats. For some reason, not all cats that are infected with the virus get leukemia. It seems that the cats that develop antibodies to the virus do *not* get the disease, which is why the vaccine works.

Forms of the Disease

There are three recognized forms of lymphosarcoma: chest, abdominal, and multicentric. The signs that your cat shows will depend on the lymph nodes or organs involved.

Chest

In this form, the enlarged chest lymph nodes compress the windpipe and esophagus, and fluid may accumulate in the chest. Your cat will experience breathing difficulties, coughing, and gagging.

Abdomen

Malignant cells may be found in the intestine, lymph nodes, liver, spleen, and kidney, causing a loss of appetite, weight loss, vomiting, diarrhea or constipation, and anemia.

Multicentric

The lymph nodes under the skin will be greatly enlarged, and tumor formation can be found in many organs, including unusual locations such as the eyes or brain. The cat may or may not have a fever.

Treatment

Many of the signs of lymphosarcoma (leukemia) are also seen in other treatable diseases; therefore, your veterinarian will have to perform some or all of the following tests to reach a *definite* diagnosis of lymphosarcoma: a complete blood count, blood chemistries, X-rays or ultrasound of the chest and/or abdomen, a bone marrow or lymph node biopsy, endoscopy, and an examination of the chest and/or abdominal fluids. There is also a specific blood test for the presence of FLV. This test should be done

1. on a new cat before it enters a household of cats or a cattery;
2. before you breed a tom or queen (be sure the cattery is *certified* FLV-free);
3. if your cat shows any of the signs of lymphosarcoma;
4. if your cat has a chronic disease, such as mouth ulcers or anemia, that does not respond to treatment (the virus seems to suppress your cat's immunologic system and make it difficult to fight off infections).

If in a multiple-cat household, one cat has lymphosarcoma or a positive test, *all* the cats should be tested. If this first test is negative, the cats should be retested in three months, because the virus has a long incubation period.

If your cat's illness is diagnosed as lymphosarcoma, some veterinarians will recommend treatment; others will recommend euthanasia. The virus can be transmitted to other cats. FLV-positive cats should be isolated until they achieve a negative status. If they do not, the cats should be removed. Many cats that are treated for lymphosarcoma with anticancer drugs or supportive therapy, such as blood transfusions, fluids, vitamins, or steroids, do not respond well. Some will be in remission for one year or longer. If your cat with lymphosarcoma passes away or is euthanized, discard its feeding bowls, litter pans, and bedding and clean the premises thoroughly (ordinary household cleaners suffice). *Note:* Do *not* bring another cat into the house for thirty days after removal of the infected cat.

The feline leukemia virus is also thought to play a role in a certain kidney ailment called *glomerulonephritis,* in reproduction problems such as infertility, and in the "kitten mortality complex"—the sudden and unexplained death of newborn and young kittens.

BREAST CANCER

Breast cancer is a disease of middle-aged and old female cats—especially Siamese cats. Ninety percent of cat breast tumors are malignant. Any hard lump near a nipple and under the skin of a breast should be examined by your veterinarian. Early diagnosis and aggressive therapy of malignant breast tumors may prolong your cat's life.

The cause of breast cancer is not known; however, it is possible that breast cancer may be averted if your cat is spayed before the first heat. So if you do not plan to breed your cat, it may be a good idea to have the ovariohysterectomy done early.

If the lump is suspicious, your veterinarian will probably recommend two procedures—a radiograph or ultrasound of the chest and a biopsy of the lump. If malignancy is present, metastasis of the cancer to the lungs is a fairly common occurrence. If there is no evidence of metastasis, surgery will be recommended. The affected breast and the adjacent lymph vessels, veins, and lymph nodes will usually be removed and examined for malignancy. If the tumor is benign, breathe a sigh of relief! Some benign tumors can become malignant if they are not removed. If the tumor is malignant, the surgery may increase your cat's lifespan and free it of discomfort or pain. Surgery may be combined with chemotherapy, radiation, or immunotherapy.

As you can see, cancer is a very complex chronic disease that, in many instances, *can* be treated. Early diagnosis is *very* important, as is close cooperation with your veterinarian during treatment. The decision between euthanasia and treatment should be made only after serious consultation with your veterinarian, always keeping in mind your cat's well-being.

VETERINARY ONCOLOGY

Oncology, or cancer detection and treatment, is a recognized specialty in veterinary medicine. If your cat develops cancer, you may want to be referred to a major veterinary medical center with an oncologist on staff. A cooperative effort between your "G.P." veterinarian and a specialist is often very beneficial in the treatment of cancer.

CHAPTER

12

Death and Euthanasia: When It's Time to Say Goodbye

Like all living things, any cat will eventually die. Death, like life, is best when it is peaceful and normal. Sometimes, unfortunately, a cat's medical condition deteriorates until it no longer enjoys life, or it poses a danger to other living creatures, and then it is time to consider euthanasia.

EUTHANASIA

This is the hardest decision to make. I know, because I had to make that decision for our dear, fourteen-year-old miniature poodle, Pepe, who was suffering with pancreatic cancer. All life is precious, but euthanasia has its time and place. If your cat has an incurable disease or is vicious and dangerous, euthanasia is usually recommended. An intravenous overdose of an anesthetic that is fast and painless is used.

Many owners want to be present when their pet is "put to sleep," and most veterinarians will assent. Although the injection is fast and painless, you should be aware that there are involuntary reflexes for a few minutes after your pet has departed.

Albert Schweitzer's reverence for life was a great influence on me when I was very young. Consequently, I will not euthanize a healthy animal or an animal that has a curable disease. Most veterinarians feel the same way. If you cannot afford the necessary care, discuss it with your veterinarian. He or she may work out a long-term payment plan or may not charge you for the time.

Final arrangements for the remains should be made prior to euthanasia. Your veterinarian may suggest cremation or a pet cemetery. Many areas have public ordinances against backyard burials.

It's very hard to lose a pet that has given you love and companionship. But you'll always have the memories, and as soon as you feel ready, I recommend finding a new family member to share your love. You'll be glad you did.

GRIEVING FOR YOUR CAT

The loss of a loved one—whether human or pet—causes great emotional pain.

The grieving process associated with human death is explained in Dr. Elisabeth Kübler-Ross's landmark book, *On Death and Dying.* We tend to go through the same series of recognized stages when we lose our cat. *Don't be ashamed* of your grief. It *is* permissible and healthy to grieve for your cat.

Denial

When we are told that our cat has a terminal illness, a subconscious protective mechanism, *denial,* occurs.

Doctor: I'm sorry to say that Speedy has tumors throughout her chest.

Mrs. Smith: I don't believe it. She caught a mouse last week. Sick cats *don't* catch mice.

This state is usually brief, but you do need *time.*

A few things might help you here.

1. Read about the disease. Perhaps your veterinarian has some literature about your cat's illness.

2. Seek a consultation or second opinion—preferably from a specialist. Getting confirmation and knowing that you did everything possible are helpful.

Anger

This stage takes the form of outward or inward anger. Many times your veterinarian is the object of the outward anger during this painful period:

"My cat only cost me $10. You charged me $500 to treat him and he still died. You're only interested in the money!"

A sensitive, understanding veterinarian will be able to help you resolve this anger. Oftentimes, an owner's anger is turned inward. This is called *guilt.*

"If I hadn't gone away for a week, Romeo wouldn't have gotten sick. He died of a 'broken heart.'"

A supportive veterinarian will be able to show you how your love and care made your cat happy and comfortable.

Grief

The sadness that accompanies the loss of a pet may last for a few days or, in some instances, a few years. Sleep, appetite, and work efficiency may be disturbed.

Find someone who will be supportive of your feelings so that you can resolve this perfectly normal stage of bereavement. Talk about your feelings with your veterinarian or a close cat-loving friend. Support may also be provided by bereavement counselors or client-support groups. Ask your veterinarian.

Specially trained social workers and mental health professionals are available to counsel you if you are having difficulty coping with the loss of your cat. Here are some centers that could refer you to a professional counselor:

The Animal Medical Center, New York City
Colorado State University, School of Veterinary Medicine, Ft. Collins
University of California, School of Veterinary Medicine, Davis
University of Minnesota, School of Veterinary Medicine, Minneapolis
University of Pennsylvania, School of Veterinary Medicine, Philadelphia
Washington State University, School of Veterinary Medicine, Pullman

Resolution

When you can remember the happy moments with your cat without great emotional pain and get back into a productive and satisfying pattern of living, you have resolved the bereavement process—not forgotten your friend. This may be the time to think about a new feline friend.

CHILDREN AND PET LOSS

Be aware of your children's feelings if their pet passes away. I still remember vividly the day that my fox terrier, Butch, got hit by a car and died when I was nine years old. My mother and I hugged each other and cried. The closeness and shared grief were very comforting.

Here are a few things that you may find helpful:

- If your cat's death is imminent, talk about feelings before the cat's demise. Depending on your children's ages, tell them what you can about the cat's illness and tell them that death will occur.
- Oftentimes, your pet is your child's best friend and confidant. The relationship is the "safe spot" in your child's life. Think about how you would feel if you lost your best friend, someone that made you feel happy.
- Express your feelings to your child, and discuss similar experiences that you had in your childhood. Listen to your child's feelings. A hug is always appreciated. Stay close and try to replace the affection that was just lost.
- Include your child in the decision making about terminating the cat's life. This will spare your child bitterness that can last a lifetime.
- If your child wants to see his or her cat after it dies or is euthanized, this should be allowed. It helps your child grasp the reality of the death.

- Give your child a mourning period. Mourning is the ritual we go through to help us feel that our loved one's death occurred with some dignity and caring. Perhaps you can bury your cat on your property and have a ceremony. Talk about the funny things that your cat did and the ways that your cat made you feel happy and enriched your lives.
- Some children, when they mourn for their cat, would rather not go to school that day. Tell your child's teacher that the family cat has died. By recognizing the death in class or having a group discussion, the teacher can show that your child's feelings of sadness are normal and, in fact, universal when a loved one dies.
- Get out photos and videos of the family cat and reminisce. Draw pictures of the cat.
- Write a eulogy or a biography of your cat with your child. This shows that the cat was important to all of the family members.
- Monitor your child's feelings and behavior for a while. Has he or she resolved the bereavement process? If not, you may see disruptive behavior, withdrawal, a reluctance to go to school, a drop in schoolwork performance, and/or a change in sleeping or eating habits. Try to help your child or seek professional help from a *sympathetic* pediatrician, your veterinarian, a mental health professional, or one of the references listed.
- If any of your child's friends' pets passes away, ask your child if he or she would like to make a condolence card.

Remember: Your children will always remember your sensitivity and caring at one of the most difficult moments of their childhood. They will be able to comfort others as you have done for them.

The following books may be helpful:

Pet Loss: A Thoughtful Guide for Adults and Children, by Herbert A. Nieburg and Arlene Fischer (New York: Harper and Row, 1982).

When a Pet Dies, by Fred Rogers (Mister Rogers) (New York: G. P. Putnam's Sons, 1988).

Index

Reader Survey

Please take a moment to fill out this survey of cat owners.

1. What type of cat do you have? _____
2. What is its name? _____
3. How old is your cat? _____
4. Where did you find your cat?
   _____ Breeder
   _____ Pet store
   _____ Humane shelter
   _____ Friend
   Other _____
5. How many times a year do you see a veterinarian for your cat? _____
6. What other companion animals or pets do you have?
   _____ Dog
   _____ Bird
   _____ Ferret
   _____ Guinea pig
   _____ Hamster
   _____ Gerbil
   _____ Mouse or rat
   _____ Rabbit
   _____ Snake
   _____ Iguana or other lizard
   _____ Tortoise
   _____ Fish
   Other _____

7. How did you find out about *The Cat Care Book*?
   _____ Saw it in a bookstore
   _____ Recommended by a veterinarian or pet-store owner
   _____ Read about it in an article
   (Where was the article? _____)
   _____ Saw it in an advertisement
   (Where was the advertisement? _____)
   _____ Heard Dr. Gerstenfeld on radio or television
   (Where did you hear him? _____)
   _____ Given to me by a friend
   Other _____

8. What parts of this book have you found most helpful? _____
   _____

9. What would you like to read more information on? _____
   _____

10. Have you read Dr. Gerstenfeld's other books?
    _____ *The Dog Care Book* (formerly *Taking Care of Your Dog*)
    _____ *The Bird Care Book*

11. Would you like to read a book about another type of companion animal?
    What type? _____

12. Would you like to be on Dr. Gerstenfeld's mailing list for booklets, news-
    letters, or notices about new products? If so, please include your name
    and address with this survey.

Please mail your completed survey to:

Sheldon L. Gerstenfeld, V.M.D.
Chestnut Hill Veterinary Hospital
Market Square
Philadelphia, PA   19118

Thank You!

Would you like to talk to Dr. Gerstenfeld about your cat or other pets—dogs, birds, rabbits, guinea pigs, ferrets, snakes and other reptiles, amphibians, fish, or other creatures great and small?

- Medical problems
- Behavior problems
- Consultation before purchasing
- Sources for purchasing healthy animals

Call Dr. Gerstenfeld's help line to set up a telephone appointment:

Telephone: (215) 242–3655

Dr. Gerstenfeld will return your call at a convenient time to discuss your question. His time can be charged by Visa or MasterCard.